Soviet Strategic Thought, 19

CSIA Studies in International Security

Michael E. Brown, Sean M. Lynn-Jones, and Steven E. Miller, series editors
Karen Motley, executive editor
Center for Science and International Affairs (CSIA)
John F. Kennedy School of Government, Harvard University

Published by The MIT Press:

Allison, Graham T., Owen R. Coté, Jr., Richard A. Falkenrath, and Steven E. Miller, *Avoiding Nuclear Anarchy: Containing the Threat of Loose Russian Nuclear Weapons and Fissile Material* (1996)

Allison, Graham T., and Kalypso Nicolaïdis, eds., *The Greek Paradox: Promise vs. Performance* (1996)

Arbatov, Alexei, Abram Chayes, Antonia Handler Chayes, and Lara Olson, eds., *Managing Conflict in the Former Soviet Union: Russian and American Perspectives* (1997)

Blackwill, Robert D., and Michael Stürmer, eds., *Allies Divided: Transatlantic Policies for the Greater Middle East* (1997)

Brown, Michael E., ed., *The International Dimensions of Internal Conflict* (1996)

Brown, Michael E., and Šumit Ganguly, eds., *Government Policies and Ethnic Relations in Asia and the Pacific* (1997)

Elman, Miriam Fendius, ed., *Paths to Peace: Is Democracy the Answer?* (1997)

Falkenrath, Richard A., *Shaping Europe's Military Order: The Origins and Consequences of the CFE Treaty* (1994)

Feldman, Shai, *Nuclear Weapons and Arms Control in the Middle East* (1996)

Forsberg, Randall, ed., *The Arms Production Dilemma: Contraction and Restraint in the World Combat Aircraft Industry* (1994)

Shields, John M., and William C. Potter, eds., *Dismantling the Cold War: U.S. and NIS Perspectives on the Nunn-Lugar Cooperative Threat Reduction Program* (1997)

Published by Brassey's, Inc:

Blackwill, Robert D., and Sergei A. Karaganov, eds., *Damage Limitation or Crisis? Russia and the Outside World* (1994)

Johnson, Teresa Pelton, and Steven E. Miller, eds., *Russian Security After the Cold War: Seven Views from Moscow* (1994)

Mussington, David, *Arms Unbound: The Globalization of Defense Production* (1994)

Soviet Strategic Thought, 1917–91

Andrei A. Kokoshin

CSIA Studies in International Security

The MIT Press
Cambridge, Massachusetts
London, England

© 1998 by the Belfer Center for Science and International Affairs
John F. Kennedy School of Government
Harvard University
Cambridge, Massachusetts 02138
(617) 495-1400

An earlier version of this work was originally published in Russian under the title
Armiia i Politika, © 1995 Mezhdunarodnye Otnosheniia.

All rights reserved. No part of this book may be reproduced, stored in a retrieval system,
or transmitted in any form or by any means—electronic, electrostatic, magnetic tape,
mechanical, photocopying, recording, or otherwise without permission in writing from
the Belfer Center for Science and International Affairs, 79 John F. Kennedy Street,
Cambridge, MA 02138.

Library of Congress Cataloging-in-Publication Data

Kokoshin, Andrei Afans'evich.
Soviet strategic thought, 1917–91 / Andrei A. Kokoshin.
p. cm. — (BCSIA studies in international security)
Includes bibliographical references and index.
ISBN 978-0-262-61138-1 (pb. : alk. paper)
1. Soviet Union—Military policy. 2. Soviet Union—Armed Forces—Political activity—History.
I. Title. II. Series.
UA770.K58824 1998
355´.033547—dc21   97-38496
                                                   CIP

Printed in the United States of America

Contents

About the Author		ix
Acknowledgments		xi
Introduction		1
Chapter 1	The Relationship between Policy and Strategy in Soviet Military Doctrine	11
	Revolutionary Military Councils and Political Commissars	12
	The Supremacy of Policy over Strategy	19
	The Evolution of a "Unified Military Doctrine"	26
	The Concept of the "Integral Military Leader"	38
	The Purges of 1937–38 and the New Generation of Soviet Military Leaders	40
	The "Genius of Stalin" and the Soviet Art of War	44
	Politics and Military Leaders in the Khrushchev Era	46
	Nuclear Weapons and the Relationship between Policy and Strategy	53
	Policy and Strategy in the 1980s	55
	Modification of Clausewitz's Formula in the Late 1980s	58
Chapter 2	Threats to Soviet Security and the Probability of a Future War	63
	Revolutionary Wars and National Wars	65
	Maneuverability in a Future War	74

	The Role of the Navy in a Future War	77
	The Political-Military Situation in the Late 1920s and Early 1930s	80
	The Theory of the Initial Phase of War	86
	The Political-Military Situation in the Nazi Era	89
	Approaches to the Great Patriotic War of 1941–45	98
	Threats to Soviet Security in the Late 1940s and Early 1950s	111
	Political-Military Conditions in the Second Half of the 1950s	116
	The Initial Phase of War and Fighting a Surprise Attack	122
	Local and Limited Wars	124
	The Political-Military Situation during the Era of Détente and Stagnation	126
	The New Role of the Soviet Navy	129
	Continuity and Revolution in the 1980s	132
Chapter 3	Offense and Defense in Soviet Military Strategy	147
	Debates on Offense and Defense in the 1920s	147
	The General Conference for the Reduction and Limitation of Armaments, 1932–34	157
	The Soviet Theory of "Deep Battle" or "Deep Operations"	160
	The Offense in Stalin's Naval Strategy	164
	Pre-war Soviet Concepts of Initial Strategic Operations	165
	Issues of Offense and Defense Immediately after the War	169
	The Enhanced Role of Offensive Operations in the 1960s	172
	Dialectics of Defense and Offense in the Nuclear Sphere	175
	The Development of the "Deep Battle" Theory in the 1970s	177
	Offense and Defense in Soviet Military Strategy in the Early 1980s	180
	"Defense Sufficiency" and the New Relationships between Offense and Defense	184

Chapter 4	In Lieu of a Conclusion: Russia's National Security and Military Power	193
	Present-Day Dimensions of the National Security Problem	194
	Building National Egoism	200
	The New Armed Forces for Russia	205 |「
Index		211
About the Belfer Center for Science and International Affairs		226

About the Author

Andrei A. Kokoshin is Secretary of the Defense Council and Head of the President's Military Inspectorate of the Russian Federation. From 1992–97, he was First Deputy Minister of Defense. Kokoshin is a graduate of the Moscow Higher Technical Institute. In 1972, he joined the Institute of the USA and Canada in the Academy of Sciences of the Soviet Union, where much of his research focused on problems of military strategy and international security. He became a doctor of historical sciences in 1982 and a professor in 1987. He is the author of many books and articles on international security and military affairs published in Russia and abroad.

Acknowledgments

My search for writings that could provide an overview of the evolution of Soviet military thinking has been unsuccessful. The most complete analysis of the topic is provided by Colonel I.A. Korotkov's *History of Soviet Military Thought: A Brief Overview, 1917–June 1941*,[1] which contains many important revelations despite the rigid constraints of the era.

In the course of my research, however, I came across many thought-provoking pieces by both Soviet and foreign authors on various aspects of the evolution of Soviet strategic and military thought in the context of Soviet political history from the October Revolution and Civil War to the collapse of the Soviet Union in 1991. Among the most interesting foreign works, I would include those of Raymond Garthoff, Michael MccGwire, Carl Jacobsen, Jacob Kipp, Dale Herspring, Harriet and William Scott, Thomas Wolfe, Stephen Meyer, David Holloway, and Peer Lange.[2]

---

1. I.A. Korotkov, *Istorriya sovetskoy voennoy mysli. Kratiky ocherk. 1917–iyun' 1941* (History of Soviet military thought. A brief overview. 1917–July 1941) (Moscow: Nauka, 1980).

2. See the following works: Raymond L. Garthoff, *Deterrence and the Revolution in Soviet Military Doctrine* (Washington, D.C.: Brookings, 1990) and *Detente and Confrontation* (Washington, D.C.: Brookings, 1985); Michael K. MccGwire, *Military Objectives in Soviet Foreign Policy* (Washington, D.C.: Brookings, 1983); Carl G. Jacobsen, "Soviet Strategic Policy Since 1945," in Jacobsen, ed., *Strategic Power: USA/USSR* (New York: St. Martin's Press, 1990), pp. 106–121; Dale R. Herspring, *The Soviet High Command, 1967–1989* (Princeton, N.J.: Princeton University Press, 1990); Harriet F. Scott and William F. Scott, *Soviet Military Doctrine: Continuity, Formulation and Dissemination* (Boulder, Colo.: Westview, 1988); Thomas W. Wolfe, *Soviet Strategy at the Crossroads* (Cambridge, Mass.: Harvard University Press, 1964); and P.H. Lange, "NATO/WTO Military Doctrine," in Robert D. Blackwill and F. Stephen Larrabee, eds., *Conventional Arms Control and East-West Security* (Durham, N.C.: Duke University Press, 1989), pp. 186–211.

I was enormously aided in my effort by the invaluable advice and remarks of a number of Russian military professionals—scholars, practitioners, and general planners—including Colonel General N.A. Lomov, Lieutenant General M.A. Milshtein, General of the Army V.I. Dubynin, Colonel General V.P. Mironov, and academician G.N. Flerov, who have all since passed away, as well as Marshals of the Soviet Union S.L. Sokolov and V.G. Kulikov; academicians B.V. Bunkin, E.A. Fedosov, and A.G. Shipunov; Generals of the Army M.A. Gareyev and V.N. Lobov; Major General I.S. Danilenko; Lieutenant General M.S. Vinogradov; Major General V.S. Belous; Professor, Doctor of Sciences (History) D.M. Proektor; Major General G.V. Batenin; Colonel General V.V. Sokolov; Colonel L.S. Semeiko; Major General, Professor M.M. Kasenkov; Colonel General V.V. Korobushin; Colonel General G.A. Mikhailov; Rear Admiral V.S. Pirumov; Rear Admiral R.A. Zubkov; Lieutenant General A.N. Vitkovsky; and others.

I am especially grateful for the thorough critique of the entire manuscript by Professor, Doctor of Sciences (History), Colonel V.M. Kulish. I particularly profited from a study we did together with Professor, Major General (Ret.) V.V. Larionov.

Many relevant ideas that touch upon problems at the junction of politics and military strategy were also discussed and put to the test in a joint seminar which I co-chaired on "Politics and Military Strategy" involving a group of scholars from the USSR Academy of Sciences and the General Staff Academy of the USSR Armed Forces. I would like to express my gratitude to the following people in the United States who helped with this project. My long-time friend and colleague Graham Allison, Director of the Belfer Center for Science and International Affairs (BCSIA) at the John F. Kennedy School of Government, Harvard University, is much appreciated for his great interest in and commitment to this project. Steven Miller, Director of the International Security Program at BCSIA, and Sean Lynn-Jones, Co-Editor of the center's book series, also supported the development of this book. Mary Albon skillfully and carefully edited a translation of the work, greatly increasing its accessibility to an English-speaking audience. Karen Motley, Executive Editor of the series, coordinated editing and production of the book and ensured that things ran smoothly; Deborah Kamen, Lynne Meyer-Gay, Dawn Opstad, Karin Shepard, and Wellington Graphics contributed valuable proofreading, research, and typesetting skills.

I would also like to express my special appreciation to my long-time assistant in preparing this work, A.K. Yusupova, as well as to O.V. Lukanina. I am most grateful to my wife, Natasha, who displayed a great deal of patience and helped maintain the pace of the whole effort, corrected a good many mistakes in the manuscript, and verified a number of ideas and historical aspects of the assessments I have made in this book.

I wrote this book as a part of my scholarly contribution and not in my capacity as a government officer. Thus, the views presented here are purely my own and by no means can be attributed to my official affiliations.

Andrei A. Kokoshin
Moscow, August 1997

Introduction

Military questions have traditionally occupied a special place in Russia's domestic and foreign policy during the centuries of the Russian Empire, as well as during the Soviet era. In the Soviet period, the proclaimed goal of surpassing the industrialized capitalist countries in labor productivity was in fact eclipsed by the objective of securing preeminent military power.

One can hardly claim that no questions have been left unanswered in the extensive writings on the origins of the high level of militarization of the Soviet Union's economy and culture. Many scholars quite rightfully refer to the following as the source of that phenomenon: the leaders of the Soviet state had emerged from the Civil War in Russia, and they had no prior experience of governing the nation in peacetime. The October Revolution of 1917 and the Civil War of 1918–22, together with the ideology of the extreme radical faction of Russian social democrats that came into power, served to implant a sort of code that gave direction to Soviet military and strategic thinking and shaped the corresponding pattern of behavior.

Proceeding from a sharply biased ideological perception of the world, Soviet policy planners and military strategists for many decades advocated doctrinal objectives that were primarily oriented toward fighting an uncompromising and decisive war until the adversary was totally defeated and the ideas of socialism were triumphant worldwide. That line of thinking continued to prevail even in the years when it no longer corresponded to actual foreign policy practice. These ideological premises predetermined the nature of most Soviet strategic concepts and plans, as well as the composition, organizational strength, and deployment patterns of the Soviet armed forces.

The Soviet armed forces were viewed not so much as an instrument of the state but more as a tool of the Communist Party, which ruled with absolute authority. The Party directly managed the military through the agency of a broad network of political organs that had grown out of the revolutionary military councils and the institution of political commissars of the Civil War years, as well as via the security services, which were also subordinate to the Party.

The degree of control that the Party leadership held over the Soviet armed forces was, as in many other sectors, unprecedented. This control not only imposed rigid political and ideological constraints on the activities of the army and the navy, but also affected the everyday lives and cultural and social pursuits of practically every member of the armed forces. Though many political workers in the military were truly worthy and dignified people, most military professionals, who loyally served their homeland rather than the given political regime, regarded that oversight as unwelcome and even humiliating. The political supervision of the Soviet military could hardly be placed on a par with the systems of civilian leadership and control of the military that began to develop in Western Europe and North America in the nineteenth century and in many countries in Asia, Africa, and Latin America in the second half of the twentieth century. However, ultimately the time came when the all-pervasive system of control over the Soviet armed forces had grown ossified and increasingly self-serving and no longer continued to bolster the leading role of the Party.

The Russian Civil War was extremely bitter. It broke out and was fought in the conditions of total collapse and overmilitarization of the national economy that World War I had engendered. The trends of previous decades to expand the civilian sector of the economy and to create a civil society and parliamentary government in Russia were abruptly terminated as a result of World War I and the Civil War.

Soviet methods for mobilizing industry, agriculture, and the population as a whole in order to tackle large-scale tasks of national economic development had for the most part been borrowed from the experiences of the Civil War but also from the United Kingdom's and especially Germany's experiences with economic management during World War I. Those practices ultimately prevailed when it had become clear under the New Economic Policy (NEP) that neither the managing cadre nor government institutions could function effectively, and that the Bolsheviks, who turned out to be ill-prepared to manage the multistructured Soviet economy, faced the risk of losing their grip on power.

In the late 1920s and early 1930s, the Soviet Union became increasingly militarized. A type of economy was developing that was primarily targeted to satisfying the goals of a military buildup. Even sectors concerned with general economic matters, far removed from the tasks of supporting the development of the army and the navy, were for the most part managed in a military style. Moreover, the political repressions under Stalin produced the extensive gulag network of labor camps that engaged millions of convicts in all sorts of economic tasks ranging from logging to building state-of-the-art (for the time) weapons systems.

The rise to power of the National Socialists under Hitler and their drastic moves to remilitarize Germany gave a powerful impetus to the militarization of the Soviet Union. To counter the threat emerging in Germany, the Soviet Union mobilized vast resources, and the leading military planners, theoreticians, and weapons designers were set to this new task.

The Soviet victory in the Great Patriotic War of 1941–45 (as Russians call World War II) made an enormous contribution to the cause of preserving world civilization and building a new system of international relationships. The incredible losses that the Soviet peoples suffered, their selfless hard work in the rear, and unyielding efforts at the front were required to break the Nazi war machine, a powerful and well-run force that had conquered most of Europe.

The Soviet victory was particularly significant because the Wehrmacht's military traditions had never been interrupted—unlike in Russia. Despite Germany's defeat in World War I, vast numbers of German professionals, including the military intellectuals constituting the backbone of the armed forces and defense industries, were not pushed out of circulation. Even the 1944 purge in Germany following Colonel von Stauffenberg's failed attempt to assassinate Hitler was dwarfed by Stalin's peacetime repressions of 1937–38.

The end of World War II precipitated a gigantic shift in world politics, the second such shift in the short period of time since World War I and the October Revolution in Russia. The countries of Eastern and Central Europe, half of Korea, and Mongolia fell under the influence and even control of the Soviet Union. China, the world's most populous nation, became the Soviet Union's ideological, political, and military ally, though Moscow kept it in a state of dependence. Russia had not enjoyed such a huge increase in its influence at the peak of Peter the Great's rule, under Catherine the Great, or even after the defeat of Napoleon in 1814 when Russian troops marched through the streets of Paris.

In the post-war years, nuclear weapons created a totally new dimension in the political-military sphere by dramatically boosting the destructive power of weapons by several orders of magnitude. Within a very short period of time both the United States and, soon thereafter, the Soviet Union had nuclear weapons, which drastically reduced the risk of their use for military purposes as well as for political pressure.

Nuclear weapons eventually came to be perceived not only as military or political-military tools but also as status symbols that countries could use to establish their standing in the global hierarchy of nations. (It was not without reason that the three other permanent members of the United Nations Security Council—the United Kingdom, France, and the People's Republic of China—joined the nuclear club.) Nuclear weapons have had a tremendous impact on political-military and strategic thinking as a whole.

Regrettably, Soviet military thinking was too slow in recognizing the implications of nuclear weapons and the vast stockpiles that adversarial countries possessed. In the Soviet Union in the post-war period, and in the Russian Federation in the 1990s, the theory of nuclear deterrence was and remains insufficiently developed and poorly understood by the political elite and military command. This has eroded the political efficacy of nuclear weapons in Moscow's quest to further its national security objectives, and visibly devalues the huge infusions of resources made by several generations of our people to build the nuclear arsenal.

The break-up of the colonial system in the aftermath of World War II created opportunities for the Soviet Union to further expand its influence in the Third World, which the Soviet leadership did not fail to exploit. In the post-war era, the Soviet leadership chose to pursue a foreign policy that was very different from the strategy employed by the builders of the Russian Empire. Imperial Russia grew through the gradual accession of adjoining lands and their integration into what was considered Russia proper. The same strategy was applied by the tsars to build up a sphere of influence that typically exists on a nation's periphery. By contrast, the Soviet Union's efforts in that regard were largely focused on regions and countries that never crossed the minds of even the most ardent champions of Russia's expanding influence in prerevolutionary times. Indonesia, Chile, Nicaragua, Angola, and Mozambique are just a few of the countries that at various times in the post-war era received tremendous infusions of Soviet resources that surely could have produced better yields if they had been used to support other objectives, even within the framework of Soviet political strategies. Not only the economic but even the pressing geopolitical interests of Russia were sacrificed just to satisfy the ideological goals of the times.

History teaches that no empire has been built without the use of an organized military force. However, while trade was the driving force behind the creation of the British and Dutch colonial empires, and capital was used to engage the national military forces to secure and consolidate their imperial gains, this was not the case with Russia. Economic interests were not the tsars' top priority; rather, matters of national security as perceived by the political elite (of which the military class constituted a major portion), and often by most of the population, predominated.

The foreign policy of imperial Russia was always rather militarized. From the sixteenth through the nineteenth centuries, the threat of force and the actual use of force were generally accepted techniques of achieving political goals. For many countries, political goals comprised concrete, selfish mercantile interests, above all of the ruling elite, but shared by a large segment of the population, with a middle class playing a special role of its own. National self-interest became a powerful factor in the rise and growth of modern industrialized nations. But in Russia, in both the tsarist and Soviet eras, national self-interest was relatively weak.

One of the principal thrusts of Soviet foreign and military policy, particularly in the late 1950s and early 1960s, was supporting a number of national liberation movements around the world and socialist-leaning countries in the Third World. Russian resources were squandered on creating, maintaining, and developing three "empires" at once: the Third World community, the people's democracies (then integrated in the socialist commonwealth), and the Soviet Union's own outlying regions, above all Central Asia. The last was a relatively new part of the Russian state and differed drastically from the core of the empire that had been consolidated by the mid-nineteenth century, not only in terms of economic development but also in ethnic, cultural, and social characteristics.

In the 1960s, the global face-off between the Soviet Union and the United States and its allies in NATO and other areas was aggravated by the development of an acute ideological and military confrontation between the Soviet Union and the Chinese giant. The growing Sino-Soviet split stemmed from a conflict of interests between the Khrushchev leadership in Moscow and the Mao Zedong leadership in Beijing. Russia appeared to have fallen into an unenviable geopolitical situation for the first time since Tsar Nicholas I was left politically and diplomatically isolated on the eve of the Crimean War of 1853–56.

No country could have withstood such an enormous strain on its resources, no matter how strong its apparatus of social control or how great its human and material resources. Those three "empires" prevented resources from being invested in building up the ancient Russian territories, the core of the Soviet Union. The Russian countryside, which for hundreds of years had produced soldiers who repeatedly impressed the world with their heroic accomplishments when statesmen and military leaders could not cope, was now falling into utter decay.

The tremendous educational and cultural capacities of the peoples of the Soviet Union were never successfully directed to achieving higher levels of economic development and improved living standards for the population. The formation of a middle class that assures steady socioeconomic and political development in any contemporary nation was never completed in the Soviet Union.

The Soviet Union achieved the capability to produce sophisticated high-tech equipment, an attainment of which few industrialized nations could boast. Yet that important Soviet/Russian achievement was barely tapped to develop the national economy as a whole and improve the well-being of the Russian people. Technological advances were primarily applied in the military and nuclear fields. And the achievements of the Soviet nuclear power industry were darkened by the Chernobyl tragedy.

By modern standards, everyday life in the Soviet Union's multiethnic and multinational culture was underdeveloped. The importance of domestic culture to a country's self-identity in the world community and maintenance of genuine sovereignty was not recognized in the Soviet Union.

By contrast, primarily because of its highly developed domestic culture (so aptly appreciated by Charles de Gaulle and his followers), France managed to preserve its individuality and sovereignty in the post-war era despite unfavorable economic, ideological, political, and strategic circumstances. That factor also affected France's defense and defense-industrial policies, enabling it to be much less dependent on the United States than any other Western nation.

Developments in the late 1980s and early 1990s produced some welcome changes and major new shifts in long-suffering Russia. The attempts to reform the economy and achieve profound political transformations rapidly led to the collapse of all three Soviet "empires."

The break-up of the three "empires" dramatically shook Russia's armed forces, which are a crucial institution in any state. The idea that Russia's military efforts, so enormous and costly, had turned out to be superfluous and even counterproductive was broadly circulated. By any historical measure, the leadership of the Soviet Union and Russia had the shortest possible time frame in which to withdraw their troops from countries of the disintegrated Warsaw Treaty Organization and Mongolia, as well as from the former Soviet republics. This was an extremely painful and difficult experience for the Russian military, given the hardships that could not be avoided. Among the most obvious consequences of this massive withdrawal are the mountains of weapons stockpiled in the countries of the Commonwealth of Independent States (CIS) and in some parts of Russia. Spending levels for procurement of weapons systems and military equipment, as well as for defense-related research and development projects, have been radically reduced. The traditional mobilization system has fallen apart and no replacement has yet emerged.

A situation that is common throughout Russian history has arisen: the pendulum has swung from extreme militarization, both direct and indirect, in the opposite direction. A clear risk has emerged that Russia could lose its defensive capability, which would have grave implications for the nation's ability to effectively preserve its sovereignty.

Determining the optimal role of the armed forces and defense industries in the new Russia during the torturous birth of a civil society and democratic political system is critical. This niche should precisely conform to Russia's actual defense needs and the goal of maintaining a favorable balance of power in various regions of the world. Despite the urgency of this task, it is by no means easy to arrive at some optimal arrangement given the economic hardships Russia is experiencing today. However, this task could be aided by a sustained effort to develop new political-military and strategic thinking based on Russia's rich military heritage, fluctuations in Soviet military thought, and the lessons of Soviet military gains and losses in the last seventy years.

It is tragic that most of Soviet military theory of the 1920s and 1930s was largely ignored, which later resulted in the heavy losses sustained in World War II by the Soviet army, navy, and nation as a whole. The overwhelming majority of Russian military scholars and strategists of that era were purged and their writings were banned. The names of such great military thinkers as Snesarev, Verkhovsky, Zaionchkovsky, and Isserson remain less familiar to the Russian educated public than the names of foreign military scholars who were active in the same period like Douhet, Mitchell, Guderian, and Liddell Hart. However, one may hope that the works of the distinguished Russian military scholars of the Soviet period will be accepted as part of Russia's cultural heritage and that they will inspire those who deal with Russian national security and preserving the country's defensive capabilities to come up with fresh viewpoints and innovative ideas.

Of the forgotten military scholars of the early Soviet period, one in particular should be reintroduced: Aleksandr Andreyevich Svechin. A career military officer, Svechin had participated in two major wars (the Russo-Japanese War of 1904–05 and World War I), and his military writings delved into foreign and domestic policy as well as economics, to the benefit of military thought. According to Colonel (Ret.) V.M. Kulish, doctor of historical sciences and a veteran of the Soviet General Staff, Svechin's book *Strategy* was secretly consulted by many General Staff officers and Red Army commanders during the Great Patriotic War as a source of concrete advice and general wisdom.

Svechin's style is distinguished by clear-cut logic and a candid, scientific approach that is entirely free of any preconceived notions. Therefore much of this book focuses on his writings. Svechin was a general in the Russian imperial army and later served in the Red Army, and during the Soviet period he was purged twice. Svechin never ingratiated himself with the new authorities or defamed the past, but he did not shy away from pointing out the dark places in the political and military history of the prerevolutionary era.

Following the political purges of the late 1930s, numerous Russian and Soviet military and political-military thinkers were for many years almost totally excluded from Soviet intellectual life. Soviet military thought not only made no advances, but also in many ways rolled back entire decades. A nuanced understanding of the interplay between military theory and practice was almost lost for good. Small wonder, indeed, that many field commanders, as well as Party and government officials, were quite skeptical about military writings from that period.

In the 1980s, some decades after the developed Western countries had already initiated a similar effort, the Soviet Union engaged civilian experts in developing a set of political-military and military-economic concepts. Retired military researchers and experts were also actively involved. For many reasons, however, that task was never completed.

This was a common trend in the social sciences at the time, with many fields actually having to start afresh. Overall, the social sciences in Russia had been particularly hard hit by Soviet ideological and political teachings, obviously suffering far more than the natural sciences, which during the Soviet period produced numerous world-class achievements.

Although practically all ideological barriers were lifted in the Soviet Union during the period of *perestroika* (restructuring), no major breakthroughs were achieved in the social sciences. Many Russian social scientists took to writing on current affairs from a political or socioeconomic perspective. Apparently that development was inevitable, and it is largely worthwhile since it has laid the groundwork for a new stage in the evolution of the social sciences in Russia.

It is my hope that this book will in some measure contribute to the complicated but absolutely necessary process of formulating new approaches to Russian political-military and strategic theory as well as to resolving the extremely critical relationship between the army and politics, which is a very sensitive issue for the Russian state and society.

The materials on which this book is based are admittedly just the tip of the iceberg of Soviet military thinking. The high level of secrecy adopted in the Soviet Union in the 1930s resulted in open publications that only contained general writings on military matters, while most sensitive points and concrete issues were totally classified. One has to read between the lines and identify the undercurrents in Soviet military science, which had been closed to the outside world, in order to make some observations based on those materials. According to many Russian analysts, only large quantities of the materials spanning several decades produce a rather explicit and detailed picture of the Soviet Union's actual political-military strategy. Based on my own practical experience, I am inclined to support that assessment.

This book could have been more substantive if it had included a detailed and comprehensive analysis of the domestic and foreign political conditions in which Soviet political-military and strategic thought evolved. Regrettably, this context will only emerge in fragments, because space does not permit such an exhaustive account.

This book covers three themes: (1) the relationship between politics and military strategy; (2) an assessment of the threats to the Soviet Union's security, the nature of future war, and methods of warfare; and (3) the relationship between offense and defense in Soviet military strategy. Of course, in many instances the boundaries between these topics, particularly between the second and third themes, will seem highly conditional, which often happens in any historical, political, or sociological study. Meanwhile, questions about the relationship between politics and military strategy in today's world, with its vast nuclear arsenals, remain thought-provoking and are often the subject of sharp domestic political debates at the highest political levels.

As I examined the evolving assessment of threats to Soviet security, as well as of the nature of future war and methods of warfare, I attempted to apply my own investigative *modus operandi*, which integrates the following techniques:

- analyzing the general Soviet perception of the world, including the existing system of international relationships, the roots of major conflicts, and contradictions in them;
- identifying the principal sources of threats and their sociopolitical features;
- defining visions of future war, giving top priority to their political attributes and an analysis of the likely political goals of war (e.g., limited or all-out warfare);
- defining the major strategic attributes of future war, including its scope, the balance between trench warfare and maneuver warfare, the pace of war (i.e., fluid or protracted), the opening stage of war, and,

in the nuclear age, the likelihood of limited nuclear conflict or a large-scale war fought exclusively with conventional weapons by countries possessing nuclear weapons, etc.; and
- comparing the roles of different branches of the armed forces and various types of troops.

Chapter 1

The Relationship between Policy and Strategy in Soviet Military Doctrine

February 23, 1918, is considered the official birth date of the Red Army, since on that date Red Army detachments took part in their first armed clash, which took place with German forces moving toward Petrograd through Narva and Pskov. (The first decrees of the Council of People's Commissars on the formulation, organization, and management of the Soviet army and navy had been issued earlier, in January 1918.) Thus, three and a half months after the October Revolution, contrary to classical Marxist concepts about universal arming of the people, the Bolsheviks created a regular military instrument of political power. The Russian Civil War, which started in 1918 and ended in 1922, was characterized by extreme violence on a huge scale. In the words of Colonel General Dmitry A. Volkogonov, the Civil War was "one of the most brutal manifestations of total violence, not only in the military arena but also in the economic, social, and spiritual ones."[1]

The Russian Civil War was also an intense ideological battle involving numerous political forces and ideologies, many more than were involved in the American Civil War in the 1860s or the Spanish Civil War in the 1930s. About forty quasi state formations claiming sovereignty and the right to have their own armed forces emerged and vanished on the territory of the former Russian Empire, which was crisscrossed by a tangled web of political and military lines. The most unexpected military alliances were formed, and while most of them were short-lived, they influenced the course of events considerably. Vibrant personalities moved to the center of the political stage. The role they played in working out the theoretical relationship between policy and strategy and implementing it in practice was most remarkable.

---

1. D.A. Volkogonov, "Devyatyi val Vandi" (The ninth wave of Vandee), *Literaturnaya gazeta*, May 30, 1990.

Many features of the Civil War have not yet been examined thoroughly by Russian historians because of endemic shortcomings in historical scholarship both in the Stalin period and later. That is why my analysis relies mainly on writings from the Civil War period and oral history—personal recollections of friends of my grandfather and father, as well as of my own friends, that I happened to hear and stored in my memory.

Revolutionary Military Councils and Political Commissars

The extent to which politics penetrated military affairs in the young Soviet Republic was most vividly demonstrated by the creation of revolutionary military councils (*revvoensovety*) and the new post of political commissar at the republic, front, and army levels in 1918. The institution of commissars was further strengthened in March 1919 by the Eighth Congress of the Russian Communist Party (Bolsheviks), which was then the supreme governing body in the country.

Leon Trotsky, then commissar for military and naval affairs and chairman of the Revvoensovet of the Republic,[2] bluntly stressed at the All-Russian Congress of Military Commanders on June 7, 1918, the right of a commissar to exercise rigid control: "If a commissar sees a threat to the Revolution emanating from a military leader, the commissar has the right to deal mercilessly with the counterrevolutionary, including having him shot."[3]

Many well-known Party members belonged to the revolutionary military councils of fronts and armies and headed their political departments (*politotdely*), including Josef Stalin, Kliment Voroshilov, Bela Kun, S.I. Gusev (Drabkin), Ia.B. Gamarnik, Sergei M. Kirov, and Sergo Ordzhonikidze. Later many of those individuals held top Party and state positions. Revolutionary military councils existed in the military in modified form during the Great Patriotic War, and in the post-war years its role was taken by deputy commanders for political work and political departments within the armed forces. It was only in 1989–90 that the elimination of these political institutions was proposed, and in 1991 they ceased to exist.

These positions, which were in large measure analogous to the

---

2. A detailed analysis of the role of Leon Trotsky (Bronstein) in the October Revolution, the Civil War and post–Civil War period can be found in D.A. Volkogonov, *Trotskii. Politicheskii portret* (Trotsky. A political portrait), 2 vols. (Moscow: Novosti, 1992).

3. Central State Archives of the Soviet Armed Forces, collection 8, inventory 1, file 360, p. 1206.

political commissars of the convention during the French Revolution, were created because many Red Army units and formations were headed by commanders who either had a purely military background and lacked the necessary political outlook or had been officers and generals in the tsarist army, or the "old army" as it was called at the time. (After the fall of the Romanov monarchy in February 1917, the army stopped taking orders from the tsar but retained its structure and personnel.)

It is worth digressing here to point out that former tsarist officers were more numerous in the Red Army than is commonly recognized. The officer corps of the old army prior to the October Revolution was 250,000 strong. After the revolution, 30 percent served neither the Red nor the White Army during the Civil War. About 75,000 officers joined the Red Army,[4] many of whom were far from supporters of Soviet power; most of them were simply drafted.[5] There were, however, quite a few who thought that Soviet power was the only realistic alternative to the tsarist regime and the Provisional Government, and the only force capable of preventing the collapse of the huge country, which had been built with the blood of generations of Russian officers. Another important motivation for former tsarist officers to join the Red Army was that much of the White leadership was extremely dependent on foreign governments, and had promised them special rights and privileges in Russia if the Whites won the Civil War.

The idea of enlisting military specialists of the old regime in the revolutionary army can be traced to Friedrich Engels, who wrote in 1851 that a victorious proletariat should draw as many officers as possible to its side. Lenin himself praised the former tsarist officers: "You have heard about the series of brilliant victories won by the Red Army. There are tens of thousands of old colonels and other officers in its ranks. If we had not taken them into service and made them work for us, we could not have created the Army."[6] Moreover, "only with their help was the Red Army able to win the victories it did."[7] Trotsky was also an active advocate of

---

4. A.G. Kavtaradze, *Voennye spetsialisty na sluzhbe respubliki sovetov, 1917–1920* (Military specialists at the service of the republic of Soviets, 1917–1920) (Moscow: Nauka, 1988), p. 55; Geller, "*Nevernoe ekho proshlogo*" (A false echo of the past), *Druzhba narodov*, No. 9 (1989), p. 233.

5. See A.S. Bubnov, S.S. Kamenev, and R.P. Eiderman, eds., *Grazhdanskaya voina 1918–1921* (The Civil War 1918–1921), Vol. 2 (Moscow: Voennyi Vestnik, 1928), p. 95.

6. V.I. Lenin, speech delivered at the First All-Russia Conference on Party Work in the Countryside, November 18, 1919, in V.I. Lenin, *Collected Works*, Vol. 30 (Moscow: Progress Publishers, 1977), p. 147.

7. V.I. Lenin, speech at the meeting of the Moscow Soviet, March 6, 1920, in Lenin, *Collected Works*, Vol. 30, p. 413.

that policy. But at times debate raged over the role of former tsarist officers in the Red Army. At the Eighth Party Congress in March 1919, it was the main theme of speeches by delegates who represented the so-called "military opposition" ("left communists" formed the core). V.M. Smirnov, a leader of the military opposition, asserted that military specialists from the old army could not be entrusted with positions of command or operational tasks, and that at most they could play a consultative role. He opposed the strict discipline imposed by the army regulations, seeing it as a vestige of autocracy and serfdom. The military opposition was in favor of electing officers, which meant preserving the Red Army's guerrilla character. At the same time, this faction supported expanding the rights of Party cells in the army and giving them greater control over military affairs. Lenin, with the support of Stalin, Okulov, and Sokolnikov, came out against the ideas of the military opposition. Although the opposition resolution received 95 votes at the Congress, 174 delegates voted against it.

While the Council of People's Commissars and Revolutionary Military Council of the Republic provided political and strategic leadership during warfare, general military affairs were under the authority of the commander in chief (*glavkom*) and the commander of the field headquarters of the Revolutionary Military Council of the Republic (the General Staff of the Red Army). During the Civil War two former colonels of the tsarist General Staff, I.I. Vatsetis and S.S. Kamenev, served as *glavkom*, while former generals of the tsarist army N.I. Rattel, F.V. Kostyayev, and P.P. Lebedev served as staff commanders.

Numerous well-known Red Army officers and commanders had formerly sworn allegiance to the tsar, including: A.A. Kork, a former lieutenant colonel in the tsarist army, who commanded the Sixth Army of the Red Army; F.K. Mironov, a former sergeant major (lieutenant colonel) who commanded the Second Cavalry; A.I. Yegorov, former tsarist colonel, who commanded first the Tenth Army, and then the southern front, and was renowned for his defense of Tsaritsyn in 1916–19;[8] V.N. Yegoriev, a former lieutenant general who commanded first the southwestern and then the southern front; B.M. Shaposhnikov,[9] a former colonel who became commander of the operational department of the field headquarters of the

---

8. Alexander Ilyich Yegorov was named one of the five first marshals of the Soviet Union in 1935. He was commander of the Red Army General Staff and a deputy people's commissar of defense. He was killed during Stalin's purges of 1937–38.

9. Boris Mikhailovich Shaposhnikov became a marshal in 1940. He was appointed commander of the General Staff twice, in 1937–40, and during the Great Patriotic War, in 1941–42.

Revolutionary Military Council of the Republic; V.M. Altfater, a former rear admiral and the first commander of the Soviet Navy; and A.B. Nimitz, a former rear admiral, who was commander of the Soviet Navy in 1920–21.[10] Many of these officers were graduates of the tsarist Nikolayevskaya Military Academy of the General Staff, which was famous for its excellent training in general subjects like history, law, and foreign languages. A considerable number of military intellectuals from the tsarist army were engaged in research and teaching at Red Army institutions.

At the time of the Polish threat in 1920, Aleksei Andreyevich Brusilov, a cavalry general under the tsar and one of the most well-known Russian officers during World War I, joined the Red Army. He became renowned for the so-called "Brusilov breakthrough," an offensive he led in June and July 1916 on the southwestern front. By some estimates, this operation brought the Austro-Hungarian Empire to the brink of military disaster. From May to June 1917, following the fall of the Russian monarchy, Brusilov was supreme commander in chief under the Provisional Government. On May 2, 1920, Order No. 718 of the Revolutionary Military Council of the Republic appointed Brusilov the chairman of a special consultative body known as the *Osoboe Soveshchanie* under the commander in chief to solve operational problems in the Polish campaign.[11] After that body was disbanded, Brusilov became inspector of the Red Army Cavalry and carried out other special missions for the Revolutionary Military Council of the USSR.

Despite his high-level position in the Red Army, Brusilov was not unequivocally pro-Bolshevik, as can be seen from the second part of his memoirs, which were published in Russia only in 1989. In them he recalls that in 1920 E.M. Sklyansky, deputy people's commissar for military affairs and deputy chairman of the Revolutionary Military Council of the Republic, approached him with the suggestion that he go to the Crimea, where the remnants of Baron Wrangel's army were on the brink of defeat from decisive blows by the Red Army. Brusilov was supposed to make an appeal to White officers not to leave their homeland. Brusilov confessed: "I thought that Wrangel's army was at my command, along with those who were loyal to me in the country and in the ranks of the Red Army. Of course I would go to the South with the pentagram,[12] but would

---

10. Some Soviet historians believe that Alexander Vasilievich Nimitz (1879–1967), also spelled Nemitz, was a distant relative of the American admiral Charles Nimitz, who was famous for his achievements in World War II.

11. See the text of Order No. 718 in *Voennoe delo*, May 10, 1920, p. 1.

12. Brusilov meant the five-pointed red star that became the symbol of the Red Army.

return with the cross and cast down the usurpers, or at least the madmen."[13] He goes on to mention that "that very evening" he had invited several people whom he totally trusted but only met rarely to his rooms" to allocate duties. We discussed everything."[14] For unknown reasons, Brusilov's mission to the Crimea did not take place, but his appeal to Wrangel's officers not to flee the country was published in *Pravda*.[15]

We learn from the memoir of General Anton Ivanovich Denikin, a prominent leader of the White movement, that as early as 1917, Brusilov was considered a suitable candidate for the position of military dictator, along with Lavr Kornilov, another White general. Denikin himself preferred Kornilov (whose banner he followed in 1918), since Brusilov's record was, as he put it, "undermined by opportunism."[16]

A good many former tsarist junior officers also served in the Red Army, notably former *poruchik* M.N. Tukhachevsky; former *podporuchiki*[17] K.A. Avksent'evsky and I.P. Uborevich; and former ensigns R.P. Eideman, T.Kh. Eikhe, I.F. Fed'ko, A.V. Pavlov, and G.D. Gai. Almost all front commanders (with the exception of M.V. Frunze) and a large proportion of army commanders were former officers of the tsarist army. Later, particularly in the 1930s, old military specialists were deliberately belittled, a mission which Voroshilov zealously pursued. That approach prevailed in Soviet military literature until the 1980s, although in the late 1950s and early 1960s, during Khrushchev's "thaw," *Voenno-istoricheskii zhurnal* (*Military-Historical Journal*), under General N.G. Pavlenko, attempted to properly reevaluate the role of the former tsarist officers.

Another group of senior Red Army commanders during the Civil War comprised former warrant officers and regulars from the tsarist army who rose through the ranks on the basis of their merits. Although many of them were excellent organizers and tacticians, as a rule, they lacked the proper educational background; they compensated for that by training at the military academies of the Red Army or by self-education. It is worth mentioning V.K. Blukher,[18] commander of the Perekop shock group (1920)

---

13. A.A. Brusilov, "*Moi vospominaniya*" (My memories), Part 2, *Voenno-istoricheskii zhurnal*, No. 12 (1989), p. 57.

14. Ibid.

15. *Pravda*, September 12, 1920.

16. A.I. Denikin, "*Ocherki russkoi smuty*" (Outlines of Russian discord), *Voprosy istorii*, No. 5 (1990), pp. 143–144.

17. *Podporuchiki* is a Russian military rank approximating lieutenant.

18. Vasily Konstantinovich Blukher became one of the five first marshals of the Soviet Union in 1935. In 1937, he participated in proceedings against Tukhachevsky, and the

and military minister and commander of the People's Revolutionary Army of the Far Eastern Republic; B.M. Dumenko, commander of the United Mounted Corp; S.M. Budennyi,[19] commander of the First Cavalry; his brother-in-arms O.I. Gorodovikov (who was for some time the ineffective commander of the Second Cavalry); D.P. Zhlob, commander of the First Cavalry Division; N.D. Tomin, commander of the Zabaikal group of the Far Eastern Republic; and S.K. Timoshenko,[20] commander of the Fourth Mounted Division.

The revolutionary military councils restricted the activities of commanders of fronts and armies and interfered in operational issues, which contradicted the tsarist traditions to which the officer corps were accustomed. Even those Red commanders and troops who had never served in the tsarist army had complicated relations with the commissars. In some cases, however, commanders who came from a worker, peasant, or Cossack background were infected by what were then called "partisan sentiments," i.e., tendencies to show off, to demonstrate their individuality, and to detest any control. Behavior of this sort undermined military effectiveness and sometimes led to bloodshed, as in the mutiny of Ivan Sorokin,[21] commander of the Eleventh Army. Such collisions arose in the

---

next year Blukher himself fell victim to Stalin's purges. He was subjected to atrocious torture and then killed.

19. Semen Mikhailovich Budennyi also became one of the first five marshals in 1935. He was passed over by the purges. In 1941 and 1942, he was given command of fronts and proved unable to cope with that mission. As a result, he was demoted to commander of the Red Army Cavalry. However, after the Great Patriotic War, Budennyi was decorated as a Hero of the Soviet Union three times. He died in 1973, at the age of ninety.

20. Sergei Konstantinovich Timoshenko was people's commissar for defense from 1940 until 1944. He attained the rank of marshal of the Soviet Union in 1940. During the Great Patriotic War, he was a representative and member of the General Headquarters and commander of fronts and a sector (groups of fronts). He was decorated as a Hero of the Soviet Union twice, in 1940 and 1965. He died in 1970, at the age of seventy-five.

21. Sorokin, a Left Socialist Revolutionary, formed a revolutionary detachment in 1918 which fought against White Guards in the Kuban region. He was appointed acting commander of the Eleventh Army. Sorokin strove for unrestricted power, and by his secret orders some of his subordinates were arrested or shot. On October 21, 1918, in Pyatigorsk, he shot members of the central executive committee and the territorial committee of the Bolshevik Party of the North Caucasian Republic. On October 30, he was outlawed by the Emergency Congress of Soviets and arrested. Sorokin was killed in prison by one of the commanders. For details see *Grazhdanskaya voina 1918–1921*, Vol. 1, pp. 28–34; and *Grazhdanskaya voina i voennaya interventsiya v SSSR. Entsiklopediya* (The civil war and military intervention in the USSR. Encyclopedia) (Moscow: Sovetskaya Entsiklopediya, 1983), p. 557.

White Army as well.[22] Relations between commanders and political commissars were not easy during the Great Patriotic War either. In the late 1980s, the role of political departments in the armed forces came into question in the context of the drastically changing role of the Communist Party.

Many members of revolutionary military councils and political commissars proved to be fearless heroes and true leaders. The opinion is rather widespread in Russia that their activities during the Civil War were on the whole justified by the specific character of that war. At the time, however, their intrusion into purely military affairs, both strategic and tactical, more often than not was seen by commanders as ineffective or professionally uninformed. In many cases commanders resented these intrusions as infringements of their powers and authority.

As far back as January 1920, Mikhail Tukhachevsky, then a twenty-seven-year-old commander who had just distinguished himself in action on the eastern and southern fronts, bluntly rejected any political role in strategic matters: "The intrusion of politics into strategy is an extreme evil. To be successful in military operations, the commander in chief should enjoy complete authority. He should be entrusted unconditionally with matters of policy."[23] He was rather critical of revolutionary committees, calling them "a thorn in the flesh of our strategy."[24] Tukhachevsky was not the only one who held these views; rather, they reflected the prevailing mood in the armed forces. An article by a writer using the pen name "Alfa" published in *Voennoe delo* (*Military affairs*), then a leading military journal, was typical. Basing his judgments on his own service on a revolutionary military council, Alfa harshly criticized the performance of this institution and pointed out that the uninformed instructions of members of *revvoensovety* with sweeping authority, often not fully clarified, merely tied the hands of commanders.[25]

However, Tukhachevsky did advocate establishing a single, unified body to run the war in order to achieve optimal interaction between policy and strategy. "Harmony between policy and strategy," he wrote,

---

22. See, for example, Ia.A. Slashchev-Krymskii, *Belyi Krym, 1920* (White Crimea, 1920) (Moscow: Nauka, 1990).

23. M.N. Tukhachevsky, *Voina klassov* (War of the classes) (Moscow: Gosizdat, 1921), p. 36.

24. Ibid.

25. Alfa, "O rabote revvoensovetov armii i frontov" (On the work of revolutionary military councils of the army and fronts), *Voennoe delo*, No. 1 (1920), pp. 10–12.

"is best achieved when leadership is exercised by one actor. In our case, that role should be taken by the *Council of Defense.*"[26]

The Supremacy of Policy over Strategy

Many consider Tukhachevsky to have been the brightest star among the Soviet military men exterminated by Stalin. The aura of martyrdom, along with his writings and deeds, gained Tukhachevsky the reputation as the preeminent commander he truly was. Tukhachevsky foresaw many features of modern warfare and repeatedly insisted on the motorization of the army. He established paratroops, initiated research and development in rocket weaponry, and developed new strategic concepts. He impressed his contemporaries with many other gifts, a broad vision, and a fine educational and cultural background. Even now Tukhachevsky remains above criticism. Journalists, professional military historians, and general historians rhapsodize about his achievements. At the same time, little is said about Tukhachevsky's approach to political-military and strategic issues, although it is on these matters that his views seem to be rather controversial—indeed, as far back as the 1920s they were the subject of sharp debates.

Although it seems paradoxical, Tukhachevsky's major opponent on the issue of the relationship between policy and strategy was Aleksandr Svechin, a former tsarist general who had gone over to the Soviet army soon after the October Revolution, rather than becoming a political commissar or party functionary. Tukhachevsky and Svechin differed on other important issues; in particular the correlation of offense and defense in future wars, which will be discussed in greater detail later. On some specific and more narrow issues—for example, the navy's role in the Soviet armed forces—their approaches were similar.

Svechin was no less prominent a personality than Tukhachevsky. He gained popularity in the 1920s for his profound research on military theories, strategy, and campaign tactics, rather than for military victories in the Civil War. However, Svechin was no armchair strategist or mere theoretician (like, for example, the U.S. naval theoretician Alfred A. Mahan). After graduating from the Academy of the General Staff in 1903, Svechin joined the army and took part in the Russo-Japanese War. He fought in World War I as well, first as commander of an infantry regiment, which gave him a chance to comprehend everyday field life and the essence of war from inside a regiment, an important element of the war

---

26. Tukhachevsky, *Voina klassov*, p. 36. Emphasis in original.

machine. He ended his career in the tsarist army as a major general and commander of the army staff. In August 1918, Svechin became the second Soviet chief of the General Staff, which was later called *Vseroglavshtab* (All-Russian Main Staff). It is worth mentioning that Svechin assumed that post at an uneasy juncture: his predecessor, also a former tsarist officer, had just deserted to the Whites and had left behind a very negative impression of tsarist military professionals. Svechin held the job for only two months; in October 1918 he got involved in research and teaching at the Military Academy of the Red Army, which, as already noted, inherited much of the legacy of the Nikolayevskaya Academy of the General Staff.

I came across a formal description of Svechin signed by R.A. Muklevich,[27] a political commissar at the Academy and a former professional revolutionary. As Muklevich phrased it, Svechin was a well-rounded military specialist. "A highly talented individual and a witty professor, Svechin is one of the most valuable professors at the Military Academy. His classes in strategy, thanks to his unfailing originality of thought, always simple and witty, are one of the biggest achievements of the graduate course this year. . . . Paradoxical by nature, obnoxious in social and human interactions, he never misses an opportunity to get in a sly dig on the slightest pretext. However, he is extremely productive."[28]

Svechin matured as a theoretician and teacher under the great influence of N.P. Mikhnevich (1849–1927), a professor at the Nikolayevskaya Academy, and an outstanding representative of the Russian school of the art of war. In his main works, *Strategy* (*Strategiya*) and *Fundamentals of the Russian Art of War* (*Osnovy russkogo voennogo iskusstva*), Mikhnevich studied the relationship between foreign policy, military affairs, and what he called state organization, i.e., the political system of a state and its economic power. He never stopped believing in Russia's great potential, and even after its defeat in the war against Japan, Mikhnevich repeatedly stated that Russia had all the necessary prerequisites for both economic success and military victories. Thirty years older than Svechin, Mikhnevich was the forerunner of Svechin's school of military thinking.

---

27. Romuald Adamovich Muklevich had been a member of the Bolshevik Party since 1906. He participated in the February and October revolutions. During the Civil War he was commissar of the staff of the western front and a member of the *revvoensovet* for the front. In 1926–31, he was head of the Soviet navy and proved to be a respected theoretician of naval organization. He supported a relatively low-cost defensive fleet, designed to protect the country's seacoast. Stalin had him killed in 1938.

28. See A.A. Kokoshin, "*Svechin o voine i politike*" (Svechin on war and politics), *Mezhdunarodnaya zhizn'*, No. 10 (1988), p. 134.

Two years after the end of the Russian Civil War, Svechin's first fundamental work, *History of Military Art* (*Istoriya voennogo iskusstva*), came out in three volumes. This work remains in many ways unsurpassed, not only in Soviet military literature, but probably in world literature on military matters. The supremacy of politics over strategy is one of Svechin's major themes, which he further developed in his main book, *Strategy*, published in 1926, with a second edition in 1927 (an English translation was published in the United States in 1992).[29] In *Strategy*, Svechin explicitly states that politics is superior and should be allowed to interfere in military strategy and operations. This stance directly contradicts Tukhachevsky's position. However, Svechin did not criticize Tukhachevsky's views directly in his book. Svechin selected French General Jules Louis Leval and three Germans, Helmuth von Moltke the elder, Erich Ludendorff, and Paul von Hindenburg, as the objects of his critical analyses. In Leval's view, wrote Svechin, war should be studied in isolation, as a gigantic duel between two nations. Political leaders should focus on policy, while generals should concentrate on strategic matters. For Leval, politics is related to war only to the extent that it determines how great a sacrifice the nation must make in peacetime to support the armed forces. In wartime, politics continues to function independently of military plans. Discussing strategic issues with politicians, Leval maintained, leads to anemia, a loss of will and energy. Politics debilitates strategy, it accumulates delusions and errors, erodes the willingness to act, and creates anxiety. A politician with a good understanding of military matters is a chimera. A military leader must not allow political issues to distract him from his immediate responsibilities.

The elder Moltke, Ludendorff, and Hindenburg, all well-known German military leaders, held similar views on the relationship between politics and strategy. Svechin contrasted their approach to that of Bismarck, who had defended the right of politics to influence strategy. "In our opinion, the claim that politics is superior to strategy is universal in nature," Svechin wrote. "It is natural for strategy to try to gain emancipation from bad politics, but strategy cannot exist in a vacuum without politics and is condemned to pay for all the sins of politics."[30] The "political brainlessness" of Germany in the early 1900s, he not unreasonably noted, helped German strategy to free itself from political directives.

The numerous references to German experiences in Svechin's works and in those of other Soviet specialists are not accidental. Throughout

---

29. Aleksandr A. Svechin, *Strategy* (Minneapolis, Minn.: East View Publications, 1992).

30. Ibid., p. 85.

world history, there has never been another state that could compete with Prussia and Germany in the organization and efficiency of its military machine—an efficiency, moreover, that was maintained and restored by several generations from the mid-nineteenth century to the mid-1940s. Russia and later the Soviet Union had to face German military might in both world wars. One should also be aware of the tradition of political-military, political, and cultural interaction between Russia and Germany to understand why Russia pays so much attention to German military thought.[31]

The impressive German military machine was the product of the efforts of the political elite, Germany's economic potential, the socioeconomic traditions of a significant part of the population, and the country's geopolitical position. As a derivative of politics and economics, however, the German armed forces had a more complex relationship to politics than mere subordination. While it would be an overstatement to say that the German military machine overrode politics, it often had a greater impact on policy than was the case in other European nations. In the final analysis it cost the German people far too much.

Germany also begot Carl von Clausewitz, the greatest military thinker, who developed the classic definition of the relationship between policy and war. In the first chapter of his well-known work, *On War*, Clausewitz wrote: "War is merely the continuation of policy by other means."[32] (Because Engels and Lenin both called attention to that particular phrase, it became very well-known in the Soviet Union.) Clausewitz went on to say that "war is not a mere act of policy but a true political instrument, a continuation of political activity by other means." With regard to specific features of war and means of war, he noted:

What remains peculiar to war is simply the peculiar nature of its means. War in general, and the commander in any specific instance, is entitled to require that the trends and designs of policy shall not be inconsistent with these means. That, of course, is no small demand; but however much it affects political aims in a given case, it will never do more than modify them. The political object is the goal, war is the means of reaching it, and means can never be considered in isolation from their purpose.[33]

---

31. Many Germans were in the service of Ivan the Terrible in the sixteenth century. Later Peter the Great invited Germans in particular to join the Russian army, as well as Scots, Austrians, Dutch, and other West Europeans.

32. Carl von Clausewitz, *On War*, ed. and trans. Michael Howard and Peter Paret (Princeton, N.J.: Princeton University Press, 1976), p. 87.

33. Ibid.

Clausewitz repeatedly pointed out that "war should never be thought of as *something autonomous* but always as an *instrument of policy*." This interpretation, according to Clausewitz, "will show us how wars must vary with the nature of their motives and of the situations which give rise to them."[34]

Lenin added his Marxist analysis to Clausewitz's interpretation, focusing on the role and interests of various classes in war, including origins, impact, and results. "Marxists regard war as a continuation of the policies pursued by certain governments representing defined classes," according to Lenin.[35] As he repeatedly pointed out, Marx and Engels considered war a continuation of the policy of certain interested states and specific classes within those states in a certain historical context.

Soviet studies of Lenin's writings that were written in the 1980s observed that there are three types of relationships between politics and armed struggle.[36] First, there is the *cause-and-effect* relationship. A war starts when aggressive policy demands military conflict and opposing political groups are not able to prevent it. Second is the *substantive* relationship. Politics defines the social and historical significance of a given war, determining whether it is progressive or reactionary. Third is the so-called *management* relationship. Politics runs war and the whole life of the country during wartime, mobilizing its full potential in order to win. The political goal greatly impacts the way war is waged. The cardinal link in this relationship is the political leadership's determining role in military strategy.

A study of Lenin's works also shows that he was mainly concerned with the genesis of war, the cause-and-effect connection between politics and war, and how this interrelationship is manifested in the character of war. As Lenin noted in a discussion among socialists on how to evaluate and approach war from a Marxist perspective, the key issues were the reasons for war and the classes that paved its way and waged it.

In the 1920s, when Soviet military doctrine was evolving, the "management" relationship between politics and war was an urgent issue. Any recourse to European political-military thought inevitably led to the

---

34. Ibid., p. 88.

35. V.I. Lenin, "In the Footsteps of Russkaya Volya," *Collected Works*, Vol. 24, p. 116.

36. The most important work is E.I. Rybkin, "*Leninskie printsipi filosofsko-sotsiologicheskogo analiza voin i sovremennost*" (Lenin's principles for the philosophical and sociological analysis of war and the present), in A.S. Milovidov, ed., *Voenno-teoreticheskoe nasledie V.I. Lenina i problemy sovremennykh voin* (The military-theoretical heritage of V.I. Lenin and problems of modern wars) (Moscow: Voenizdat, 1987), pp. 51–52.

works of German military thinkers. Indeed, military men in many countries and with varied social orientations were receptive to the views of Moltke the elder on the management relations between politics and military affairs, the essence of which are contained in his *Military Lectures of Field Marshal Count Moltke*. As mentioned above, Tukhachevsky and a number of other Soviet commanders in his circle held views that were similar to Moltke's.

Basically accepting Clausewitz's approach, Moltke wrote: "Thus politics, unfortunately, is inseparable from strategy." For Moltke, however, the scope of political interference in strategy is limited: "Politics is used to achieve the aims of war, and it has a decisive impact on war's *beginning and end*." At the same time, however, Moltke recognized the right of politics "to raise its demands or be content with less success during the war."[37] He held that "politics must not interfere with operations," underscoring that

the course of war is guided by military considerations, while political ones are at the forefront only if they demand nothing militarily unacceptable. A military leader should never be guided only by political motives, but should make success in war the primary concern. How politics should use victory or defeat is none of the military leader's business—this is the business of politics.[38]

In drawing this particular conclusion, Moltke does not seem absolutely sincere. His disputes with Bismarck over how to use German victories in the Austrian-Prussian War of 1866 and the Franco-Prussian War of 1870–71 were sharp indeed.[39]

It is worth mentioning that the first Soviet edition of Moltke's *Military Lectures*, which came out in 1938, omitted the chapters on "War and Peace" and "War and Politics." In the preface to the Soviet edition, Moltke's ideas on these subjects were harshly criticized: " . . . Moltke's view on war and the interaction between war and politics inspired the German military clique which, among other things, impacted the methods of Chief of Staff von Schlieffen prior to the imperialist war."[40] The

---

37. *Voennye poucheniya feldmarshala grafa Moltke* (Military lectures of Field Marshal Count Moltke) (St. Petersburg: Empress Catherine the Great Military Printing House, 1913), p. 14. Emphasis added.

38. Ibid.

39. For more details, see A.A. Kokoshin, "Bismark i Moltke" (Bismarck and Moltke), *Mezhdunarodnaya zhizn'*, No. 7 (1990).

40. Field Marshal Moltke, *Voennye poucheniya. Operativnaya podgotovka k srazheniyu* (Military lectures. Operational preparation for battle) (Moscow: Voenizdat, 1938), p. 9.

authors of the preface drew a line from Moltke to Ludendorff, and from Ludendorff to the leaders of Nazi Germany:

Later Moltke's approaches manifested themselves in the demands of the German military clique that "all politics should serve war" (Ludendorff, *Conducting War and Policy*, Berlin: 1922). From there it is but one more step to the fascist interpretation of the slogan of "total war," which makes the core and foundation of politics the preparation for and waging of a predatory war for a new partition of the world, and an extremely brutal terroristic regime at home.[41]

Underlining the superiority of politics over strategy and the political leadership's right to intervene in decisions on strategic and tactical matters, Svechin repeatedly stated that political decisions must also be consistent with strategy and military potential, and that political leaders must listen to the opinions of military professionals and learn how the military machine and the government's mobilization mechanisms function:

Responsible politicians should be familiar with strategy. . . . [A] politician who sets a political goal for military operations must have an idea of what is feasible for strategy given the resources available and how politics may affect the situation for better or for worse. Strategy is one of the most important tools of politics, and even in peacetime political calculations must to a great extent be based on the military capabilities of friendly and hostile nations.[42]

Svechin also pointed out that studying strategy was important to all commanders of the armed forces. He wrote that

the study of strategy by just a small circle of commanders, such as the general staff, leads to the creation of a 'strategic caste' . . . and it creates an undesirable gap between strategists and tacticians among commanders and destroys mutual understanding between staffs and line units. Strategy should not become a kind of Latin which separates the believers and the nonbelievers![43]

Svechin maintained that the art of strategy should be studied by all command personnel, since not only commanders of fronts and armies but commanders of corps would also fail to carry out their missions successfully if they were incapable of clear strategic thinking.

Elaborating on institutional aspects of the relationship between

---

41. Ibid.
42. Svechin, *Strategy*, p. 74.
43. Ibid., p. 76.

politics and strategy, Svechin paid particular attention to the specific role of general staffs, which "introduced the spirit of systematic routine to preparations for war, which is the main achievement of bourgeois thought." In his view, "in the epoch of imperialism . . . the General Staff should evaluate all peacetime life from a special perspective—the perspective of planning war." He explained that

[if] the balance between the General Staff and political leadership is upset, a threat to peace emerges. The General Staff from its own perspective would always be inclined toward the idea of preventive war . . . toward declaring war at the moment when we enjoy maximum advantages in preparedness in comparison with the competing state, advantages which could be brought to zero as a result of the latter's efforts in coming years, or could even turn into disadvantages.[44]

Svechin noted that in 1875, when the Prussian General Staff demanded a preventive war against France in the face of France's efforts to rebuild its military power, on the one hand, and a possible Russian-French alliance, on the other, Bismarck successfully "managed to resist those attempts to turn politics into a servant of strategy."[45]

Arguing against some Soviet and foreign authors, Svechin pointed out that "mistaken policies will also bear the same pitiful fruit in war as they do in any other field, but one should not confuse protests against political errors with refusal to acknowledge the right and obligation of politics to determine the basic direction of a war."[46]

The Evolution of a "Unified Military Doctrine"

Intermittent discussions between 1920 and 1923 on a "unified military doctrine" for the Red Army probably played a central role in the formulation of an overall scheme for managing the interaction between politics and military strategy. Some participants in these discussions recalled the tsarist army's attempts to develop and adopt a unified military doctrine prior to World War I. Both advocates and opponents of such a doctrine had participated actively in the prerevolutionary debates on the issue.[47]

---

44. Svechin, "Recent Times, 1814–1914," in *Istoriya voennogo iskusstva* (History of the art of war), Part 3 (Moscow: Supreme Military Council, 1923), p. 112.

45. Ibid.

46. Svechin, *Strategy*, pp. 84–85.

47. See P. Zhilin, "*Diskussiya o yedinoi voennoi doktrine*" (Discussion on a unified military doctrine), *Voenno-istoricheskii zhurnal*, No. 5 (1961), pp. 12–23.

General V.E. Borisov suggested that A.V. Suvorov's *Science Triumphs* (*Nauka pobezhdat*) should serve as the basis for a unified doctrine,[48] with the new historical situation taken into account. According to Borisov, the core of Russian military doctrine should be a bold offensive strategy and tactics that, in his opinion, corresponded to the nature of the Russian soldier and could bring victory in a future war. Generals A.G. Elchaninov and A.A. Neznamov also espoused a unified military doctrine. Neznamov, a professor at the Nikolayevskaya Military Academy, advocated a unified military doctrine that envisaged broad preparations on the part of the nation, the state, and the people for a forthcoming war.[49] Quite a few generals and senior officers of the tsarist army, including L. Zaionchkovsky, E. Krivtsov, N. Adaridi, and F. Ogorodnikov, opposed the concept of a unified doctrine. They argued that such a doctrine could paralyze the thinking and initiative of the military leadership.[50] After the October Revolution, some of the participants in these debates—e.g., Neznamov and Zaionchkovsky—became well-known theoreticians in the Red Army.

A number of doctrinal principles were included in the tsarist army's field regulations and in a 1912 directive "On the Field Operation of Troops." Immediately after the release of this directive, a special decree prohibited any further discussion of military doctrine. This decree of 1912 was based on Tsar Nicholas II's order to the chief of the Academy of the General Staff, the chief of the General Staff, and the editor in chief of *Russkii invalid*, which was then the main military theoretical journal. As the tsar bluntly phrased it in his order to General R.R. Yanushkevich, who headed the Academy, "Military doctrine is what I say it is. I ask you to convey to Neznamov that it should no longer be discussed. I shall ask *Russkii invalid* to do the same."[51]

---

48. Generalissimo Prince Alexsandr Vasilievich Suvorov (1730–1800) is rightly regarded as one of the greatest Russian military leaders. He won celebrated victories in Catherine the Great's wars against Turkey, and when he was well advanced in years, against revolutionary France in northern Italy. He inflicted defeats on such outstanding generals as Moreau, Joubert, and Macdonald. He helped put down the Polish revolt of 1768 and Emelian Pugachev's uprising in Russia in 1774.

49. *Historiya pervoi mirovoi voiny 1914–1918* (History of World War I, 1914–1918), Vol. 1 (Moscow: Nauka, 1975), pp. 182–183.

50. Ibid., p. 183.

51. *Voennoe delo*, No. 2 (1920). It was Svechin who fueled the discussion of the Red Army's military doctrine. In 1920, he wrote a report entitled "Military Doctrine"(*"Voennaya doktrina"*), which was later published in the second issue of *Voennoe delo*. Unfortunately, I have not been able to find a complete text of that work, and in referring to it, I am relying on the recollections of Svechin's colleagues. (It is important to bear in

The most interesting ideas on the essence and underpinnings of military doctrine were generated by A. Neznamov, I. Vatsetis, and I. Uborevich. Neznamov, for example, recommended incorporating the following three points into the doctrine:

- *The view on war* of a given society and government, or better still, of the whole people if it is mature enough for that. Foreign policy will be conducted and the armed forces organized (including economics and the rearing of children) in accordance with this approach.
- *Modern, purely military approaches to the use of the armed forces in war.* This is what is found in "Main Instructions for Senior Commanders of Troops" in the German case and in "Règlement sur la conduite des grandes unités" in the French case.
- As a product of the two preceding points:
  (a) *field regulations*, the modern catechism for second-tier commanders, and
  (b) *other regulations*, rallying points for the masses in the army.[52]

In other words, Neznamov suggested that matters of supreme political-military importance and matters of strategic and tactical importance should be systematically combined within the framework of military doctrine. Uborevich disagreed: "This definition seems too broad because it embraces fields not directly related to doctrine." In his view, "doctrine is instruction, and military doctrine is military instruction; but this definition is too general. A more particular one is that military doctrine is an understanding by the intellectual forces of a given military world of the essence of war and of the options of troops in various situations."[53]

Vatsetis, for his part, avoided considering questions of high military and strategic significance. He stressed the need to develop unified tactical approaches, giving special emphasis to an increasing role for new technological means of waging war. In this regard Vatsetis sharply criticized pre-war Russian traditions of the "cold steel doctrine," i.e., reliance on the infantry's bayonet charge and the cavalry's attack with drawn swords,

---

mind that during and after Stalin's purges of 1937–38, all publications in any way related to the victims were removed from Soviet libraries and destroyed. Many materials used in this book were given to me by the owners of private libraries and collections of papers who had kept them at the risk of arrest.)

52. A. Neznamov, "*Voennaya doktrina*" (Military doctrine), *Voennoe delo*, No. 4 (March 22, 1920), p. 98.
53. I. Uborevich, "*O voennoi doktrine*" (On military doctrine), *Voennoe delo*, No. 10 (1920), p. 291.

which resulted in great losses during World War I.[54] Vatsetis's conception of military doctrine seems fairly close to what is currently accepted in the West, including in the United States.

Quite a few Red Army commanders and political workers were unable to take part in this debate because they were at the front, but the dialogue resumed after the Civil War and the Soviet-Polish war had ended. At that stage, the pronouncements of Mikhail Frunze, then commander in chief of Ukraine and the Crimea, were particularly noteworthy.

Frunze was a professional revolutionary who became a prominent military leader and military theoretician. To call him the "Soviet Clausewitz"[55] would probably be an overstatement, although the range and depth of his theoretical analysis of military issues were impressive. He was born in 1885 into the family of a military medical attendant and was educated at the St. Petersburg Technical Institute. For his revolutionary activities Frunze was twice sentenced to death; both times the sentence was reduced to lifetime exile, from which he escaped. Frunze participated in the October 1917 armed uprising in Moscow. As a commander of the southern group of the eastern front and later commander of the eastern front, he led a number of successful offensive operations against the White Admiral Alexander Kolchak's troops in 1919. Afterward Frunze effectively commanded the Turkestan front and became famous for his performance as a commander of the southern front, where he inflicted the final blow against the White Army under Wrangel in the Crimea in 1920.

Frunze assumed that there was no clear definition of a "unified military doctrine," and instead tried to focus on a series of "general ideas and practical steps stemming from them" that would comprise that concept. He believed that the military apparatus, guided by general state policy, would ensure the unity of the armed forces, instilling a common outlook on the nature of military missions and how to conduct them. As Frunze noted, military doctrine first and foremost should indicate the nature of military confrontation that awaits the country and the kinds of actions it should take in organizing its armed forces. Doctrine should address the question of whether the nation should prepare for a passive defense or should develop forces capable of offensive operations.[56]

---

54. I. Vatsetis, "*Doktrina shtyka i ognya*" (The doctrine of bayonet and fire), *Krasnaya armiya*, No. 16–17 (1920), pp. 33–34.

55. See W.D. Jacobs, *Frunze: The Soviet Clausewitz, 1885–1925* (The Hague: Martinus Nijhoff, 1969).

56. M.V. Frunze, *Izbrannye proizvedeniya* (Collected works), Vol. 2 (Moscow: Voenizdat, 1957), p. 7.

After summarizing the views of various military writers, Frunze pointed out two dimensions of doctrine, the technical and the political. The technical dimension, he wrote, comprises everything relating to the organization of the Red Army, the kind of preparation for combat that troops should undergo, and the means of achieving combat goals. The political dimension includes the dependence of the technical dimension on the general structure of the state, which defines the social environment for military work and the nature of military missions.

Frunze was well versed in history. Unlike many other commanders of the Red Army who had not been trained at the Nikolayevskaya Academy, Frunze was able to incorporate the experience of other states in his conception of a unified military doctrine. His appraisal of Germany under the kaisers is worth quoting: "Until now Germany has been a state with a very powerful military apparatus, a well-balanced system of military organization, and a clear-cut military ideology shared both by leading elements like the army and by the entire nation."[57] The clearly articulated offensive character of the technical dimension of German military doctrine seemed to appeal to Frunze. "The major feature of German military doctrine in its technical (i.e., purely military) dimension is an extremely pronounced offensive spirit. . . . Training and education of troops were conducted on the basis of offensive tactics and, in the final analysis, yielded a perfect military force . . . which later demonstrated its outstanding fighting capabilities on the gigantic battlefields of the imperialist war."[58] His appraisal of the German General Staff's performance was also extremely positive.

Frunze explained the reasons for the high level of German military development prior to World War I as follows:

Economically and politically, [Germany] was a powerful capitalist state with a pronounced imperialist complexion, which pursued a predatory policy and sought world domination on the basis of its material and cultural resources. Its major competitors among the imperialist states (France, Britain, Russia, and others), which historically had become nation-states earlier than Germany and had already grabbed the best parts of the world as prey, made Germany put all its strength into the struggle for a global position.[59]

In Frunze's view, the French military machine and doctrine were not as strong as their German counterparts: "Despite the French army's rich

---

57. Ibid., p. 8.
58. Ibid., p. 9.
59. Ibid., p. 11.

military traditions, from the great Turenne to Napoleon, and despite their excellent models of the art of war based on daring offensive strategy and tactics, the military doctrine of the Third Republic was no match for that of the Germans."[60]

Svechin gave a high, but more critical, appraisal of the German military machine and military doctrine in World War I. He pointed out many deficiencies, and in his subtle and acute manner, reasonably concluded the following: "The German military leadership was talented. It was probably only one inch shorter than the height needed for victory, but it is precisely that missing inch which differentiates the genius from an ordinary mortal."[61] (This remark of Svechin's also seems to apply to the German military leaders' performance during World War II. They planned and carried out a number of highly successful and even brilliant operations, but at many critical points they were not at their best.) In general, however, Germany's military doctrine, military strategy, and approach to war received high marks from many Soviet writers.[62]

The admiration (sometimes mixed with envy) with which many Soviet military commanders viewed German military achievements in large measure made possible the cooperation between the Red Army and the Reichswehr of the Weimar Republic in the late 1920s and early 1930s. During this period the Soviet Union and Germany, which had both been seriously affected by the Versailles peace treaty, were drawing closer to each other on a number of political and military issues.

Forbidden by the Treaty of Versailles from operating officer training centers on its own territory, Germany established such centers, as well as tank and aviation training centers, in the Soviet Union. A.M. Vasilevsky, marshal of the Soviet Union and chief of the General Staff during World War II, recalled that the Soviet maneuvers of 1932, which were supposed to demonstrate the merits of large (for the time) mechanized units—i.e., tank brigades—were attended by the military attachés of several countries, including Germany. The German guests were shown everything,

---

60. Ibid.

61. A.A. Svechin, "*Itogi grazhdanskoi strategii*" (The results of civilian strategy), *Voennoe delo*, No. 20 (1919), p. 659.

62. In 1926, G. Isserson, a promising young Soviet theoretician, made a significant comment in his book on Samsonov's army: "The superiority of German strategic thought manifested itself not only in the East Prussian operation, but throughout the imperialist war of 1914–1918. Learning from the actions of our former adversary can serve to instill in our command staff a high level of strategic thinking, boldness, a will to win, and accuracy and clarity in operational work." G. Isserson, *Kanny mirovoi voiny (gibel' armii Samsonova)* (The Cannae of the world war [The ruin of Samsonov's army]) (Moscow: Gosvoenizdat, 1926), p. 3.

whereas the representatives of other armies were allowed to watch only part of the exercise. The Germans were taken by different routes in separate cars to places kept secret from the other foreign guests. Von Brauchitsch, who was present at the maneuvers (he later became a general field marshal and a commander of an army group during the German invasion of the Soviet Union in 1941), complimented the Red Army by declaring that everything he had observed was done "in the best traditions of the German military school." Everyone seemed pleased to hear that remark, Vasilevsky recalled.[63]

After Hitler seized power in 1933, the Soviet Union's relationship with Germany drastically changed. The German military training centers were closed down, and the military relationship between the two countries became increasingly hostile. Military plans were reconsidered. Many of those who had participated in earlier contacts between the two sides became irreconcilable enemies on the battlefields of World War II.

In 1922, Frunze suggested the following definition of "unified military doctrine," which later came to be considered its classic formulation:

"Unified military doctrine" comprises the teachings adopted by the army of a particular state which establish the character of the development of the armed forces and the methods used in combat training and troop management based on the state's prevailing views on the nature of the military missions lying before it and the means of executing them, which reflect the class nature of the state and are determined by the country's level of economic development.[64]

Frunze emphasized, however, that his definition should not be considered final, complete, and logically perfect.[65] Despite his authority in political and military matters, Frunze's concept of a unified military doctrine was not accepted immediately. Indeed, there was a time when it was on the verge of being rejected. In April 1922, during the 11th Congress of the Russian Communist Party (Bolsheviks), the military delegates held their own meeting, where they discussed fifteen theses on the unified military doctrine that had been proposed by Frunze and adopted at an earlier gathering of officers from Ukraine and the Crimea. Leading theoreticians

---

63. K.M. Simonov, "*Besedy s Marshalom Sovetskogo Soyuza A.M. Vasilievskii*" (Conversations with Marshal of the Soviet Union A.M. Vasilevsky), in *Glazami cheloveka moego pokoleniya* (Through the eyes of a person of my generation) (Moscow: Novosti Press, 1989), pp. 442, 448.
64. Frunze, *Selected Works*, Vol. 2, p. 8.
65. Ibid.

of the day, like Neznamov and Svechin, were neither delegates to the congress nor members of the Party. Although they actually initiated the discussion of a unified military doctrine, they did not participate in the debate at the congress, which made the discussion less interesting and not as far-reaching.

What was the essence of this "unified military world view" corresponding to Frunze's proposals? It was that

the existence of deep and principled contradictions between the structure of proletarian statehood, on the one hand, and the surrounding bourgeois capitalist world, on the other, makes confrontation and struggle between these two feuding worlds inevitable. Thus the aim of political education in the Red Army is to maintain and enhance its constant preparedness to fight against world capital.[66]

Leon Trotsky, who was then the people's commissar for military and naval affairs and chairman of the national *revvoensovet*, was critical of Frunze and his supporters (who included important political functionaries such as S.I. Gusev and K.E. Voroshilov). His report analyzing the theses was characteristically caustic.[67] He called the authors of the fifteen theses "the champions of scholasticism and utopianism" and added:

The history of war, like the history of architecture, could be rewritten from the Marxist point of view since history is a [social] science. But the so-called theory of war is quite another thing. . . . With the help of Marxist methodology one could explain the sociopolitical and international orientation [*orientirovka*] in a positive way. . . . But one cannot base field regulations on Marxism. The mistake here is that under a military doctrine or, even worse, a "unified military world view," they understand our general state line, both foreign and domestic, our practical military methods, rules, and suggestions for regulations, and interpret them anew with the help of Marxist methodology. But our state orientation has long been formed by Marxist methodology and there is no need to form it again in the bosom of the military administration.[68]

---

66. *Voennyi vestnik*, No. 5–6 (1922), p. 33.

67. See *Osnovnaya voennaya zadacha momenta: Diskussiya na temu o edinoi voennoi doktrine* (The basic military mission of the moment: Discussion on the subject of the unified military doctrine), verbatim report of the second day of the meeting of military delegates of the 11th Party Congress, April 1, 1922, stenographic notes (Moscow: *Visshii Voennyi Redaktsionnyi Sovet* [Supreme Military Editorial Council], 1992). (The report carried the notice, "Not for sale. Sale will be prosecuted by law as plundering of public property.")

68. Ibid., p. 64.

Tukhachevsky's speech at the meeting mainly supported Frunze: "We shall certainly need unity. I believe that we should make achieving such unity a goal.... If we content ourselves with polishing boots and sweeping floors, we shall not reach all our objectives because our objectives are broader than the tactics of a petty few—there is still strategy."[69] It is worth mentioning that in this speech and later observations, Tukhachevsky did not repeat his views on the autonomy of the strategist from politics and did not criticize the revolutionary military councils. He seemed to have divorced himself from the ideas he had put forward in January and now held more balanced views on the relationship between politics and strategy. Thus, in his work entitled "On the issue of modern strategy"("*K voprosu o sovremennoi strategii*"), Tukhachevsky wrote: "War is a continuation of politics by other means. However, this principle does not mean that politics comes to a halt during wartime. Comrade Lenin stated this principle the following way: 'war is a continuation of politics! And politics continues during war.'" Moreover, unlike Moltke and Ludendorff, Tukhachevsky acknowledged that "diplomacy does not stop once war is declared."[70] He underscored that war is "a most decisive and powerful means of implementing policy, and therefore it was necessary to upgrade the level of organizational preparedness for war in every possible way. Without that, even a strong economy did not assure success." He continued: "British imperialism crushed German imperialism, but the victory was worse than Pyrrhic. Germany endured much greater strain than Britain and France, but thanks to an exceptionally high level of combat training in the army and a relatively high level of national preparedness, it cost the German bourgeoisie less, and now economically Germany is growing faster and with more success than the victors."[71]

Unfortunately, Tukhachevsky's opposition in the late 1920s to political interference in military strategy, which he voiced so fervently and resolutely, remained in the memory of those who later developed the case against him, a case that ended with his execution by firing squad in 1937.

Trotsky's speech at the 11th Party Congress itself was in the same spirit as his speech at the meeting of the military delegates. He stated: "I think that a unified military doctrine, new means of waging war, and all debates on these issues are of secondary importance. What is more

---

69. Ibid., p. 69.

70. M.N. Tukhachevsky, "*K voprosu o sovremennoi strategii*" (On the question of modern strategy), in *Voina i voennoe iskusstvo v svete istoricheskogo materializma* (War and the art of war in light of historical materialism) (Moscow: Gosizdat, 1927), p. 121.

71. Ibid., pp. 121–122.

important, much more important and much more difficult, is to reach the point at which no Red Army man has a single louse. This is our direct and immediate doctrine."[72] Then he formulated the key task of the Red Army for the immediate future:

It is the development and training of a corps of junior commanders, who in the old army were called noncommissioned officers [*unter-ofitsery*] and in our army are called squad leaders. . . . And if I were asked what the Red Army's focus is, my answer would be: it is focused on the training of worker and peasant squad leaders who are competent and skillful and have practical knowledge. This is the prime target of the Red Army and the Communist Party for the immediate future.[73]

Trotsky maintained this critical approach to the concept of a unified military doctrine for the next few years. His statement at the celebration of the fourth anniversary of the Red Army in February 1922 was significant in this regard:

I happened to speak out against the delusions caused by the terms "new military doctrine" and "unified military doctrine," but this does not mean, comrades, that I am truly afraid of a new word in military affairs. What I am most afraid of is that it could give rise to superficiality, which reassures and soothes with high-minded phrases and allows people not to learn because somebody has promised them he will pull a new military doctrine out of his waistcoat pocket for them.[74]

Trotsky's criticism of the unified military doctrine was immediately supported by a number of writers who formed a group around the journal *Voennyi vestnik* (*Military Herald*). Sometimes their comments seem to be merely flattery. Thus D. Petrovsky, commenting on the meeting of military delegates mentioned above, wrote in *Voennyi vestnik*:

Comrade Trotsky called upon the delegates to reject doctrinairism, not to make a fetish out of concepts of maneuverability, offense, etc., not to canonize

---

72. "*Doklad t. Trotskogo o Krasnoi Armii na XI s'ezde RKP*" (Comrade Trotsky's report on the Red Army at the 11th Congress of the RCP), *Voennyi vestnik*, No. 7 (1922), p. 49.

73. Ibid.

74. "*Rech' tov. Trotskogo na prazdnovanii 4-i godovshchiny Krasnoi Armii na voenno-akademicheskikh kursakh vysshego Kommandnogo Sostava RKKA*" (Comrade Trotsky's speech at the celebration of the 4th anniversary of the Red Army at the Academic-Military School for the Supreme Command Personnel of the Red Army), in *Voennaya nauka i revolyutsiya* (Military science and revolution), Vol. 1 (Moscow: Goslitizdat, 1922), p. 281.

our past, but to proceed expeditiously, to study our past experience thoroughly and discriminately. With all the power of his brilliant talent, Comrade Trotsky presented the meeting with the urgency and great importance of the task, of training sound, reliable squad leaders.[75]

The debates on these issues showed that there was no consensus on either the definition of a "unified military doctrine" or the value of introducing such a doctrine. Several years passed before Mikhail Frunze's concept was widely accepted as basic. In 1928, the first edition of the Big Soviet Encyclopedia *(Bol'shaya Sovetskaya entsiklopediya)* carried Frunze's definition of military doctrine.[76] By that time, Trotsky was no longer people's commissar or chairman of the Revolutionary Military Council, and was losing his position in the top political leadership because of his defeat in a fierce political struggle with Stalin, Zinoviev, and Kamenev. Frunze replaced Trotsky in both positions in 1924, only to die during a botched surgical operation at the Kremlin hospital in 1925. (Some believe this was the way Stalin chose to do away with him.) While serving as the top Soviet military official, Frunze put substantial effort into carrying out military reforms, the impact of which can be detected even now. Frunze's reforms were as profound and broad as the famous reforms of the tsarist army carried out by Dmitry Miliutin in the 1860s and 1870s, or the reform of the navy by Prince Konstantin Nikolayevich in the same period.[77]

Kliment Yefremovich Voroshilov became people's commissar for military and naval affairs after Frunze's death. Voroshilov's life was long and rather eventful. Born into a poor family, he started working at age seven and was illiterate until age twelve; he attended school for two winters and educated himself by reading Marxist literature, classical fiction, and books on science and even the arts. During the February and October

---

75. D. Petrovsky, "*Soveshchaniye voennykh delegatov XI s'yezda RKP*" (Meeting of military delegates of the 11th Congress of the RKP), *Voennyi vestnik*, No. 8 (1922), p. 14.

76. *Bol'shaya sovetskaya entsiklopediya* (The big Soviet encyclopedia), 1st ed., Vol. 12 (1928), p. 163.

77. See N.A. Mal'tsev, "*Kadrovaya ili militsionnaya? (O printsipakh komplektovaniya Sovetskikh Vooruzhennykh Sil)*" (Regular or militia? [On the principles of the composition of the Soviet armed forces]), *Voenno-istoricheskii zhurnal*, No. 11 (1989), pp. 30–40; P.F. Vashchenko and V.A. Runov, "*Voennaya reforma v SSSR*" (Military reform in the USSR), *Voenno-istoricheskii zhurnal*, No. 12 (1989), pp. 33–40; G.P. Meshcheryakov, *Russkaya voennaya mysl' v XIX veke* (Russian military thought in the 19th century) (Moscow: Nauka, 1973), pp. 166–173; and A.P. Shevyrev, *Russkii flot posle Krymskoi voiny: liberal'naya byurokratiya i morskie reformy* (The Russian fleet after the Crimean War: Liberal bureaucracy and naval reforms) (Moscow: Moscow State University, 1990).

revolutions, at the age of thirty-six, he carried out a number of important missions. Thus in February 1917, because of his close ties to the soldiers, Voroshilov succeeded in getting the Ismailov Regiment of the Imperial Guard, one of the oldest in the country, to join the uprising.[78] That was no easy task, since the Imperial Guard possessed rather impressive military strength, though less impressive than prior to World War I.[79] During the Civil War Voroshilov commanded the 5th Ukrainian Army, the Ukrainian group of troops, and the 10th and 14th Armies. After that he was only the chief of the 61st Infantry Division and then headed a group of troops within the 61st Infantry Division and the 11th Cavalry Division.

According to some sources, Voroshilov failed as a commander of large formations of troops. At the same time he won fame for his courage and his organizational ability and was popular with the Red Army rank and file. Voroshilov's career began to advance again in November 1919, when he was appointed chairman of the Revolutionary Committee of the First Cavalry, where he won his first military decoration, the Order of the Red Banner. Toward the end of his life (he died in 1969), Voroshilov was twice decorated as a Hero of the Soviet Union (1956 and 1968) and as a Hero of Socialist Labor (1960), and he was awarded eight Orders of Lenin and the Order of Suvorov, first rank. Voroshilov was promoted to top positions in the state leadership: he was deputy chairman of the Council of Ministers of the USSR (1946–53) and chairman of the Presidium of the Supreme Soviet of the USSR (1953–60). He was a member of the Politburo (earlier known as the Presidium) of the CPSU (Communist Party of the Soviet Union) Central Committee for a remarkable thirty-four years, from 1926 to 1960.

Voroshilov was one of the first Party and state leaders to glorify Stalin's accomplishments in the Civil War, and thus he helped to create Stalin's cult of personality, dictatorship, and brutally repressive regime. In 1929, Voroshilov wrote a book entitled *Stalin and the Red Army* on the occasion of Stalin's fiftieth birthday. It was an important text, interpreting the history of the Red Army and the relationship between the state (political) leadership and the military command, between policy and strategy. For the next sixty years, the Party and state leadership drafted

---

78. See A. Khorev, "Narkom Voroshilov" (People's Commissar Voroshilov), *Krasnaya zvezda*, January 14, 1989.

79. On account of its poor administration, the Russian Imperial Guard sustained great losses during World War I and its troops were no longer first-rate. Prior to World War I, the Imperial Guard comprised sixteen infantry regiments, thirteen cavalry regiments, three artillery brigades, an engineer battalion, a naval detachment, and a few warships.

political and ideological guidelines for each and every realm of life, including purely military matters. The result was a deteriorating relationship between policy and military strategy.

When Voroshilov was appointed people's commissar, a reshuffling of the Red Army took place. Some historians have reasonably argued that the unstated intention was to upset the established commanders' network, to remove some commanders from their comfortable perches, and thus to weaken any opposition to the new leadership. As a result, Tukhachevsky became chief of staff of the Red Army. Voroshilov and Tukhachevsky clashed repeatedly, often as a result of Voroshilov's incompetence.

Even after taking this important government position, Tukhachevsky continued to engage in theoretical studies, including various aspects of the relationship between policy and military strategy.[80] In all probability he kept in mind the testing of the unified military doctrine and the sharp criticism to which its advocates had been subjected, and thus he offered another name for the discipline that was to integrate policy and military strategy—polemical strategy (*polemostrategiya*). Tukhachevsky and his followers thought this would lay the foundation for a new doctrine of war, encompassing the nature of war, methods and means of preparing for warfare, and the most effective use of the country's forces and resources to achieve victory. Tukhachevsky assumed that the supreme command running the war as a whole could not be guided only by military strategy, or "pure strategy" of the old type; what was required was a new, comprehensive, and superior strategy.[81] But polemical strategy did not find supporters. As some critics noted, in constructing the concept, Tukhachevsky strove not so much to subordinate strategy to policy, but to adjust policy to strategy.

The Concept of the "Integral Military Leader"

Svechin, who had developed highly detailed conceptions of not only the interrelationship between policy and strategy, but also the triad of policy, strategy, and operational art, proposed the concept of the "integral military leader." In his view, "war is waged by the supreme authority of a state, because the decisions which must be made by the leaders of a war

---

80. See *Voina i revolyutsiya* (War and revolution), No. 10–11 (1927), p. 26; and V.D. Ryazanov, "*Marksizm i voennoe delo*" (Marxism and military affairs), *Voennyi vestnik*, No. 3 (1926), pp. 14–15.

81. See M.A. Gareyev, *M.V. Frunze—voennyi teoretik* (M.V. Frunze—military theoretician) (Moscow: Voenizdat, 1985), p. 394.

are too important and critical to be entrusted to any agent of executive authority."[82] As he wrote in *Strategy*:

Our notions of leadership have been perverted by the use of the term supreme commander in chief because we associate it with a person to whom the active armies and navy are subordinate and who has supreme authority in a theater of operations. In fact, this kind of commander in chief is not supreme, *because he does not direct foreign and domestic policy or the entire rear of the active armies, because he does not have all power over the entire state.* A strategist and commander in chief is only part of the leadership of a war, and sometimes decisions are made without his knowledge and sometimes completely against his will. Giving full power to a chosen military leader is an obsolete formula which never reflected any kind of reality.[83]

The idea of an integral military leader was supported by Boris Mikhailovich Shaposhnikov, a future chief of the Red Army General Staff, in his fundamental work *The Brain of the Army* (*Mozg armii*), which came out in three volumes published between 1927 and 1929. Although it was not as profound as Svechin's *Strategy*, in some respects Shaposhnikov's opus was a landmark in the development of a theory of strategy and management for the Red Army. Frequently citing Svechin, Shaposhnikov supported his ideas: "Clausewitz also considered a commander in chief to be a military leader without the additional word 'supreme'; for us, the chief of the General Staff is considered a strategist and commander in chief who is only part of the leadership in war."[84]

Shaposhnikov's *The Brain of the Army* fared much better than Svechin's *Strategy*. It has always been cited as a standard text by almost all Russian military writers and historians, and is still included in the curriculum of the Academy of the General Staff in the 1990s. One reason for this reliance on Shaposhnikov's text was probably that it focused on the General Staff of the Austro-Hungarian Empire, which had disappeared from the political map in 1918. Shaposhnikov did not touch upon the Russian General Staff or the Soviet Supreme Command during the Civil War, or the German General Staff.

Beginning in the second half of the 1930s, for many years the discussion of the relationship between policy and military strategy came to a halt in the Soviet Union because of the dictatorship and personality cult of Stalin, who had concentrated enormous power in his own hands.

---

82. Svechin, *Strategy*, p. 100.

83. Ibid. Emphasis added.

84. B.M. Shaposhnikov, *Mozg armii* (The brain of the army), Vol. 1 (Moscow: Voennyi Vestnik, 1926), p. 113.

Indeed, military strategy itself was interpreted as the exclusive prerogative of Comrade Stalin. As for the concept of the integral military leader, it proved its viability in the course of World War II, when supreme commands were set up not only in the Soviet Union, but in the United Kingdom, the United States, and Germany.

The Purges of 1937–38 and the New Generation of Soviet Military Leaders

World War II introduced correctives into the relationship between policy and military strategy, though it by no means achieved its optimal character immediately. The concentration of power within the Soviet political leadership, which directed the conduct of war, devised strategy, and implemented it operationally, was unavoidable in the context of the total war unleashed by Nazi Germany. Despite his unparalleled despotic power, Stalin turned out to be poorly prepared for the war, which started in a way he had never anticipated. A.M. Vasilevsky wrote in his memoirs that, at the start of the war, Stalin "was unreasonably arrogant and overestimated his capacity to direct the war. He paid little attention to the General Staff, failing to draw on the knowledge and expertise of its members. He frequently changed top military officials for no apparent reason." In Vasilevsky's opinion, "only during the battle of Kursk [i.e., in the summer of 1943, after two years of bloodshed] did he start to fully master the ways and means of running the military conflict in a new way."[85]

The Soviet-Finnish War of 1939–40 scarcely prepared Stalin and his associates for the coming war with Germany. Finland was defeated, but the war did not proceed as had been envisaged by the military command headed by Voroshilov. The Red Army sustained huge losses (many troops perished of frostbite), and the international prestige of the Red Army, the Communist Party, and the country as a whole was badly damaged even in the eyes of many sympathizers abroad.

Brutal purges of the Red Army command, which were a part of the broader purges of Party and state leaders, and indeed of anyone who could be considered a "potential threat" to Stalin's regime, had an extremely negative impact on the nation's defenses. The purges deformed the relationship between policy and strategy, depriving military leaders of any initiative and the ability to make independent decisions within reasonable limits. The most notorious case was the purge of

---

85. A.M. Vasilevsky, *Delo vsei zhizni* (The business of a whole life) (Moscow: Politizdat, 1974), pp. 126–127.

Tukhachevsky and a number of other military leaders in 1937.[86] The following year many military officers who had served as judges in Tukhachevsky's trial were also executed, including V.K. Blukher, marshal of the Soviet Union.

At the time, the military was the only force that might have been able to effectively oppose Stalin's dictatorship. Thus the fate of many of the most popular commanders was sealed by the very logic of Stalin's regime. That Tukhachevsky became the military's first victim was the result of not only his great authority within the Red Army but also his personal relations with Stalin. In the 1920s and 1930s, quite a few people within the Party and Red Army leadership knew that Tukhachevsky blamed Stalin for military failures in the Warsaw region in August 1920 when the western front was under Tukhachevsky's command. At that time Stalin was a member of the revolutionary military council of the adjacent southwestern front. Stalin and Yegorov, commander of the southwestern front, did not turn over in time three armies that S.S. Kamenev, commander in chief of the Soviet Republic, had ordered to be put under Tukhachevsky's command.

After 1938 the purges subsided, but did not stop altogether. G.M. Stern, commander of the national air defense, P.V. Rychagov, commander of the air force, and Ia.V. Smushkevich, chief inspector of the air force, were all arrested. Some generals, including K.A. Meretskov, K.K. Rokossovsky, and A.V. Gorbatov, were arrested but later freed.[87] Some historians, both in Russia and abroad, believe that the forged documents showing that Tukhachevsky had been collaborating with the Germans, which played no small role in his trial, were concocted by German political intelligence under the direction of Reinhard Heydrich and Walter Schellenberg and surreptitiously left for Stalin by Czechoslovakia's President Edvard Beneš.[88]

The scale of Stalin's purges of Red Army officers was immeasurable. It would not be an exaggeration to state that the impact of the purges is still felt in the Russian military. Repressive actions were taken not only against military commanders who theoretically might have challenged Stalin; they swept away many senior and middle-ranking officers as well.

The dimensions of Stalin's purges of military command personnel are

---

86. In April–May 1937, M.N. Tukhachevsky, I.E. Yakir, I.P. Uborevich, A.I. Kork, R.P. Eideman, and B.M. Feldin were arrested. V.M. Primakov and V.K. Putna had been arrested shortly before that.

87. *Voenno-istoricheskii zhurnal*, No. 6 (1988), p. 6.

88. See, for example, A.M. Nekrich, *1941. 22 yunya* (June 22, 1941) (Moscow: Nauka, 1965), pp. 86–87.

summarized in Table 1.[89] Almost the entire command staff was shot or died in prison. Members of the Party as well as nonmembers, former noblemen, workers, peasants, former tsarist senior officers, and Red commanders all fell victim to the purges. Military intellectuals who preserved the best of the tsarist army's intellectual heritage were mowed down; the first blows against this group were delivered as early as the late 1920s and early 1930s. The devastation undoubtedly caused a collapse in morale among those who survived and continued their military service. It is a wonder that, after all the Red Army had suffered, it did not fall apart altogether during its grimmest hour in 1941. The purges had another consequence for the Soviet military: in just one year, 1938, 38,702 people were promoted to higher positions in the armed forces, ranging from battalion and division leaders to commanders of military districts. Some brilliant careers began to take off. Those who had been eclipsed by military stars more popular with the public and the press now had a chance to shine. It was a time of triumph for Georgy Konstantinovich Zhukov over Japanese forces in the Khalkhin-Gol area of Mongolia in 1939. Not many of the newly promoted military men withstood the test of World War II as well as Zhukov. In addition to Zhukov, the "big ten" commanders of fronts (and army groups) during the war, who continued to play an important role in the Soviet armed forces until the 1960s, included I.S. Konev, A.M. Vasilevsky, K.K. Rokossovsky, K.A. Meretskov, F.I. Tolbukhin, R.Ya. Malinovsky, L.A. Govorov, A.I. Yeremenko, and I.Kh. Bagramyan. Of this group four men stood out: Konev, Vasilevsky, Rokossovsky, and, above all, Zhukov. Zhukov started his military service as a regular soldier and did not hold important posts during the Civil War. Only three years younger than Tukhachevsky, Zhukov was merely a platoon leader and later led a troop of cavalry. After the Civil War he consecutively headed a cavalry regiment, a brigade, a division, and a corps, and then briefly served as a deputy inspector of the cavalry. When the decision was made to send Zhukov to the Far East to rebuff the Japanese in the Khalkhin-Gol region, he was the deputy commander of a military district. Upon his return from Mongolia, Zhukov was appointed commander of the Kiev special military district, and later made chief of the General Staff and deputy people's commissar for defense of the Soviet Union.

An evaluation of Zhukov's performance as commander of the 2nd Cavalry Brigade of the 7th Samara Cavalry Division can be found in the

---

89. V. Karpov, "*Marshal Zhukov, yego soratniki i protivniki v gody voiny i mira*" (Marshal Zhukov, his associates and adversaries in the years of war and peace), *Znamia*, No. 9 (1989), p. 40.

Table 1. The Impact of Stalin's Purges (1937–38) on Military Command Personnel.

	Number before purges	Number executed or imprisoned
Marshall of the Soviet Union	5	3
Commissar of the Army, 1st rank	2	2
Flag officer of the Navy, 1st rank	2	2
Flag officer of the Navy, 2nd rank	2	2
Flag officer, 1st rank	6	6
Flag officer, 2nd rank	15	9
Commander of the Army, 1st rank	4	2
Commander of the Army, 2nd rank	12	12
Commissar, 2nd rank	15	15
Corps commander	67	60
Corps commissar	28	25
Division commander	199	136
Brigade commander	367	221
Brigade commissar	36	34

certification of character given to him by his boss K.K. Rokossovsky, Division Commander, in 1930 and published in 1990. It reads:

Has a strong will. Decisive and firm. Often demonstrates initiative and skillfully applies it. Disciplined. Demanding and persistent in his demands. A somewhat ungracious and not sufficiently sympathetic person. Rather stubborn. Painfully proud. In professional terms well trained. Broadly experienced as a military leader. Loves the military profession and steadily accumulates knowledge. His capacity for further development is quite noticeable. Is held in respect. In political terms is well educated. MEETS THE REQUIREMENTS of the job he holds. Might be used effectively as a deputy division commander or a commander of a mechanized formation provided that he gets through appropriate specialized classes. Absolutely cannot be used in staff or teaching jobs since constitutionally he hates them.[90]

Rokossovsky's path later crossed Zhukov's more than once. Zhukov's performance as deputy inspector of the cavalry was greatly appreciated by Semen Budennyi, a member of the Revolutionary Military Council of the Soviet Union and Red Army inspector of the cavalry. Budennyi underlined Zhukov's dutifulness, thirst for knowledge, and creativity. He

---

90. "*Epokha v autobiographiyakh* (The epoch as reflected by autobiographies), Georgy Konstantinovich Zhukov," *Voenno-istoricheskii zhurnal*, No. 5 (1990), p. 22.

did not overlook Zhukov's weaknesses and rightly pointed out that he was "a determined, self-disciplined, and exacting leader, but displays too much toughness and rudeness in relations with his subordinates."[91] Zhukov's negative traits were displayed during World War II, when a great many reports of his excessive toughness circulated among both officers and the rank and file, and his rude character was often contrasted with the humanity of Konstantin Konstantinovich Rokossovsky. Rokossovsky's arrest in 1938 dropped him below Zhukov on the promotion ladder for a long time. While Zhukov was rising, Rokossovsky was enduring outrages in prison or in labor camps. After he was released, Rokossovsky went to war as a commander of a mechanized corps. He ended the war as a front commander, and took part in the assault on Berlin. On June 24, 1945, at the Victory Parade in Moscow, Zhukov reviewed the troops while Rokossovsky commanded them.

The "Genius of Stalin" and the Soviet Art of War

After the Soviet victory in World War II until the death of Stalin in 1953, Stalin's cult of personality as well as the nature of the Soviet political regime itself remained unchanged. Although there were no mass purges of officers like those of 1937–38, after the war some military leaders found themselves in disgrace, and they were discharged from service, demoted, or arrested. Marshal Zhukov was one of the first to be persecuted. As far back as December 1941, after the Red Army's victory over the Germans on the outskirts of Moscow, Zhukov was the most popular commander on the western front—a fact that pleased neither Stalin nor Lavrenty Beria, chief of the secret police. Compromising material started to be filed on Zhukov. An important step in the campaign to discredit Zhukov was the arrest in the spring of 1942 of Major General V.S. Golushkevich, chief of operations of the western front headquarters. Using reliable information from Lieutenant General N.G. Pavlenko, Beria hoped to get at Zhukov through Golushkevich's testimony. But despite all the tricks and traps set for him during his interrogations, Golushkevich did not testify against Zhukov.

Another step was taken against Zhukov after the war. At a meeting in the Kremlin, Stalin openly accused Zhukov of taking credit for all the Soviet war victories. The final action was taken in early 1946, at another meeting of military leaders chaired by Stalin. The testimony of two

---

91. Ibid., p. 23.

military officers under arrest, A.A. Novikov, chief marshal of aviation, and General N.F. Telegin, was read to the audience by S.M. Shtemenko, then chief of the General Staff. In their testimony, both officers attacked Zhukov. Some participants in the meeting—Konev, Rybalko, Sokolovsky, and others—came out in support of Zhukov, and presumably their speeches helped to avert his arrest, which Stalin had already planned. General F.I. Golikov spoke against Zhukov (during the war Golikov held the post of commander of the army and front, and before that he had been chief of the intelligence directorate of the General Staff).[92] Zhukov avoided arrest, but he was forced to resign from his appointment as deputy minister of the armed forces and commander in chief of the army and to take relatively insignificant posts, first as commander of the Odessa military district and then as commander of the Urals military district.

Those marshals and generals who kept their posts extolled Stalin, not only as the political and state leader but as a "military genius." They credited him with and praised him for every achievement in strategic planning, strategic operations management, and any significant area of military activity. "A solid theoretical foundation for the post-war development of the Soviet armed forces has been laid thanks to Comrade Stalin's further developing Soviet military science. In this period, Comrade Stalin is formulating major theoretical principles of the Soviet art of war, developing them with due attention to the economic and moral potential of our country," wrote Marshal of the Soviet Union Alexander Vasilevsky.[93] Admiral A.E. Golovko noted in 1949 that "there existed no issue to which Iosif Vissarionovich [Stalin] did not attend." Golovko mentioned as an example that in the course of his direct guidance of the navy, "Iosif Vissarionovich examined the Kola Gulf coast and selected the sites for future bases of the northern fleet, batteries of the coastal defense, and other strong points."[94] Chief Marshal of Artillery N. Voronov eulogized Stalin's genius in specific professional matters: "Stalin's genius as military leader enabled many to see the light of reason on the issue of equipping division artillery with howitzers. . . . Comrade Stalin gave a

---

92. See *"Beseda s general-leitenantom N.G. Pavlenko"* (Conversation with Lieutenant-General N.G. Pavlenko), *Sovetskaya kul'tura*, August 22, 1988.

93. A. Vasilevsky, *"Tovarishch Stalin—stroitel' Vooruzhennykh Sil Sovetskogo gosudarstva"* (Comrade Stalin—builder of the armed forces of the Soviet state), *Voennaya mysl'*, No. 12 (1949), pp. 24–25.

94. A.E. Golovko, *"I.V. Stalin—sozdatel' Sovetskogo Voenno-Morskogo Flota, organizator yego pobed"* (I.V. Stalin—creator of the Soviet navy and organizer of its victories), *Morskoi sbornik*, No. 12 (1949), pp. 81–82.

direct order to fit out an infantry division with light cannons in appropriate proportion to light howitzers, enabling the division to successfully implement all missions on the modern battlefield."[95]

In this torrent of glorification of the dictator, Stalin's "faithful brother-in-arms" Voroshilov did not go unmentioned, despite the fact that at the outset of World War II while he was part of the top military command, nearly all his missions were failures. In 1951, General of the Army V. Kurasov called Voroshilov "one of the most prominent founders and leaders of the Red Army" and enumerated both his real and imaginary services to the nation, including missions in which Voroshilov had proved to be utterly inadequate.[96]

Politics and Military Leaders in the Khrushchev Era

In the second half of the 1950s and early 1960s, the head of the Communist Party and the Soviet government, Nikita Sergeyevich Khrushchev, was actively engaged in formulating military policy, decisively outlining his design for building up the Soviet armed forces, and making extremely important political-military decisions.

Khrushchev focused on developing missile weaponry of all kinds, and he often spoke against the necessity of large surface warships, aviation, and massive ground forces, thus meddling significantly in military affairs. His opinions were not those of a dilettante: Khrushchev was a member of the military councils of several fronts during the Great Patriotic War, although his contribution to resolving operational and strategic matters was by no means outstanding. Khrushchev did not exaggerate his own wartime record, especially since he shared the blame for the dramatic defeats of the Red Army in the initial phase of war.

In the Khrushchev era, as earlier, Soviet military men highlighted their loyalty to the Party and to the top state leadership, praising them for their role in formulating Soviet military doctrine. However, their praise was not unrestrained and boundless like that displayed in Stalin's time.

In 1955, Khrushchev appointed Zhukov minister of defense;[97] two

---

95. N. Voronov, "*Stalin i sovremennaya artilleriya*" (Stalin and modern artillery), *Voennaya mysl'*, No. 12 (1949), pp. 105–106.

96. V. Kurasov, "*Vydayushchiisya voennyi deyatel' stalinskoi shkoly*" (An outstanding military leader of the Stalinist school), *Voennaya mysl'*, No. 2 (1951), pp. 23–38.

97. In 1934, the People's Commissariat for Military and Naval Affairs was transformed into the People's Commissariat for Defense. In 1946, it was renamed the

years later he discharged Zhukov from that post in spite of their joint efforts to fight those who opposed the debunking of Stalin's personality cult. Zhukov was accused of antiparty behavior—of attempting to lead the armed forces away from political (Party) control and "Bonapartism."[98] These charges were mentioned in the Soviet military press as long as Khrushchev was in power. A quotation from an editorial in *Military Thought* (*Voennaya mysl'*), the main theoretical journal of the Ministry of Defense, reviewing the 22nd Party Congress is typical:

The resolution "On Improving Party and Political Work in the Soviet Armed Forces and Fleet" adopted by the October 1957 plenary meeting of the Central Committee of the CPSU [Communist Party of the Soviet Union] played a great role in further enhancing the armed forces. The plenum firmly condemned the antiparty activity of former Minister of Defense G.K. Zhukov, who spread the cult of his personality, violated Lenin's principles on directing the armed forces, pursued a policy of curtailing the work of the party organization, political bodies, and military councils and of nullifying the guidance of and control over the army and navy by the Party, the Central Committee, and the Soviet state.[99]

The commander in chief of the navy, Admiral N.G. Kuznetsov, was the next to be removed from his post, after arguments with Khrushchev over the structure and composition of the navy. Kuznetsov was blamed for the wreck of the battleship *Novorossiisk*. (The reasons for the wreck remain unclear to this day, as do the reasons for the wreck of the battleship *Empress Maria* of the Russian Imperial Fleet in 1916.) For both Zhukov and Kuznetsov, that was their second dismissal from the top levels of power.

In 1947, Kuznetsov, who was then also commander in chief of the navy, had been removed by Stalin and appointed chief of the education department of the navy. Soon after that Kuznetsov and his fellow officers Heller, Alafusov, and Stepanov were brought before a "court of honor"

People's Commissariat of the Armed Forces of the USSR, and later that year, Ministry of Armed Forces of the USSR. In 1950, it was divided into two government departments: the Ministry of the Army of the USSR, and the Ministry of the Navy of the USSR. In 1953, the two departments were merged to form the Ministry of Defense of the USSR.

98. According to people who knew Zhukov, the accusations of "Bonapartism" were quite groundless. However, it was widely known in army circles that Zhukov disliked political workers, whom he often called "priests."

99. "*Leninskii kurs XXII s'yezda KPSS*" (The Leninist course of the 22nd Congress of the CPSU), *Voennaya mysl'*, No. 4 (1962), p. 13.

and accused of having committed "antistate and antipatriotic acts by passing to the former wartime allies the blueprints for and documents on naval weaponry on the pretext of exchanging information."[100] On the second day the work of the "court of honor" was over. Despite the absurdity and unsubstantiated nature of the charges, the judgment was definite: the men were to be handed over to the Supreme Court of the Military Collegium of the USSR for having forwarded state secrets to foreign intelligence services. The Military Collegium sentenced Admirals Alafusov and Stepanov to ten years and Admiral Heller to four years in prison. On Stalin's personal instruction, only a so-called administrative penalty was inflicted on Kuznetsov: he was reduced in rank to rear admiral and demoted to running schools for naval personnel. After Stalin's death, two of the admirals were rehabilitated; Heller, however, had died in prison in 1950, before he could be rehabilitated.[101] As for Kuznetsov, he became head of the newly formed USSR Ministry of the Navy in 1951, and he retained that post until 1953, when the ministry was closed down. In 1953–56, Kuznetsov served as first deputy minister of defense as commander in chief of the navy. In 1955, he was promoted to the highest naval rank, admiral of the fleet of the Soviet Union. When Kuznetsov was discharged by Khrushchev, he was reduced in rank to rear admiral for the second time and retired.

Rodion Yakovlevich Malinovsky (1898–1967), marshal of the Soviet Union, replaced Zhukov as minister of defense in 1957. Malinovsky had fought in World War I, the Russian Civil War, and the Spanish Civil War in 1936–39. From 1939 to 1941, he taught at the Frunze Military Academy. He was promoted to the rank of Marshal of the Soviet Union in 1944. During the Great Patriotic War, Malinovsky commanded several fronts rather successfully. After the war, he commanded the Baikal-Amur military district. From 1947 to 1956, Malinovsky commanded forces in the Soviet Far East, and later he was the commander of the Far Eastern military district. In 1956–57, he was commander in chief of Soviet ground forces. Malinovsky headed the Ministry of Defense after Khrushchev was pushed out in October 1964 until his death in 1967.[102] In his 1962 book

---

100. Quoted from L. Mikhailov, "*Sud bez chesti*" (Court without honor), *Krasnaya zvezda*, June 16, 1990.

101. Ibid.

102. Some sources indicate that Malinovsky took part in Khrushchev's ouster. Malinovsky and Brezhnev spoke to Khrushchev by telephone, insisting that he return immediately to Moscow from his vacation to take part in a session of the Presidium of the Party Central Committee. Although not a member of the Presidium, Malinovsky attended its meeting, as did Andrei Gromyko and several secretaries of regional Party

entitled *Vigilantly Safeguarding Peace* (*Bditel'no stoiat' na strazhe mira*), Malinovsky wrote, "The New Program of the Party has provided the answer to the fundamental questions of ensuring the security of the construction of communism against aggressive actions of the imperialist states and their political-military blocs. It has defined in exhaustive detail the tasks of our country's armed forces at the current stage."[103]

Marshal of the Soviet Union and chief of the General Staff of the Soviet armed forces S. Biryuzov made similar statements: "Within the last few years, our military thought has advanced a great deal. As a result of enormous work done by the Central Committee of the CPSU with comrade N.S. Khrushchev at its head, and by our military cadres, we now have a quite modern military doctrine, determined by the nature of the state, which is building communism."[104] P.A. Rotmistrov, chief marshal of armored troops and one of the most popular tank army commanders during World War II, also echoed Malinovsky:

A deep analysis of the nature of modern warfare, which is at the foundation of Soviet military doctrine, was made by N.S. Khrushchev in his report to the fourth session of the Supreme Soviet of the USSR in 1960. In this report, the features of future war, the nature of its initial phase, the role of fire power and means of delivery, the relationship between various services and branches of forces, the role of surprise, etc., were creatively revealed. All of that made a major contribution to Marxist-Leninist scholarship on war and the army.[105]

The relationship between policy and military strategy was analyzed in a book called *Military Strategy* (*Voennaya strategiya*) written by a team of authors headed by Marshal of the Soviet Union V.D. Sokolovsky, who headed the General Staff in 1952–60. A number of witnesses maintain that Sokolovsky resigned from that post because he disagreed with Khrushchev's decision to reduce the armed forces by 1.2 million troops.

Sokolovsky had an impressive service record. In the Civil War he served as leader of a company, a deputy leader of a regiment, chief of

---

organizations. See Nikita Sergeyevich Khrushchev, *Materialy k biografii* (Materials for a biography) (Moscow: Politizdat, 1989), pp. 194–195.

103. R.Y. Malinovsky, *Bditel'no stoyat' na strazhe mira* (Vigilantly safeguarding peace) (Moscow: Voenizdat, 1962), p. 5.

104. S. Biryuzov, "*Novyi etap v razvitii Vooruzhennykh Sil i zadachi obucheniya i vospitaniya voisk*" (A new stage in the development of the armed forces and the tasks of training and developing troops), *Kommunist Vooruzhennykh Sil*, No. 4 (1964), p. 18.

105. P.A. Rotmistrov, "*Prichiny sovremennykh voin i ikh osobennosti*" (Reasons for modern wars and their specific features), *Kommunist Vooruzhennykh Sil*, No. 26 (1963), p. 29.

staff of an infantry division, and chief of staff of a cavalry division. During World War II, he first headed the staff of a front and later commanded a front. After the war, Sokolovsky was commander of the group of Soviet forces in Germany (1946–49). He was considered one of the most knowledgeable Soviet military leaders. Before his military service in the tsarist army, Sokolovsky had graduated from a teachers college. In 1918–21, with some intervals, he took classes at the Academy of the General Staff, where he was taught by brilliant teachers. M.V. Zakharov, Sokolovsky's successor as chief of the General Staff in 1960–63 and again in 1964–71, was less educated than Sokolovsky, though he had taken classes in two departments at the Frunze Academy (in 1928 and 1933) and at the Academy of the General Staff in 1937. Malinovsky was not highly educated either. But even Sokolovsky could not match the military leaders of the 1920s and 1930s in either general education or historical knowledge.

Military Strategy was published in three editions in 1962, 1963, and 1968. The book was translated into several foreign languages and was frequently cited in the Western military literature. In the Soviet Union, it was a sourcebook for many works of military history. One of the primary implicit goals of the book was to impress Westerners with Soviet military power. As some contemporaries have recalled, Khrushchev directed the team of authors (via Malinovsky) "to frighten them to death." "The recognition of war as a means of policy defines the relationship between military strategy and policy which is based on the principle of complete subordination of the former to the latter," the authors stated in the introduction to the book.[106] They did not delve deep into a detailed analysis of the relationship between policy and strategy as Svechin, Shaposhnikov, and Tukhachevsky had, instead confining themselves to the assertion that "the goals and tasks of strategy are defined by and directly stem from the aims and goals of state policy, of which military strategy is one means."[107]

Authors of another Soviet military study, *On Soviet Military Science* (*O sovetskoi voennoi nauke*), evaluated policy and strategy in a similar fashion, but did not limit themselves to this standard thesis. They put as strong an emphasis as they could on the subordination of strategy to policy, which was probably an echo of earlier debates over whether strategy had increased its impact on policy or not. In brief, their message was as follows: policy and strategy are not equal categories; policy plays a leading and determining role with regard to military strategy; policy

---

106. *Voennaya strategiya* (Military strategy), 2d ed. (Moscow: Voenizdat, 1963), p. 24.
107. Ibid.

outlines tasks for strategy and strategy fulfills them. In turn, policy takes into account the achievements and demands of strategy, but the priority of policy always remains foremost.[108]

Colonel General N.A. Lomov, chair of the strategy department at the Military Academy of the General Staff and one of the most prominent theoreticians in the field of strategy at the time, did not deny policy's predominance over military strategy within the framework of military doctrine. However, he noted that "there is an internal link between the substance of military doctrine and strategy . . . principles of military strategy are an extremely important, integral component of the substance of military doctrine."[109]

To substantiate similar views on the relationship between policy and military strategy during the 1960s, some analysts used the tragic lessons of the opening stage of the Great Patriotic War. Colonel B. Kulish presented a detailed analysis in a 1962 article in *Voennaya mysl'*. Ostensibly, Kulish's article was mainly about the dismantling of Stalin's cult of personality, i.e., it followed the Party line. However, it also carried an implicit message to the political leadership about the necessity of observing the demands of military strategy and its impact on policy. According to Kulish,

shortly before the Great Patriotic War began, Stalin viewed the interrelationship between policy and military strategy rather one-sidedly. He and, under his influence, the leaders of the People's Commissariat of Defense, underestimated the objective requirements of strategy in that period. Afraid to provoke fascist Germany's attack against our country, they did not attach due importance to the danger of preemption in preparation for war, especially in strategic deployment by the enemy. . . . Thus the policy of averting fascist Germany's attack against our country was not supported by military strategy, which only encouraged the aggressor rather than stopped it.[110]

Critiquing some of his colleagues, Kulish observed that "sometimes . . . military strategy is deprived of any independence and becomes a blind instrument of policy."[111]

Quite a few Soviet military writers of this period emphasized their

---

108. S.N. Kozlov, M.V. Smirnov, I.S. Biaz', and P.A. Sidorov, *O sovetskoi voennoi nauke* (On Soviet military science) (Moscow: Voenizdat, 1964), p. 255.

109. N. Lomov, "*Sovetskaya voennaya doktrina*" (Soviet military doctrine), *Voennaya mysl'*, No. 1 (1963), p. 16.

110. V. Kulish, "*O vzaimosvyazi politiki i voennoi strategii*" (On the interconnection between policy and military strategy), *Voennaya mysl'*, No. 4 (1962), p. 31.

111. Ibid.

negative attitudes toward the ideas of various "extreme militarists" who denied the predominance of policy over strategy. They often mentioned the names of the German military theorists Bernhardi, Schlieffen, and Ludendorff in this regard. *Military Strategy* pointed out the erroneousness of their viewpoints, according to which "policy, having done its business in unleashing war, becomes a passive observer when military actions start."[112]

Generals M. Milshtein and A. Slobodenko, who belonged to the older generation of instructors at the General Staff Academy, shared this attitude in their book entitled *On Bourgeois Military Science* (*O burzhuaznoi voennoi nauke*), which was also published in the 1960s. They subjected Ludendorff's book *Total War*, which had come out in 1935, two years after the Nazis had taken power, to detailed criticism. In their view, Ludendorff demanded that policy should be subordinate to war and not vice versa.[113]

Colonel General M. Povaly expounded his approach to the subject in *Voennaya mysl'*: "Based on an evaluation of world political and class forces, and the moral and political potentials of potential adversaries, policy defines the political mission of war, i.e., its political substance. Policy evaluates the role of its own coalition, the coalition of adversarial states, and neutral countries."[114] Moreover, Povaly asserted that

> policy defines the most important interim targets of military actions stemming from the general mission, the order of entry into the war, and the timing and priorities of the attacks to be launched in various theaters or strategically important areas of the world. Policy also defines the composition of the armed forces at the beginning of the war and throughout its duration, as well as their groupings and missions, taking into account the significance of the theaters of military action and the forces of the enemy.[115]

What then is the function of military strategy and military command? Povaly responded with a quotation from Shaposhnikov's *The Brain of the Army*: "Strategy's task is to achieve the set goals." The strategic leadership develops a concrete plan of war against both apparent and potential adversaries, Povaly wrote. In the bitter struggle between the two social

---

112. *Voennaya strategiya*, pp. 23–24.

113. See M.A. Milshtein and A.K. Slobodenko, *O burzhuaznoi voennoi nauke* (On bourgeois military science), 2d ed. (Moscow: Voenizdat 1961), pp. 113–118.

114. M. Povaly, "*Politika i voennaya strategiya*" (Policy and military strategy), *Voennaya mysl'*, No. 7 (1970), p. 11.

115. Ibid.

systems of communism and capitalism, this plan should be flexible enough to respond to various political scenarios.[116]

Nuclear Weapons and the Relationship between Policy and Strategy

The adherence of Soviet military professionals throughout the 1960s and 1970s to the principle of strategy's subordination to policy implicitly suggests that they did not see any changes in the character of war in the nuclear age. *Military Strategy*, for example, quoted British Marshal Edgar J. Kingston-McCloughry, whose book *Global Strategy* was published in Russian in 1956,[117] on Clausewitz's formula: "But take his most famous pronouncement that 'war is the continuation of policy by other means,' viz. by force, and consider it in the light of present-day conditions. Nothing would seem further from the truth in the event of nuclear warfare. Such a war, if wholly unleashed, would be the end of all policies and an utter mutual annihilation."[118]

The authors of *Military Strategy* were rather categorical in their response to Kingston-McCloughry's argument: "It is quite clear that such views are the product of a metaphysical and unscientific approach to a social phenomenon like war, and are the result of the idealization of the new weapon." Furthermore, "it is well known that the essence of war as the continuation of policy does not change as a result of developments in technology and armaments."[119]

In keeping with the spirit of the times, the Soviet authors drew a stunning conclusion about the purpose of assertions like those of Kingston-McCloughry: they "were needed by the military ideologues of imperialism to justify their course of preparations for a new war and to put the development of the economy, science, and technology at the service of the military organization."[120]

Kingston-McCloughry's formulation is deficient because he did not specify that in the nuclear age, nuclear war cannot be a *rational*

---

116. Ibid.

117. It is worth mentioning that in the second half of the 1950s and the early 1960s, a good many Western books on military matters were translated into Russian. Later, the practice was discontinued. As a result, most Western military writing was unavailable to Soviet military leaders, who generally did not read English.

118. Edgar J. Kingston-McCloughry, *Global Strategy* (New York: Frederick Praeger, 1957), p. 248.

119. *Voennaya strategiya*, pp. 24–25.

120. Ibid., p. 25.

continuation of policy. But such a war could be a continuation of a "bad" (*durnoi*, using Svechin's word) policy, such as a policy of actively using nuclear weapons to blackmail, exert pressure, etc.

The idea that nuclear war is a continuation and instrument of policy was most vividly expressed in an article by V. Shilyag, M. Popov, and T. Kondratkov that appeared in *Voennaya mysl'* in 1966, in which the authors stated that

historical experience and contemporary wars—control of policy over the course of war in Korea and Vietnam, prevention of nuclear war during the crisis in the Caribbean [i.e., the Cuban missile crisis]—provide definite grounds to assume that in the event of global nuclear conflict, weapons of mass destruction will be under the control of and directed by policy.[121]

(They noted, however, that this did not mean that such a war would necessarily be of a limited type.) They did not exclude the possibility that policy would prohibit the use of nuclear weapons, or would limit or stop their use in the course of war. According to their argument, "politics is not only relations between states, but also relations between classes within states. And while the ruling exploiting classes conduct one policy, the oppressed classes have completely different political interests that clash with the reactionary policy of monopoly capital."[122]

Nevertheless, some Soviet authors of the 1950s and 1960s did call attention to drastic shifts in military strategy that resulted from the emergence of nuclear weapons. As General Svyatoslav N. Kozlov and his co-authors noted, the range of strategic options would greatly increase in a nuclear war. Strategy had ceased to be merely an organizer and a manipulator of the systems of operations: "Now strategy has the chance to achieve its aims directly rather than through an aggregation of tactical and operational steps. This opportunity is secured by nuclear weapons. Indeed, the impact of strategic strikes directly and more or less immediately defines the situation, the development and results of all other efforts. ... This should be considered one of the most important theses for the art of war in contemporary conditions."[123]

According to participants in closed discussions that took place at that time, several Soviet military theoreticians revised the traditional approaches to the art of war differently, arguing that the enormous number

---

121. V. Shilyag, M. Popov, and T. Kondratkov, "*Politika i yadernaya voina*" (Policy and nuclear war), *Voennaya mysl'*, No. 12 (1966), p. 11.

122. Ibid.

123. Kozlov et al., *O sovetskoi voennoi nauke*, p. 255.

of victims and massive destruction caused by nuclear weapons put their use beyond the bounds of warfare altogether. But at that time these views were not officially accepted.

In the second half of the 1960s and throughout the 1970s, Soviet military thought, and particularly the conception of relations between policy and strategy, scarcely changed. A.A. Grechko, minister of defense from 1966 to 1976, emphasized in his book *The Armed Forces of the Soviet State* (*Vooruzhennye sily Sovetskogo gosudarstva*) that "the Communist Party's leadership of the Soviet armed forces is the main principle of Soviet military development."[124] This book, as well as Grechko's other statements in the media, were full of praise for the Party's achievements in the military sphere.

During this period, excessive praise of Leonid Brezhnev, Khrushchev's successor as head of the Party and the state, escalated in Soviet propaganda. An increasing number of high-ranking military officials joined the campaign, issuing panegyrics in pieces on purely professional military matters. Similarly, the first half of the 1980s did not seem to promise any changes in the established formulas on policy, war, and military strategy. The leading military analysts merely repeated theses formulated decades earlier.

Policy and Strategy in the 1980s

In the 1980s, the "management" interaction of policy and strategy was discussed in a number of works by well-known Soviet military figures, including Nikolai Vasilievich Ogarkov, marshal of the Soviet Union and chief of the General Staff (1977–84), and his deputy, Makhmut Gareyev, who was responsible for the development of military science.

Ogarkov is considered one of the most prominent chiefs of the Soviet General Staff in the post-war period. He took the job in 1977, when he was sixty, after twenty-two years of military service. A graduate of the Kuibyshev Military Engineering Academy, Ogarkov served in the ground forces as a military engineer during the Great Patriotic War. After the war ended, he held a series of important posts: first, commander of a division in the group of Soviet forces in Germany, then deputy commander of the Belorussia military district, and later commander of the Baltic military district. From 1968 to 1974, Ogarkov was the first deputy chief of the General Staff. He also participated in the U.S.-Soviet negotiations on strategic arms.

---

124. A.A. Grechko, *Vooruzhennye sily Sovetskogo gosudarstva* (The armed forces of the Soviet state), 2d ed. (Moscow: Voenizdat, 1975), p. 32.

In his book *History Teaches Vigilance* (*Istoriya uchit bditel'nosti*), Ogarkov underscored the prime importance of the sociopolitical dimension of military doctrine, but also emphasized that there is a close interdependence between this aspect of military doctrine and military technology. According to Ogarkov, "the political mission of war must fully correspond to the military potential of the state, the combat resources of the armed forces, and the methods of conducting military actions. The latter should reliably ensure the attainment of the set goals."[125] It is noteworthy that Ogarkov's ideas about a technological component of military doctrine were somewhat atypical of Soviet military traditions since the 1930s. He pointed out, for example, that the substance of the technological dimension of the military doctrine of socialist and capitalist countries shared some similar features rooted in common trends in the development of military technology, the level of scientific and technological progress, and the experience of past wars.[126]

In his monograph *M.V. Frunze—Military Theoretician*, Makhmut Gareyev noted that Frunze himself had attached cardinal importance to policy.[127] According to Gareyev, the sociopolitical dimension of military doctrine is based on the principles of Marxist-Leninist teachings on war and the army and on other social sciences, whereas its military-technological dimension is based on military science and military aspects of other sciences. He contested the views of some Soviet authors who asserted that military doctrine could be worked out only within and by military science. As Gareyev stated, "it is absolutely clear that the political part of military doctrine cannot be based only on the achievements of military science."[128] Thus the deputy chief of the General Staff accentuated policy's dominance over military strategy and military affairs even more clearly and explicitly than had earlier Soviet military thinkers.

Reflecting on the issue of whether war could be a continuation of politics in the nuclear age, Ogarkov concluded:

The appearance in 1945 and the subsequent rapid development of nuclear weapons with incredible destructive capacities threw a new light on the issue of *the expediency of war as a means to achieve a political goal*. Only if one lost one's common sense entirely could one try to find arguments and set goals that could justify unleashing world war and thus risking the complete

---

125. N.V. Ogarkov, *Istoriya uchit bditel'nosti* (History teaches vigilance) (Moscow: Voenizdat, 1985), p. 59.

126. Ibid.

127. Gareyev, *M.V. Frunze*, p. 394.

128. Ibid., p. 419.

annihilation of the human race. Thus it is an indisputable conclusion that it is criminal to consider thermonuclear war as a rational and seemingly "legal" means of continuing policy.[129]

This kind of declaration represented a huge step forward from the perceptions that had dominated Soviet military scholarship since the 1960s. It is important to note that Ogarkov considered it possible that thermonuclear weapons could be unleashed by irrational political forces. The history of the nuclear era unfortunately includes several examples of nuclear blackmail as an instrument of policy employed by both the United States and the Soviet Union, which led to tense confrontations and the real possibility of nuclear war.[130]

An analysis of the political behavior of the superpowers in the 1970s and 1980s, when military strategic parity was maintained, shows that the political leadership of both countries much more rarely and much less openly resorted to nuclear blackmail. Even the Reagan administration, despite its initial bellicose image, never in eight years resorted to direct nuclear blackmail. Nor did the Soviet Union use this double-edged weapon in this period.[131]

In analyzing the relationship between policy and war in a nuclear confrontation, another problem should be noted, i.e., the possibility of "accidental" war resulting from a combination of unintentional actions by both sides that create a *sui generis* situation of "strategic resonance." There are four major sources of danger that could lead to unintentional, accidental nuclear war: (1) technical malfunctions in the early warning and monitoring systems for nuclear weapons; (2) poor organizational principles for channeling information in the decision-making network; (3) human errors in assessing the military-strategic situation as a result of a misinterpretation of incoming data; and (4) mechanical defects or mistakes due to the mental breakdown, illness, or exhaustion of the responsible person(s). Any combination of these factors is even more dangerous.[132]

The outbreak of nuclear war was discussed by Soviet military analysts as far back as the early 1960s. In the 1980s, it became the number one topic. The top state and Party leadership focused on this concern, and

---

129. Ogarkov, *Istoriya uchit bditel'nosti*, p. 88. Emphasis added.

130. A detailed analysis of the problem can be found in Richard K. Betts, *Nuclear Blackmail and Nuclear Balance* (Washington, D.C.: Brookings, 1987).

131. See A.A. Kokoshin, *V poiskakh vykhoda* (In search of an exit) (Moscow: Politizdat, 1989), p. 63.

132. Ibid., p. 159.

a number of civilian political scientists turned their attention to political-military studies and the problem of nuclear war.

Modification of Clausewitz's Formula in the Late 1980s

In the second half of the 1980s, the Soviet discussion of the relationship between policy and war received a new impetus thanks to the recognition first by the political leadership and then by the top military command that it is impossible to win a nuclear war. General Secretary Mikhail Gorbachev concluded in a February 1987 speech at an international forum, "For a Nonnuclear World, for the Survival of Humanity," that "after Hiroshima and Nagasaki, world war was no longer a continuation of politics by other means. The authors of such a policy will be incinerated in a nuclear war."[133] This thesis was not immediately universally accepted, however. It was secretly criticized behind the scenes. The official standpoint of the Soviet military, voiced by Minister of Defense Dmitry Yazov in his 1989 book, *Loyal to the Fatherland* (*Verny otchizne*), was that the unleashing of a nuclear war by aggressive reactionary quarters "would be the direct result of an absurd, criminal policy which this circle conducted right up to the beginning of war." However, Yazov emphasized, "the outbreak of such a war would be the end of any policy since it would be a global catastrophe and the annihilation of all humanity. . . . The policy of military force and its extreme manifestation—war—have exhausted themselves."[134] With this argument, Yazov was following the Soviet tradition of citing the opinion of the top political leadership. He wrote that "there is no terrestrial or cosmic roof to take shelter under if the nuclear thunderstorm breaks out. M.S. Gorbachev has clearly stated this idea more than once. The most important principles of the documents of the 27th Congress of the CPSU and the Party Program are imbued with it."[135]

Statements by Gorbachev, Yazov, and other Soviet political and military leaders provoked increased discussion of nuclear war. Specifically, a question was raised about the legitimacy of using the very term "war" with regard to such a hypothetical phenomenon as nuclear war. Thus scholars at the Institute of Military History of the Soviet Ministry of Defense reflected a widespread view when they wrote the following

---

133. M.S. Gorbachev, *Za bez'yadernyi mir, za gumanizm mezhdunarodnykh otnoshenii* (For a nonnuclear world, for humanism in international relations) (Moscow: Politizdat, 1987), p. 10.

134. D.T. Yazov, *Verny Otchizne* (Loyal to the fatherland) (Moscow: Voenizdat, 1988), p. 284.

135. Ibid.

about nuclear warfare: "If one overcomes the inertia of old ideas and looks at it through the prism of new political thinking, one would understand that nuclear war lacks a number of significant features inherent in war as a specific social phenomenon."[136] They noted that in a "nuclear-missile war," war itself becomes obsolete in purely military terms since its "natural" end result—victory—for which wars have in fact always been waged, becomes impossible:

Ultimately, war is not only an armed confrontation. It implies other means of supporting armed struggle, but relatively independent and 'nonmilitary' forms of conflict: economic, diplomatic, intelligence, scientific and technological, ideological, etc. But with the total destruction of human and physical resources, nuclear catastrophe would not leave room for these forms of opposition.[137]

On the basis of that argument they concluded: "Thus, the formula that war is a continuation of politics is so distorted by the realities of the nuclear age that in terms of both substance and functions, it is useless to the understanding of what used to be called a nuclear-missile war."[138]

Similar ideas were expressed by Yu.Ya. Kirshin, V.M. Popov, and R.A. Savushkin, military analysts from the same institute, in their book *The Political Substance of Contemporary Wars* (*Politicheskoe soderzhanie sovremennykh voin*). In their words, "modern weaponry, due to its destructiveness, has objectively developed beyond the expediency of its utility for achieving political goals."[139]

In a discussion sponsored and published by the journal *International Life* (*Mezhdunarodnaya zhizn'*) in 1988, all the participants but one, N. Grachev, supported the above line of thinking. Grachev, however, opposed it and reiterated the arguments of the 1960s and 1970s:

Nuclear missiles are created, accumulated, and improved at the order of political leaders, they are the manifestation of a quite intentional policy. Policy has made and will continue to make decisions on the use or nonuse of nuclear weapons. Aggressive forces in the United States have wanted to

---

136. B.K. Kanevsky and P.N. Shabardin, "*K voprosu o sootnoshenii politiki, voiny i raketno-yadernoi katastrofy*" (On the issue of the correlation of policy, war, and nuclear-missile catastrophe), *Mezhdunarodnaya zhizn'*, No. 10 (1987), p. 121.

137. Ibid., p. 122.

138. Ibid.

139. Yu.Ya. Kirshin, V.M. Popov, and R.A. Savushkin, *Politicheskoye soderzhanie sovremennykh voin* (The political substance of contemporary wars) (Moscow: Nauka, 1987), p. 35.

use nuclear weapons against the USSR and other countries more than a dozen times. Nothing at the level of principles has happened to prevent these weapons from being instruments of war. The accidental start of nuclear war due to a technical mishap does not eliminate its political substance since it is the policy that has prepared for war that is responsible for the "accident" itself. Moreover, retaliatory measures would not be accidental in this unintentional war and the decision to take them would be made by the political leadership.[140]

Arguing against Grachev, Daniil Proektor, a well-known military historian and theoretician, wrote that "no one with even a minimum of common sense would use nuclear weapons to wage war and to achieve victory."[141] However, he also underscored the political role of nuclear weapons. He wrote that

it is becoming, so to speak, a rather "political" weapon, exceeding the limits of the traditional means of war. In the past, a weapon was above all a means of warfare and only secondarily a means of "indirect" actions. With nuclear weapons, it is vice versa. They are first of all a means of "indirect" actions and only secondarily, in an extreme and almost unthinkable case, a means of warfare.[142]

Proektor defined the line dividing policy and nuclear conflict, which must not be considered a continuation of politics, as "the processes of international political struggle, the growth of political tension, preparations for war and even moves toward it—all of these are politics. Nuclear war is an entirely different state which cannot be considered politics since it has none of its characteristics. It is not policy."[143]

Proektor also considered that "if we are talking about small, 'limited' or local wars outside the East-West confrontation which are being waged by conventional means, then Clausewitz's ideas on war as a policy which replaced the pen with a sword continue to be confirmed. . . . Nevertheless, a more thorough analysis of the possibilities for resolving political problems by force shows that they are steadily decreasing in this area as well."[144]

---

140. N. Grachev, "O raketno-yadernoi voine i yeye posledstviyakh" (On nuclear-missile war and its aftermath), *Mezhdunarodnaya zhizn'*, No. 4 (1988), p. 80.

141. D. Proektor, "O politike, Klauzevitse i pobede v yadernoi voine" (On politics, Clausewitz and victory in nuclear war), *Mezhdunarodnaya zhizn'*, No. 4 (1988), p. 80.

142. Ibid.

143. Ibid., p. 84.

144. Ibid.

These debates undoubtedly will continue in Russia and elsewhere, since the use of various forms of military force remains a part of international relations, and political institutions that generate ideas about the use of force to resolve international problems exist in almost every country.

Chapter 2

Threats to Soviet Security and the Probability of a Future War

Making predictions in the political-military sphere is an extremely difficult undertaking. Throughout history, few forecasts have been correct, and those that were rarely affected the development of policy or military strategy. Often the predictions that came true had been made by outside observers who were not involved in the consuming everyday routine of political and military institutions.

In the 1920s, Soviet assessments of threats and of the nature of a future war were directly influenced by World War I and the Russian Civil War, and the ideological guidelines formed by the imperatives of world revolution played a dominant role. Despite the suppression of revolutionary outbursts abroad, many Party and Red Army leaders sincerely believed that world revolution was inevitable—although not in the immediate future. The belief that the Soviet Union was the first broken link in the chain of imperialism and that similarly structured states would soon appear worldwide was an important component of the political mentality of workers and even some peasants in addition to the Party and Komsomol zealots. It was that belief that helped many to endure the adversity of the civil war and the post-war political and economic blockade by the Entente. For a significant portion of Party functionaries and Red Army commanders, this belief also meant the export of revolution. The general revolutionary population considered the necessity to support revolutionaries abroad not at all unnatural and quite fair, since during the Russian Revolution and civil war, France, the United Kingdom, the United States, Japan, and other members of the Entente provided military support to the counterrevolutionaries. Their armed intervention, financial support, and major supplies of arms and ammunition to the Whites prolonged the civil war and intensified the disorder and famine in Russia. The brutal suppression of revolutions in Germany and Finland in 1918 by German troops, and in Hungary with the help of the Entente in 1919, as well as the suppression of revolutionary activities in Poland in 1918–19, were received with indignation and pain by political activists in the young Soviet Union.

In the 1920s, debates, sometimes quite sharp, on world revolution took place within both the Party and the Communist International, or Comintern (an international revolutionary organization of communist parties controlled by Moscow, which acted in 1919–43). Lenin himself concluded that Europe was not yet mature enough for a proletariat revolution. While not denying in principle that such a revolution was the goal, Lenin had reservations about its methods and timing. In a letter dated August 5, 1921, to G.A. Miyasnikov, a member of the Workers' Opposition, Lenin wrote: "Indeed, whoever fails to understand the substitution of the slogan of 'civil peace' for the slogan of 'civil war' lays himself open to ridicule, if not something worse."[1]

Lenin's remark was aimed at both foreign and domestic policies. The New Economic Policy (NEP) was now at the core of Soviet domestic policy; in Lenin's view, NEP represented "a totally different method, a reformist method: not to *break up* the old social-economic system . . . but to *revive* trade, small businesses, and capitalism while cautiously and gradually getting the upper hand over them, or making it possible to subject them to state regulation *only to the extent* that they revive."[2] Lenin criticized the dogmatism of those who ardently championed world revolution at any price.

Despite Lenin's great authority within the Party, most of his closest associates did not listen to him. Many leftists whose thinking had been formed by the long struggle against tsarism, time spent in penal colonies, exile or emigration, as well as the civil war, were unprepared for governing the new Soviet state and formulating wise and balanced peacetime domestic, foreign, and military policies.[3]

It is true that Lenin developed the thesis that the struggle between the bourgeoisie and the proletariat was the key feature of world politics after the victory of the October Revolution in Russia: "There are two forces on earth that can decide the destiny of humankind. One force is international capitalism. . . . The other force is the international proletariat."[4] Moreover, "without the slightest exaggeration, two camps quite

---

1. V.I. Lenin, *Collected Works*, Vol. 32 (Moscow: Progress Publishers, 1977), p. 504.

2. Ibid., Vol. 33, p. 110.

3. See V. Sirotkin, "*Puti mirovoi revolyutsii*" (The paths of world revolution), *Izvestia*, September 2, 1988.

4. Lenin, *Collected Works*, Vol. 30, p. 215.

consciously oppose each other on a worldwide scale."[5] This oversimplified formula was canonized and lay as the basis of Soviet appraisals of a future war and the political-military situation until the late 1980s. However, it is important to note that Lenin, in polemicizing with his Party colleagues, differentiated between "wise capitalists" and "sensible representatives of the bourgeoisie," on the one hand, and representatives of the "military party" and "adventuristic elements," on the other. In his view, the Soviet Union could interact with the former group to pursue the policy of peaceful coexistence of states with different social systems.

Revolutionary Wars and National Wars

As mentioned above, in the 1920s Red Army commanders and Soviet military theoreticians primarily based their political and military-strategic approaches to a future war on World War I (which was called the "Imperialist War" in Soviet Russia) and the Russian Civil War. In many cases, some antagonism was evident between those who relied more on the World War I experience and those who thought that the civil war was more appropriate to an understanding of future warfare. As a rule, the first group comprised former tsarist officers, and the second included Red Army commanders who had risen through the rank and file and the noncommissioned officer corps of the tsarist army.

The expectation of a decisive battle between the Soviet Union—the first socialist state—and a combination of capitalist states underlay Soviet military and political characterizations of a future war. However, it would be incorrect to say that concepts of world revolution and its export dominated the thinking of the Red Army command. In fact, these ideas coexisted with defense concepts in which the primary task of the Red Army was the defense of the Soviet Union against foreign encroachment. Although the defense of socialism in the interest of the proletariat and working people all over the world was said to be the main mission of the Red Army, many former tsarist officers who were at the service of the new regime interpreted the defense of the motherland in traditional terms of Russian patriotism.

Mikhail Frunze's conception, eloquently depicted in his 1921 article "Unified Military Doctrine and the Red Army," was indicative:

At the first convenient moment, the waves of the bourgeois capitalist ocean surrounding our proletarian island will rush in to attempt to sweep away all the achievements of the proletarian revolution. At the same time the flames

---

5. Ibid., p. 450.

of revolutionary fires are erupting more and more frequently in various countries of the bourgeois world, and the formidable tramp of proletarian columns preparing for the attack reveals in part the plans of the other side. This contradiction can be eliminated only by force in a bloody battle between class enemies. There is and can be no other way out.[6]

Mikhail Tukhachevsky shared this viewpoint in a collection of his articles published in 1921 under the title *War of the Classes* (*Voina klassov*). As he put it, "Soviet Russia is a disseminator of socialist revolution for the entire world."[7] Tukhachevsky's general conclusion about the prevailing character of international relations was that "it is absolutely impossible to imagine that the world, shaken to its very foundation by the world war, could quietly divide into two parts—socialist and capitalist—capable of living in peace and perfect harmony. It is absolutely clear that such a time will never come and the socialist war will not end until the victory of one or the other side."[8]

The idea of a "revolution by bayonets" (*revolyutsiya na shtykakh*) was likely of key importance for Tukhachevsky in the early 1920s. It was reflected in Order No. 1423, dated July 2, 1920, for troops on the western front, which ended with these rousing words:

Fighters of the workers' revolution! Fix your eyes on the West. It is in the West that the fate of the world revolution is being decided. Over the dead body of White Poland lies the way to the world fire of revolution. Let us bring peace and happiness to the working people by bayonet. To the West! To the decisive battles, to resounding victories![9]

The order was signed by Tukhachevsky, commander of the armies of the front; I.T. Smilga and I.S. Unshlikht, members of the revolutionary military council of the front and lifelong revolutionaries; and Shwartz, chief of the front staff. Thus Tukhachevsky entirely rejected the concept of peaceful coexistence of states with different social systems that Lenin advocated.

Calling on the Party leadership and the nation as a whole, Frunze emphasized that "our country continues to be like a besieged fortress, and it will remain in this position as long as capital prevails in the

---

6. M.V. Frunze, *Selected Works*, Vol. 2 (Moscow: Voenizdat, 1957), p. 14.

7. M.N. Tukhachevsky, *Voyna klassov* (War of the classes) (Moscow: Gosizdat, 1921), p. 61.

8. Ibid., p. 69.

9. Central State Archives of the Soviet Army, collection 104, inventory 5, file 65, p. 843.

world."[10] The "besieged fortress" concept was maintained and in circulation in the Soviet Union until the 1980s. In 1922, Frunze developed the concept in his report to a meeting of the commanders of Ukraine and the Crimea, and later it was used as the basis for the theses "Training Troops. Military and Political Training in the Red Army," mentioned in Chapter 1. On the function of the Red Army, these theses state the following: "The Red Army will later carry out its combat mission in the conditions of a revolutionary war, either defending against the attack of imperialism or waging a common struggle with the working people of other countries."[11]

In the 1920s, the Red Army leaders who thought that future wars in which the Soviet Union engaged would be revolutionary in character assumed that the rear of the adversarial states would be extremely unstable, and that that would increase the Red Army's possibilities. Tukhachevsky explicitly emphasized the importance of this factor in *War of the Classes*: "A state ruled by the workers does not set its political goal in war on the basis of its armed forces and means, but should instead develop the forces necessary for conquering the bourgeois states of the world." He stressed that "the proletariat of the entire world regardless of nationality will be the source for bringing the army up to strength."[12]

This was not a purely theoretical assumption or a slogan unsupported by practical steps. During the Soviet-Polish War of 1920, the Red Army entered Poland after rebuffing the Polish assault on Soviet territory. The Provisional Revolutionary Committee of Poland (*Pol'revkom*) was established by the Polish Bureau of the Central Committee of the Russian Communist Party (Bolsheviks) chaired by Feliks Dzerzhinsky and including F.Ia. Kon, Iu.Iu. Markhlevsky, E.Ia. Prukhnyak, and Iu. (I.S.) Unshlikht as members.[13] Besides introducing agricultural reforms on the territory under Red Army control, the Provisional Revolutionary Committee also started to form Red units of Polish volunteers. Courses for over one thousand Polish Red commanders were set up first in Bobruysk, then in Smolensk, and later in Moscow.

Certainly the Soviet-Polish War amounted to more than merely implementing the idea of a "revolution by bayonets." In its initial stage, when Polish troops penetrated deep into the territory of Belorussia and

---

10. Frunze, *Selected Works*, Vol. 2, p. 15.

11. *Voennyi vestnik*, No. 5 (1922), p. 33.

12. Tukhachevsky, *Voina klassov*, p. 139.

13. *Grazhdanskaya voina i voennaya interventsiya v SSSR. Entsiklopediya* (Civil war and military intervention in the USSR Encyclopedia) (Moscow: Sovetskaya entsiklopediya, 1983), p. 467.

Ukraine, the war was exclusively defensive and provoked a rise in patriotic sentiments among various strata of the Russian population, including former tsarist officers. General Alexis Brusilov, head of the *Osoboe Soveshchanie* (a provisional body set up under the commander in chief to run the war with Poland), pointedly remarked in a letter to the chief of the All-Russian General Headquarters (*Vserosglavshtab*): "In the last few days I have been reading in the newspapers daily about the rapid and large-scale offensive of the Poles, who probably want to seize all the lands which had been part of the Polish Kingdom prior to 1772, or may not limit themselves to them."[14] In his opinion, the first measure that the Soviet Union had to take to repel this aggression was to stimulate people's patriotism, for without it the army would not be able to achieve great combat efficiency.[15] This was by no means an appeal to old imperial sentiments, which had been fed by the idea of "Slavic unity."

Our people should understand that the old fallen government was not right to have forcibly kept a part of the fraternal Polish people under its dominance for more than a century. Free Russia did the right thing when it immediately removed the chains from all the peoples dependent on it. But having released the Poles and given them the opportunity for self-determination and to live according to their wishes, Russia could righteously demand the same from them. The Polish invasion of lands which have belonged to the Russian orthodox people from time immemorial should be driven out by force.[16]

In the "Appeal to All Former Officers Wherever They Are," Brusilov and other members of the *Osoboe Soveshchanie* appealed to patriotism and national unity in the face of foreign aggression:

At this critical historic point in the life of our nation, we, your senior comrades in arms, appeal to your love of country and loyalty to it, we call to you and ask you to forget all your injuries regardless of who inflicted them on you and where they were inflicted and enlist in the Red Army voluntarily, eagerly, and with dedication at the front or in the rear. And wherever the government of Soviet Workers' and Peasants' Russia might send you, serve not out of fear but out of conscience, to defend our dear Russia, and with your honest service and not begrudging your life, do not allow Russia to be plundered since it might vanish forever. Then our descendants will rightfully curse us for not using our combat expertise and knowledge, for forgetting

---

14. "*Pis'mo A.A. Brusilova k n-ku Vserosglavshtaba*" (Letter of A.A. Brusilov to chief of the *Vserosglavshtab*), *Voennoe delo*, No. 10 (May 10, 1920), p. 291.

15. Ibid.

16. Ibid.

our dear Russian people, and ruining our Mother Russia out of selfish feelings of class struggle.[17]

In 1920, a significant appraisal of the Soviet-Polish War appeared in the magazine *Voennoe delo* in an article by an anonymous author:

The spring has come and notwithstanding the incredibly hard winter campaign and splendid victories of the Red Army, its weapon is again bared in the West where the cannonade roars ceaselessly and an ancient dispute with the *lyakhi* [Poles] is being solved. A few more months of efforts by the Red fighters of Russia will be needed to put an end to the wars that have broken out in the 20th century! Combat trumpets are sounding in Russia, calling the fighters for the last battle with the *lyakhi* for dear life! *Hey, Russia! Forward to the defense of your ancient rights! Arise as one against the enemy!*[18]

Although many responded positively to the appeal of the *Osoboe Soveshchanie* headed by Brusilov, according to some historians it was not all that successful. Moreover, Brusilov and his associates' characterization of the war did not prevail. More typical was an interpretation by Nikolai Kakurin, then a well-known Red Army commander:

The struggle between Russia and *panskaya* Poland is the first international clash between a proletarian state's policy and that of a capitalist state . . . . The Polish-Soviet War is not a struggle between two nations, it is a struggle of the proletariat that has already shed its shackles for the freedom of the proletariat that has not yet succeeded in throwing off the yoke of its enslavers.[19]

It is noteworthy that Kakurin came from the ranks of the senior officers of the tsarist army. He graduated from the Academy of the General Staff in 1910 and rose to the rank of colonel. During the Soviet-Polish War he was an acting commander of the army and then an assistant to the commander of the western front. Kakurin was neither a political worker nor a former junior officer of the old army, i.e., he did not belong to the groups noted for their ideological interpretation of war.

---

17. "*Vozzvaniye. Ko vsem byvshim ofitseram, gde by oni ni nakhodilis*" (Appeal to all former officers wherever they are), *Voennoe delo*, No. 13 (July 7, 1920), p. 1.

18. "*Obzor boevykh deistvii Krasnoi Armii v mae mesyatse 1920 g.*" (Survey of military actions of the Red Army in May 1920), *Voennoe delo*, No. 13 (1920), p. 410. Emphasis in original.

19. N. Kakurin, "*Bor'ba Sovetskoi Rossii c panskoi Pol'shei*" (The struggle of Soviet Russia with *panskaya* Poland), *Voennyi vestnik*, No. 7 (1922), p. 3. *Panskaya* refers to the Polish word *pan*, meaning lord or master.

The political interpretation of the Soviet-Polish War by the leadership of the Red Army is evident in a comment by Serge S. Kamenev, commander in chief of the armed forces of the republic, in his work *Struggle with White Poland*. When the forces of the western front led by Tukhachevsky formed a semicircle around Warsaw, Kamenev wrote, "a moment came when the working class of Poland could in fact have helped the Red Army, which could have given the workers' and peasants' Russia a guaranteed peace with no danger of new attacks. But there was no helping hand. Probably the more powerful hands of the Polish bourgeoisie had hidden this helping hand somewhere."[20]

Svechin was among the main opponents of the idea that future wars would be mainly class-based and revolutionary in character. Without excluding entirely the possibility of a revolutionary war, Svechin developed the idea that basing policy and military strategy on this political-military expectation was both erroneous and dangerous. It could result in inappropriate political guidelines and an overestimation of the capabilities of strategic offensive operations, and thus could bring catastrophe to the offensive side. To justify his position, Svechin turned to history. One of his examples was Napoleon's Egyptian campaign, the ultimate goal of which, according to Svechin, was the conquest of India, with the support of an anti-British rebellion of Indian patriots. In Svechin's view, that campaign was an adventure. "Tippoo Sahib, an Indian patriot who had organized a rebellion in India against English exploitation, played a major role in Napoleon's plans. A key role in Hannibal's plans was played by the promises of the Gauls, who had just been conquered by Rome, to launch a rebellion against the Romans and assist the Carthaginian leader. In the campaign of 1920 great faith was placed in the Polish proletariat."[21] Generalizing on the lessons of both the distant and not-so-distant past, Svechin concluded: "Historical revolutionary wars often involve such hopes and impel leaders to take strategic risks."[22]

On the whole, Svechin's judgments on the nature of a future war turned out to be correct, since they were based on deep analysis and an understanding of history rather than merely extrapolating from the experience of the Russian Civil War. Localized armed conflicts with Chiang Kai-Shek's forces in 1929, with the Japanese at the Khalkhin-Gol River and Lake Khasan in 1938 and 1939, in the Soviet-Finnish War of 1939–40,

---

20. S.S. Kamenev, *Zapiski o grazhdanskoi voine I voennom stroitel'stve* (Notes on the civil war and military development) (Moscow: Voenizdat, 1963), p. 167.

21. Aleksandr A. Svechin, *Strategy* (Minneapolis, Minn.: East View Publications, 1992), p. 266.

22. Ibid.

and in the greatest test of the first socialist state, the war with Germany and its allies in 1941–45, did not corroborate the opinion of Svechin's opponents that all future wars involving the Soviet Union would be revolutionary wars. Nevertheless, attempts to make these wars revolutionary did not stop. For a number of historical reasons Hitler, the Nazi Party, and the government apparatus subordinated to it managed to make the bulk of the German population fight against the Soviet Union.[23]

Relying on an analysis of the potential of states and of long-term historical trends, Svechin emphasized that a future war would be a painful undertaking for the Soviet Union, that it would most probably be protracted, and that it would demand the staged mobilization of huge resources and the exertions of the whole nation. He warned against hopes for rapid progress and the success of the so-called "strategy of destruction," which, it was asserted, could decide the outcome of war between the Soviet Union and its major capitalist adversaries through a series of glorious offensive operations within a short period of time. Actually Svechin's understanding concurred with Lenin's definition: "War tests all the economic and organizational forces of a nation."[24] It also corresponded to Engels's ideas about wars of attrition in the coming era of imperialism, which he defined in a series of outstanding works written between 1880 and 1890 in which he brilliantly forecast the nature and results of World War I.[25]

As a result of his thorough study of the political, economic, and military-technological resources of states, Svechin concluded that in modern conditions, when powerful states and coalitions of states confront each other, wars between them inevitably will be long and the forms and methods of warfare will vary. It was in this context that Svechin used the term "strategy of attrition." However, he noted that "the term attrition is a very poor expression of all the diverse shades of different strategic methods outside the realm of destruction."[26] But Svechin's critics preferred to ignore this and many of his other interpretations. The strategy of attrition, as Svechin understood it, "in no way renounces in principle the destruction of enemy personnel as a goal of an operation. But in this

---

23. M.A. Gareev, *M.V. Frunze—Voennyi teoretik* (M.V. Frunze—military theorist) (Moscow: Voenizdat, 1985), p. 229.

24. Lenin, *Collected Works*, Vol. 30, p. 154.

25. Engels's most brilliant prediction concerning World War I can be found in his preface to a book by S. Bokheim, *Zur Erinnerung für die deutschen Mordspatrioten 1806–1807* (In remembrance of the fallen German patriots of 1806–1807) (Zurich: Hottingen, 1888).

26. Svechin, *Strategy*, p. 246.

it sees only a part of the mission of the armed front rather than the entire mission."[27] In modern conditions, not only the orientation of the efforts but also their proportion must be pondered. Svechin emphasized that a strategy of attrition could pursue most of the same decisive military and political goals as a strategy of destruction.[28]

Svechin's political-military and strategic analysis of a future war was closely linked with an economic and geographical analysis. More than once he pointed out the necessity to consider a possible annexation of Soviet territory by the enemy in the event of aggression from the West, and the consequential importance of military and strategic considerations in locating new industrial enterprises. For example, "the construction of powerful sources of electrical power, such as the Dneprostroi and Svirstroi, which in the future will be used to industrialize entire regions, will also require competent strategic analysis as well as technical and economic analysis."[29] In this regard, Svechin considered the Urals to be an area where industry could be relatively safely concentrated. The fate of Leningrad greatly concerned him. Svechin called the city the "Sevastopol of a future war," remembering the role Sevastopol had played in the Crimean War in the mid-nineteenth century. He warned against further concentration of industry and population in Leningrad:

The tsarist government decided to crowd many plants into Leningrad without being bothered by the fact that it conflicted with nature. In 1925 Leningrad had 11.6 percent of all Soviet industry, including 56 percent of the rubber industry, 48 percent of the electrical industry and more than 13 percent of the metal industry, which is so important for building engines, machine tools and equipment . . . . The disadvantages of Leningrad's strategic location are made even greater by its distance from sources of fuel, grain and raw materials.[30]

Svechin did not pay much attention in his works to the role of tanks and strike aviation in a future war. It was Tukhachevsky who turned to these means in some of his writings, including his critical reviews of Svechin's concepts. For example, Tukhachevsky pointed out that by 1918, France, Britain, and the United States had undertaken the large-scale and rapid development of tank and aviation technology in preparation for major operations in the closing stages of World War I when they had

---

27. Ibid.
28. Ibid., p. 96.
29. Ibid., p. 90.
30. Ibid., p. 89.

expected to end the war in 1919 rather than in 1918.[31] Svechin foresaw the large-scale use of artillery, tanks, and aircraft in the West by some potential adversaries of the Soviet Union. At the same time, he thought it was unrealistic to expect that the Red Army could be equipped with high-quality combat weaponry in sufficient quantity in the near term. Svechin proceeded from the assumption that the level of industrial and economic development of his country, despite all the efforts to industrialize it, would not allow the Soviet Union to match the West in terms of fighting equipment or the ability to properly apply it strategically and in military operations. "It would be a grave mistake and a disassociation from reality to forget about the vast virgin expanse on which the Dneprostroi and the Nizhny Novgorod autoplant are mere dots."[32] However, Svechin never expressed solidarity with advocates of strategic cavalry. Rather, he supported primarily focusing on the development of the infantry and safe and efficient equipment for it to use in nearby battles. Svechin was sharply criticized for these views by many, including Tukhachevsky, who asserted that Svechin underestimated the Soviet Union's chances for industrialization and thus wished to preserve the technological gap between the Red Army and its potential enemies.

On June 30, 1928, the first five-year plan for the development and reconstruction of the Soviet armed forces was adopted. Among other things, the plan envisaged building 1,075 tanks by the end of the plan's term.[33] In 1929, "thanks to successes in socialist construction" and the acceleration of the tempo of industrialization, by order of the government, the Revolutionary Military Council of the USSR revised the plan to develop the armed forces. Attaining superiority in three fields—aviation, artillery, and tanks—became the cornerstone of the Red Army's task.[34] Even before these instructions had been given, the target for tank production had been raised from 1,075 to 3,500 units. At the end of 1931, the Red

---

31. M. Tukhachevsky, "*O strategicheskikh vzglyadakh prof. Svechina*" (On the strategic views of Prof. Svechin), in *Protiv reaktsionnykh teorii na voenno-nauchnom fronte. Kritika strategicheskikh i voenno-istoricheskikh vzglyadov prof. Svechina. 25 aprelya 1931 g.* (Against reactionary theories in the military scientific field. A critique of the strategic and military-historical views of Prof. Svechin. April 25, 1931) (Moscow: Gosvoenizdat, 1931), p. 14.

32. A. Svechin, "*Mezhdu koryem i traktorom*" (Between the horse and the tractor), *Krasnaya zvezda*, No. 135 (1929).

33. A. Ryzhakov, "*K voprosu o stroitel'stve bronetankovykh voisk Krasnoi Armii v 30-e grody*" (Towards the question on the building of armored troops of the Red Army in the 1930s), *Voenno-istoricheskii zhurnal*, No. 8 (1968), p. 106.

34. Central Archives of the Ministry of Defense, collection 15-A, inventory 165, file 3, pp. 4–7.

Army received 900 tanks. In the second half of 1931, tank production rose, and the increase continued in 1932 and beyond. Beginning in 1932, the Red Army received 3,000 tanks and light tanks annually.[35]

The increase in tank and other armaments production in the Soviet Union in the 1930s began within the framework of putting into practice Stalin's concept of "intensive building of socialism in the areas of industry and agriculture." At the 16th Party Congress, Stalin proposed doubling or even tripling many of the plan's targets (even though the original targets had been rather difficult to achieve); his proposals passed without any serious debate or criticism. None of the targets was reached, although Soviet industrial development did increase remarkably by draining resources from the agricultural sector and lowering the standard of living.[36] It was in this period that the foundation was established for the buildup of the Soviet defense industry that continued until the 1980s. Soviet investments in the defense industries proved to be justified during World War II, but were far too costly in human terms.

Maneuverability in a Future War

Like many other top Soviet military leaders of that period, Frunze assumed that a future war would be a war of maneuver. He did not deny the special role that strategic cavalry had played in the Russian Civil War, which had proved to be highly maneuver-oriented, but he took issue with overly ardent advocates of cavalry, stressing that "the experience of the civil war alone is not sufficiently convincing, and thus this issue is by no means clear for everyone."[37] On the whole, Frunze argued, the experience of the civil war was largely one-sided because in the course of both the civil war and the Soviet-Polish War, Russia had to face an enemy either equal to or somewhat superior to the Red Army in terms of technology. The theses on "Training Troops" stated the following: "The circumstances of future revolutionary wars will have a number of peculiarities which will approximate civil wars. In this regard these will be mainly wars of maneuver."[38]

However, Frunze's and like-minded people's skepticism could not

---

35. Svechin, "*Mezhdu koryem i traktorem*," p. 106.

36. L. Gordon and E. Klokov, "*Tridtsatye—sorokovye*" (The thirties and forties), *Znanie—sila*, No. 4 (1988), pp. 24–25.

37. Frunze, *Selected Works*, Vol. 2, p. 19.

38. "*Obuchenie voisk. Voennoye i politicheskoye vospitanie Krasnoi Armii*" (Training troops. Military and political training in the Red Army), *Voennyi vestnik*, No. 5 (1922), p. 33.

convince the Red Army command to take a critical approach to cavalry. Military leaders with a cavalry background occupied rather important positions in the army after the civil war, and they tirelessly promoted the key role of the cavalry and large formations of strategic cavalry in future warfare. They persistently tried to prove that cavalry could have had an impact on many military operations in World War I. "Cavalry failures or inactivity were not a result of modern firepower depriving the cavalry of the ability to act in mounted formations on the battlefield," wrote Yushkov in *Voennyi vestnik* in 1922 shortly before the Cavalry Congress. "Rather, they were caused by a lack of faith in their own weapons, the misapplication of cavalry by the supreme command, and poor command of cavalry due to an absence of talented leaders."[39]

Contrary to widespread opinion, not only cavalry service people but also some military leaders advocated using cavalry. Even Shaposhnikov, an outstanding commander of the early 1920s (who had, however, once served in the cavalry),[40] stated: "We insist that the cavalry should be independent in its operational activity in the future, i.e., it should be able to carry out its tactical missions without assistance from the infantry."[41] Thus major formations of cavalry were needed: "We recognize the expediency of having strong unified formations of cavalry—cavalry masses—since only they have the force and firepower needed to blaze forward, even in the enemy's rear."[42] A knowledgeable military professional, Shaposhnikov did not, however, avoid highly ideological pronouncements in his defense of strategic cavalry: "I welcome the vibrant idea of a proletarian cavalry with only one aim: to point out the proper paths to victory! As to cavalry's significance to the Red Army, it is correctly defined by the historic slogan: 'Proletarian, to the Horse!'"[43]

Semen Budennyi, a famous commander of the First Cavalry, was without a doubt one of the most zealous supporters of strategic cavalry. He believed that even in World War I strategic cavalry could have fulfilled an extremely important mission. Tsarist Russia had had forty first-class cavalry divisions armed with about 300,000 sabres, and in Budennyi's

---

39. Yushkov, *Sovremennaya organizatsiya konnitsy za rubezhom i zadachi konnitsy v sovremennoi voine* (Contemporary organization of cavalry abroad and missions of cavalry in modern warfare), *Voennyi vestnik*, No. 7 (1992), p. 92.

40. See B.M. Shaposhnikov, *Vospominaniya. Voennye trudy* (Memoirs. Military works) (Moscow: Voenizdat, 1982), pp. 195–372.

41. B.M. Shaposhnikov, "*Dva opyta*" (Two experiences), *Voennyi vestnik*, No. 7 (1922), p. 14.

42. Ibid.

43. Ibid., p. 15.

view, if they had been sent deep into the rear, they would have "terrorized" the enemy. "The First Cavalry never had more than 14,000 sabres. Now compare 14,000 and 300,000. If we had had 300,000, we could have simply smashed a corridor through the enemy's forward area with our horses' hooves."[44]

It is likely that Budennyi's view of the cavalry's role was quite rational in the 1920s. However, turbulent developments in military technology in the period between the two world wars should have finished off any plans for using the cavalry in future wars.[45] Although Tukhachevsky and his supporters insisted on this, their opponents did not yield, and used every possible pretext to promote the idea of strategic cavalry and everything related to its development, above all providing the cavalry with front-line horses. In a characteristic speech at the 17th Party Congress in 1934, Budennyi stated: "Spring is the time for sowing grain as well as mating horses. But in our country, when they start sowing, they immediately forget about mating horses. This has continued for three years running."[46]

Even in the late 1930s, on the eve of World War II—a "war of engines," as Stalin later called it—the proponents of the cavalry maintained their position. "In all the armies of the world, the cavalry is going through, or rather has gone through, a crisis and has come to nought. . . . We hold another opinion. . . . The Red cavalry continues to be a victorious and destructive armed force. It is able to carry out and will carry out tactical tasks on all fronts," wrote Voroshilov in 1938.[47] This was not

---

44. S.M. Budennyi, "*Konnitsa v sovremennoi voine*" (Cavalry in modern war), in *Zapiski. Kommunisticheskaya akademiya. Sektsiya po izucheniyu problem voiny* (Notes. The Communist Academy. Section on studies of the problems of war), Vol. 2 (Moscow: Komakademiya, 1931), p. 17.

45. At the same time it should be remembered that in the 1920s and 1930s, the cavalry was used effectively in the prolonged struggle against the *basmachi* nationalist counterrevolutionaries in the republics of Central Asia. This partisan movement battled with the Soviets until 1922, and was completely eliminated in the early 1930s. See A.I. Zevelev, Iu.A. Poliakov, and A.I. Chugunov, *Basmachestvo: Vozniknovenie, sushchnost', krakh* (The *basmach* movement: Its emergence, essence, and failure) (Moscow: Nauka, 1981), pp. 136–137, 140, 166.

46. *XVII s'ezd Kommunisticheskoi partii (b)* (The 17th Congress of the Communist Party [Bolsheviks]), stenographic notes (Moscow: Partizdat, 1934), p. 513.

47. K.E. Voroshilov, "*XX let Raboche-Krest'yanskoi Krasnoi Armii i Voenno-Morskogo Flota*" (Twenty years of the Workers' and Peasants' Red Army and Navy), *Voennaya mysl'*, No. 3 (1938), p. 13.

simply rhetoric: from 1934 to 1939, the number of Soviet cavalry personnel increased by 52 percent.[48]

During World War II, Soviet cavalry divisions and corps were widely used in mounted-mechanized formations to exploit strategic successes. However, the cavalry was never employed successfully for attack, and all such attempts had pitiful results.

The Role of the Navy in a Future War

The role, structure, and composition of the navy played a significant part in defining the future of the Soviet armed forces. After the civil war, the navy was in a lamentable position. The newly founded Soviet state did not have naval forces in the Black Sea, the Pacific Ocean, or in the North. Only in the Baltic did it manage to maintain the very small naval force of the former tsarist fleet. Economic problems were central to the situation of the Soviet navy. A well-known Soviet naval specialist, I.M. Ludri, noted that the Red Army and the Red Fleet (as the Soviet navy was known) had been moving in different directions for a number of years.[49] However, he pointed out that competition between naval and army commands was universal, occurring not only in revolutionary times, but also in tsarist Russia, and it never abated in capitalist countries.

In the Soviet armed forces, the navy's tendency toward independence stemmed from, in Ludri's view, the presence in the top naval institutions of a great number of tsarist officers who had been trained in the spirit of an independent fleet. That independence had been institutionally secured: the navy's general staff had functioned in parallel with the general staff of the armed forces. According to Ludri, institutional defects were overcome in the Soviet armed forces: the Revolutionary Military Council of the Republic, which included representatives of the navy and the air force, was a commanding body that covered all kinds of weaponry. He wrote, "As to its operational department—the staff of the RKKA [Red Army]—this brain of the army, from which the threads of operational guidance should stretch in all directions, has done a great deal in recent years to achieve unity. At least no one dreams about a separate naval general staff."[50]

---

48. K.E. Voroshilov's speech at the 18th Congress of the Communist Party, in *XVIII s'ezd Kommunisticheskoi partii (b)* (The 18th Congress of the Communist Party [Bolsheviks]), stenographic notes (Moscow: OGIZ, 1939), p. 192.

49. I.M. Ludri, "*Krasnyi Flot v sostave Vooruzhennykh Sil Respubliki*" (The Red Fleet within the armed forces of the republic), *Morskoi sbornik*, No. 10 (1927), p. 23.

50. Ibid., pp. 24–25.

Ludri also highlighted another reason for the navy's struggle to maintain its independence. In his view, the navy was reacting to "liquidationist attitudes," which were especially strong after the Kronshtadt mutiny, when the view that Soviet Russia did not need a navy began to gain force.[51] Ludri, who later became a deputy chief of the Soviet naval forces, formulated a guiding principle on the navy's role, which prevailed for at least a decade and, according to some specialists, is still influential: "It should never be forgotten that the navy does not have its own separate and independent missions within the Red Army. The fleet can and must fulfill independent operations, but within the range of tasks set forth by the army command."[52]

Many agreed with Ludri on the need to critically reevaluate the underlying philosophy that guided the tsarist navy. K.I. Dushenov, a former noncommissioned officer in the crew of the legendary cruiser *Aurora* who rose to the position of chief of staff of the Black Sea Fleet and later to commander of the Northern Fleet, wrote that it was necessary to exorcise everything from the past that negatively affected the Red Fleet. Dushenov singled out the following as the most characteristic features of the development of the tsarist navy:

- a discrepancy between the plans for naval development and Russia's level of economic development;
- a dysfunction between the rate of the navy's growth and the policy of the ruling classes in various periods of Russian history; and
- a complete lack of coordination between the army and the navy in the general preparation of the tsarist armed forces.

Dushenov wrote: "What did the tsarist government and sailors of the old fleet strive for? For 'the expanse of the ocean,' for 'broad sea lanes.' Since all the outlets from Russian waters were in the possession of other states, it was necessary to capture those outlets. . . . This line of conduct of the tsarist government and the sailors of the old fleet was accurately described by Comrade Kozhanov as the concept of an 'active strait.'" As a result, Dushenov concluded, "they prepared for war according to one plan, but it was fought according to another, and they were defeated everywhere."[53]

---

51. Ibid., p. 28.
52. Ibid.
53. K.I. Dushenov, "K istorii voprosa o 'maloi voine' na more" (Toward a history of the question of a "small war" at sea), *Morskoi sbornik*, No. 4 (1928), p. 31.

"Considering the enormous cost of modern ships," A.M. Yakimychev, another Soviet naval theoretician, wrote in 1928, "our state cannot afford a powerful battleship fleet in the immediate future. By building a *'small (weak) battleship fleet'* we would play right into the hands of our potential enemies."[54] Yakimychev argued that in waging a "small war," it was necessary to give top priority to those means that are not vulnerable to blockade, such as aviation, submarines, motorized torpedo boats, and other rapid submarine forces.[55] Quite reasonably, he noted that it was unwise to reject the concept of "conquest by sea" because it was a "symbol of belief" of the probable enemy (at that time, Britain), and it weighed upon Russians like the "specter of communism" weighed upon our enemies.[56]

What then was the essence of the theory of naval power according to Yakimychev? His answer was quite definite: "*If we must go to war with a state that has a powerful fleet, then to wage naval warfare we must build either a battleship fleet in no way inferior to that of the adversary, or the means for waging a 'small war' that is capable of paralyzing the enemy's fleet.*" However, "for a long time to come the USSR will not be able to build a battleship fleet capable of engaging in battle with the powerful fleet of our potential adversaries. Therefore we should first of all build the means for waging a 'small war.' A third option does not exist since any other alternative would entirely serve our enemies' interests."[57]

In the early 1930s, several young researchers in the Naval Academy's department of strategy and operational art, I.S. Isakov, A.R. Aleksandrov, and V.A. Belli, stressed the growing role of submarines and aircraft in naval warfare. They advocated using submarines in tandem with air power against large surface ships.[58]

As Admiral Kuznetsov witnessed, these debates were rounded off by Romuald Muklevich, who headed the Soviet navy in that period. Muklevich rejected both the idea of securing supremacy at sea (struggle for

---

54. At the time, most Soviets considered Britain the Soviet Union's main potential adversary. See A.M. Yakimychev, "*Voina 'malym (slabym) flotom' i 'malaya voina' v epokhu parovogo flota*" (War with a "small [weak] fleet" and a "small war" in the epoch of the steam-powered fleet), in *Voprosy strategii i operativnogo iskusstva v sovetskikh voennykh trudakh (1917–1940 gg.)* (Issues of strategy and operational art in Soviet military writings [1917–1940]) (Moscow: Voenizdat, 1965), p. 701. Emphasis in original.

55. Ibid.

56. Ibid., p. 703.

57. Ibid. Emphasis in original.

58. A.P. Aleksandrov, I.S. Isakov, and V.A. Belli, *Operatsii podvodnykh lodok* (Operations of submarines), Vol. 1 (Leningrad: Naval Academy, 1933), pp. 401–402.

the straits) and the concept that the naval forces should comprise smaller ships and motorized boats (gulf defense). In his view, the fleet should first and foremost be oriented to defensive missions related to and defined by the Soviet Union's coastal theaters. Ships of various classes were thus needed in addition to battleships and heavy cruisers of the so-called Washington type.[59]

The Political-Military Situation in the Late 1920s and Early 1930s

A basic conception of the official (and declared) appraisals of the Soviet Union's political-military situation in the late 1920s and early 1930s is provided in statements by Kliment Voroshilov, people's commissar for defense. For instance, in his 1926 article "Eight Years of the Red Army," Voroshilov considered in detail various aspects of international relations and the domestic situation in the United States, Great Britain, France, and Germany.[60] In his view, smaller states like Poland, Czechoslovakia, Romania, and others were totally dependent upon their great "benefactors." A number of major global problems "which might be solved by arms" were at the center of the global political-military situation, according to Voroshilov, including the struggle between Britain and France for dominance in the Mediterranean, competition between the United States and Japan in the Pacific, and a conflict in the Middle East between Turkey and Mosul (Iraq). And all of these tensions, Voroshilov wrote, were "complicated by the powerful growth of the liberation movement of the peoples of the East, the scope of which is steadily growing."[61]

It is important to note that in this article Voroshilov barely touched upon the themes of world revolution and the coming inevitable clash between the Soviet Union and the capitalist states. A considerable part of his article was devoted to the disarmament policies of the leading capitalist states. Voroshilov sharply criticized them, emphasizing the Soviet Union's adherence to the cause of disarmament and reminding the reader that People's Commissar for Foreign Affairs Georgi Chicherin had proposed a program for disarmament at the 1922 Genoa Conference. As Voroshilov wrote in 1926, the Soviet Union "called together our neighboring states to try to get an agreement on arms reductions and perhaps

---

59. See N.G. Kuznetsov, *Nakanune* (On the eve) (Moscow: Voenizdat, 1966), p. 52.

60. K.E. Voroshilov, *Oborona SSSR. Izbrannye stat'i, rechi i pis'ma* (Defense of the USSR. Selected articles, speeches and letters) (Moscow: Voenizdat, 1937), pp. 17–20.

61. Ibid., p. 18.

disarmament." But under pressure from Britain and other states, "our neighbors refused not only to disarm but to discuss this subject further."[62]

Voroshilov provided data on the sizes of the armed forces of some states whose military activities concerned the Soviet Union. For example, he said that France presently had 685,000 troops in ground forces while in 1913 it had had 546,000; Great Britain now had 329,000 (compared to 441,000 during World War I); Italy had 291,000 troops (400,000 prior to World War I) plus 295,000 "fascist troops." Voroshilov also noted a huge increase in the U.S. armed forces, up from 226,000 in 1913 to 408,000 in 1925. Although Japan had reduced its armed forces, there were said to be tens of thousands of clandestine armed individuals in the country. Those five states put together now had 1,918,000 troops compared to 1,880,000 in 1913. Voroshilov also included the Soviet Union's neighbors—Finland, Estonia, Latvia, Poland, Romania—in his analysis (though he neglected to include Lithuania).[63] Finland increased its army by 3,000 troops between 1923 and 1925, and now had 33,000 troops. Estonia's armed forces increased from 12,000 to 14,000; Latvia's from 20,000 to 22,000 troops; Poland's from 264,000 to 325,000 troops; Romania's from 153,000 to 158,000 troops.[64] Thus the total armed forces of the Soviet Union's neighboring states in the West numbered about 552,000 troops. Only the Soviet Union decreased the size of its army, from 5.5 million troops to 562,000, Voroshilov noted.[65] "The USSR is not increasing the Red Army, but it

---

62. Ibid., pp. 20–21.

63. In a series of archival materials from a slightly later period, I discovered evidence that, in the late 1920s, Lithuania and the Soviet Union established secret relations in the military sector. This relationship was connected with the peculiarities of both countries' relationships with Poland.

64. Ibid., p. 25.

65. According to the authors of *The Civil War, 1918–1921*, published in 1928, the size of the Red Army, about 5.5 million strong in 1920, did not guarantee sufficient combat power. As they wrote, by October 1, 1920, there were 5,498,00 *edoki* (eaters) in the Army, i.e., people who were officially on the Army list of food supply. About half of them were stationed in the military districts, i.e., not at the fronts. There were 391,000 people in the reserve army; 159,000 in the labor army. On the western and southwestern fronts (the most important fronts), 360,000 and 221,000 troops were respectively stationed, i.e., only 10 percent of all Soviet troops. Within each front the ratio of fighters to "eaters" was highly unfavorable. In the Red Army as a whole there were 700,000–800,000 combat troops, and of these, 400,000–500,000 were armed; in other words, for each bayonet at the front, there were ten "eaters" in the rear. "Such an Army devoured huge resources, yet at the same time its utility was infinitesimal," according to the authors of "*Voennoe iskusstvo Krasnoi Armii*" (Military art of the Red Army), *Grazhdanskaya*

cannot decrease it either as long as we are encircled by such 'friendly' nations," he concluded.[66]

An exchange of opinions between Svechin and Shaposhnikov not long before the Nazi victory in Germany was indicative of Soviet appraisals of the political and military situation and the character of a future war. Svechin sent Voroshilov a classified memorandum, "Future War and Our Military Missions," and Shaposhnikov, then chief of the operational department of the Red Army, commented on it. In a section on the "Political Background of Future War," Svechin indicated that a coalition of states could unleash a future war against the Soviet Union. In this scenario, the leading role would be played by Great Britain and France. The United States would provide financial support to the coalition, but would initially refrain from direct military involvement.[67] Germany would have to conclude a military convention on the transit of cargo and troops through its territory to Poland, and would use its rolling stock to strengthen the Polish and Romanian rail networks. Svechin thought that Germany would condition its direct assistance to Poland on the territorial concession of the Danzig corridor by Poland. According to Svechin, Poland would only accept such a condition in an extreme situation, e.g., if the Red Army were to take Warsaw. Estonia, Latvia, and probably Finland would be called upon to mobilize their armed forces to tie down some Soviet troops, but would temporarily remain neutral. Their task, in anticipation of progress in the military theaters and reinforcements from France, Britain, and possibly Sweden, would be to provoke the Soviet Union to violate their "armed neutrality." Such a violation would be welcomed by the coalition.

Svechin paid special attention to the potential attitude of the coalition toward various nationalities and regions of the Soviet Union. In his view, the coalition would "use the national issue most actively in Ukraine and Transcaucasia, and exploit the difficulties the Soviets had in the black-earth regions in the South and in the Cossack regions of the Don and the Kuban."[68] As Svechin noted, "Ukraine, the Donets Basin, the northern Caucasus, and Transcaucasia are particularly rich areas, producing

---

voina 1918–1921 gg. (The civil war, 1918–1921), Vol. 2 (Moscow: Voennyi vestnik, 1928), p. 89.

66. Ibid., p. 25.

67. A. Svechin, *Budushchaya voina i nashi voennye zadachi* (Future war and our military missions), Central State Archives of the Soviet Army, collection 33987, inventory 3, file 347e, p. 13.

68. Ibid., p. 14.

important exports like wheat, oil, ore, and coal, and they are very attractive markets for imperialist nations." Moreover, since there is easy access to these regions from the sea, turning them into colonies and exploiting them would be "especially convenient... profitable and tempting." Therefore, Svechin concluded, those areas would be the immediate target of an anti-Soviet coalition.

"For the next 15 years, we will not be able to rely on the quantitative or qualitative superiority of Red Army technology in our struggle with the imperialist coalition," Svechin warned.[69] In his view, it was necessary to abandon the bold hopes of technologically surpassing the West so ardently promoted by Triandofilov and Tukhachevsky. Svechin expected that the coalition would focus its efforts on creating a continuous front from Polesye to the Caspian Sea. The prime task of Poland's main forces and Romania's entire army would be to attack and consolidate the Dnieper line.[70]

According to Svechin, at the beginning of such a war, the mission of the Red Army would be to seize the weakest link in the chain of the enemies' fronts, achieve an immediate major success, and rapidly restore the freedom of maneuver to its main forces. This task could be fulfilled only by directing the first strike at Romania. In sociopolitical and military terms, he wrote, Romania was both the weakest and the most important component of the coalition.[71]

In his commentary on Svechin's memorandum, Shaposhnikov played down Svechin's faculties as a military thinker, though he acknowledged the usefulness of the views of outsiders. As he noted, without sufficient data, these thinkers quite often made mistakes, but their judgments were nevertheless interesting and fresh since they were not concerned with these issues as a full-time occupation and thus noticed mistakes more quickly.[72] Svechin's analysis was helpful in checking Soviet plans for waging a future war, outlining the structure of the Red Army in wartime, and teaching operations and tactics, Shaposhnikov noted. He shared Svechin's assumptions that in a future war the Soviet Union would confront a coalition of states and that France would play the leading role in the coalition. As for Britain, however, Shaposhnikov did not consider

---

69. Ibid., p. 16.

70. Ibid.

71. Ibid., p. 21.

72. B. Shaposhnikov, *Otvet na zapisku A. Svechina, "Budushchaya voina i nashi voennye zadachi"* (Response to Svechin's memorandum on "Future War and Our Military Missions"), Central State Archives of the Soviet Union, collection 33987, inventory 3, file 347e, p. 32.

it one of the Soviet Union's major adversaries. In accordance with Lenin's theory of two types of bourgeoisie (aggressive and more inclined to peaceful solutions), Shaposhnikov pointed out that Svechin had overlooked the fact that the Labour Party held power in Britain. However, if the Conservatives or a coalition government of liberals and conservatives came to power, this would undoubtedly increase the role of Great Britain in the coalition.[73]

Shaposhnikov disagreed with Svechin's appraisal of the U.S. role: "America is presently enduring an economic crisis and would hardly throw money at Europe, and especially not at states like Poland and Romania, whose solvency is not high in the world market."[74] Shaposhnikov also excluded Italy from the list of potential enemies of the Soviet Union. "Svechin says nothing about Italy and he is right since Italy's expansion does not affect the Soviet Union."[75] Shaposhnikov agreed with Svechin's thoughts about the "main initiators" of an anti-Soviet coalition, except the idea that they would send major troop formations to the front line, which did not seem plausible to him. In Shaposhnikov's view, it would be much more advantageous for them to wage war by proxy, leaving the bloodshed to other states.[76] He agreed with Svechin that the coalition's mission would be to "defeat the proletarian state and set up 'colonies' as a reward for the war."[77] However, Shaposhnikov immediately specified that there was no military force large enough to occupy such a huge colony, as had been proved during the Russian Civil War. And without a central authority, he added, no profits could be derived from the colonies.[78]

Shaposhnikov criticized Svechin for disregarding the increasing role of workers' movements and communist parties in other countries. Unlike participants in the later campaign against the "Svechin school,"[79] Shaposhnikov did not call Svechin a heretic or blame him, but instead discussed the issue. Shaposhnikov noted that the growth of workers' movements and communist parties was increasing the hatred of the

---

73. Ibid., p. 34.
74. Ibid., p. 35.
75. Ibid.
76. Ibid.
77. Ibid.
78. Ibid., p. 36.
79. See *Protiv reaktsionnykh teorii na voenno-nauchnom fronte. Kritika strategicheskikh i voenno-istoricheskikh vzglyadov prof. Svechina*.

bourgeois states for the Soviet Union.[80] If the economy had given these states a stable rear, then Russia would have been at war with them long ago. Shaposhnikov argued that

> on the contrary, the economies of the large West European countries cannot achieve the balance needed for a war with us. Unemployment is growing, more and more often workers are protesting in the street, and it is not so easy for the bourgeoisie to inspire the multimillion masses to fight against the Soviet Union. However, they are using every means to try to make the idea of war popular among the proletarian masses, but if there is no economic stability in a country, it is impossible to secure enthusiasm for war on the basis of high emotions alone.[81]

Shaposhnikov further concluded that the bourgeoisie were aware of the impossibility of correcting the domestic situation by war and achieving civil peace. "This route is taken only by political adventurists; capitalism is still far from this path."[82] His judgment of which countries were potential enemies of the Soviet Union stems from this analysis: "One cannot exclude that the large European states might employ major military forces of *other states* within their sphere of influence against the Soviet Union. First of all Poland and Romania, then Finland and Sweden, are these states."[83] In his view, "these smaller states, politically and economically dependent on larger European states, are immediate neighbors of the Soviet Union, and above all fear the 'red menace' and thus are most interested not only in preserving their borders but in expanding them to the East."[84]

One cannot fail to recognize that both Svechin and Shaposhnikov made penetrating analyses. In their discussions of the likelihood of one or another state's participation in a war against the Soviet Union, both men took into account the domestic situations of other countries, the inclination toward adventurism of foreign leaders, geopolitical factors, and foreign perceptions of the "red menace." Shaposhnikov seemed to be more insightful, and demonstrated an ability to differentiate and to make unbiased judgments.

---

80. Shaposhnikov, response to Svechin's memorandum, p. 37.
81. Ibid., p. 36.
82. Ibid.
83. Ibid., p. 37.
84. Ibid.

The Theory of the Initial Phase of War

Already in the late 1920s some Soviet military experts were focusing on the initial phase of war, analyzing the experience of World War I. The initial phase of World War I was defined as the period starting from the day that war was officially declared along with a general mobilization, to the beginning of battle at the border involving the main forces, which were deployed in the theater of military actions according to the war plan. The primary features of that period were the mobilization, strategic deployment, and strategic concentration of the main part of the armed forces of the belligerent powers.[85] For Germany and France, the initial phase of war lasted from sixteen to seventeen days.[86] S.I. Ventsov, chief of the Mobilization Department of the Red Army, drew attention to the period preceding mobilization in a speech at a December 1925 conference of military leaders and political personnel of the Ukrainian military district, pointing out that "when there is a threat of war, a series of steps should be taken to accelerate mobilization readiness."[87] Various methods of mobilization and strategic deployment were discussed. For example, there was a suggestion to establish "screen forces" (*voiska zavesy*) comprising cavalry reinforced by infantry and technical troops (armored forces, artillery, machine-gun units, and aviation) and a network of fortresses, individual forts, and fortifications.[88] Svechin contributed a great deal to that discussion. In 1926, he introduced two new notions: (1) the "premobilization period," starting before the declaration of war and general mobilization when preparatory measures are taken; and (2) a "special period of war," lasting from the declaration of war to the beginning of major operations when general mobilization is carried out and armed forces are concentrated and deployed for the first major operations. It is this special period that Svechin identified as the initial phase of war. By rejecting the old terminology and developing a new one, Svechin took an important step forward.[89] At the same time, according to his interpretation, the initial phase was basically a preparatory period for major military

---

85. I.A. Korotkov, *Istoriia sovetskoi voennoi mysli 1917–Iiun' 1941* (History of Soviet military thought 1917–June 1941) (Moscow: Nauka, 1980), p. 129.

86. Ibid.

87. S.I. Ventsov, "*Itogi i perspektivy mobilizatsionnoi raboty*" (Results and perspectives of mobilization activity), *Mobilizatsionnyi sbornik*, No. 2 (1926), p. 17.

88. G. Sokolov, "*Sovremennaya zavesa i voprosy strategicheskogo prikritiya*" (The modern screen and issues of strategic covering), in *Voina i revolyutsiya* (War and revolution), Book 4 (Moscow: Gosizdat, 1928), p. 17.

89. Svechin, *Strategy*, pp. 201–203.

operations, and included all those measures that had been earlier classified as "preparatory (preliminary) operations" in the terminology of G.A. Leer, a distinguished nineteenth-century Russian military theoretician.[90] Although Svechin thought that individual battles and skirmishes would take place during that period, he did not foresee the possibility of any major battles.

Shaposhnikov was studying that issue in parallel to Svechin, and argued that mobilization is directly connected to the strategic plan of operations. His main work, *Mozg armii*, published in 1929 in three volumes, includes a chapter entitled "Mobilization is the Opium of War." There he noted that in World War I, the belligerents intended to wage war according to the principles of the "strategy of destruction." That strategy required the rapid buildup of as large a military force as possible, its rapid concentration, and almost simultaneous introduction into action in order to achieve a quick and decisive victory.[91] Shaposhnikov believed that the dependence of mobilization on political and strategic factors would become apparent before the beginning of a new war. In his opinion, a future war would be no less tense and protracted than the previous one, and governments would have to resort to additional mobilizations in the course of the war. Nevertheless, mobilization carried out before the war would enforce the first echelon and prevent failure in the initial operations.

In drawing this conclusion, Shaposhnikov proceeded from the fact that the mobilization on the eve of World War I had been equivalent to a declaration of war. Therefore, Shaposhnikov wrote, if a state decided to mobilize, it should realize that, by taking this step, it was starting down the road to war. Since that had been the case in World War I, added to the complexity of mobilizing millions-strong armies, governments were forced to organize a special preparatory period, or premobilization as they began to call it. Within that period, they attempted to implement as many mobilization steps as possible (e.g., measures targeted at converting industry to military production), but secretly and without issuing a call up for active military service. Prior to a future war, Shaposhnikov deduced, a similar premobilization period would be necessary but would start earlier, especially in the economy. However, both sides might shorten the premobilization and actually start to mobilize their forces. "In any

---

90. G. Leer, *Opyt kritiko-istoricheskogo issledovaniya zakonov iskusstva vedeniya voiny* (The experience of critical-historical study of the laws of the art of war conducting) (St. Petersburg: Nikolaevskaya Engineering Academy, 1869), pp. 99–148.

91. B. Shaposhnikov, *Mozg armii* (The brain of the army), Vol. 3 (Moscow: Voennyi vestnik, 1926), p. 283.

case, we will see a certain gradualism and advance steps in preparing mobilization in all spheres to a much greater degree than in 1914." With this remark, Shaposhnikov had in fact singled out a trend which still continues in one fashion or another.[92] Behind it lies the desire of the state to deploy its main forces before the enemy does, and thus be stronger in the initial battles.[93]

In the 1930s, Soviet interest in the initial phase of war further increased. The issue was raised by the extensive motorization and mechanization of the army, and the visible improvement in mobilization methods. Anticipating the enemy in strategic deployment was of particular interest. The most important features of the initial phase of war were dramatically affected by the emergence of new means of war, particularly aircraft and tanks.[94] R.P. Eideman, a prominent Soviet military figure of the period, examined that issue in his 1931 article, "On the Issue of the Nature of the Initial Phase of War." Eideman argued that the initial phase of a future war would be characterized by bitter ground and air fights to secure the advantage to deploy forces first. These clashes would develop at an increasing pace, and the scope of fighting would be much greater. The first hours would be marked by the opening of an air war.[95]

Since aviation was developing rapidly in those years, more and more attention was paid to its role in the initial phase of war. A.N. Lapchinsky, a well-known Soviet aviation theoretician, thoroughly discussed this issue in his 1932 work, *The Air Force in Air Battle and Operation*. According to Lapchinsky, during the initial period of war, aviation would solve three tasks: (1) immediately after the declaration of war, the air force would strike deep in the enemy's rear in order to destroy its mobilization and concentration; (2) it would defend the country against air and chemical attack by the enemy, protecting the mobilization and concentration of its own troops; and (3) it would assist troops on the battlefield. Lapchinsky stressed that these missions could be carried out successfully by establishing air supremacy over the enemy. The struggle to achieve supremacy in the skies should begin in the first days of war using all available means—assault aircraft, bombers, infantry, destroying air bases or disrupting their operation, long-range field artillery, cavalry, motorized units,

---

92. Ibid., pp. 288–289.

93. See S.P. Ivanov, ed., *Nachal'nyi period voiny* (The initial phase of war) (Moscow: Voenizdat, 1974), p. 75.

94. Ibid., p. 92.

95. "*K voprosu o kharaktere nachal'nogo perioda voiny*" (On the issue of the nature of the initial phase of war), *Voina i revolyutsiya*, No. 8 (1931), p. 12.

and acts of sabotage by guerrillas. He attached special importance to bombers, which would mainly disrupt the movement of troops to regions of concentration and thus upset the enemy's plans.[96]

The Political-Military Situation in the Nazi Era

When Hitler came to power in Germany in 1933, the nature of the threat from abroad began to appear in a new light, and Germany became the Soviet Union's most probable major adversary. By that time, the failure of the General Conference on Disarmament of 1932–34 had become obvious. In the early 1930s, a threat to Soviet security began to grow in the Far East. The main source of the danger was Japanese aggression against China and the occupation of Manchuria by Japanese troops.

At the 17th Party Congress in 1934, Stalin proclaimed that everything is for a new imperialist war. He justified this conclusion by stating that the "unprecedented aggravation of the political situation" in the capitalist countries both domestically and internationally was the result of the prolonged international economic crisis.[97] According to Stalin, the potential enemies of the Soviet Union wanted "to defeat the USSR, to divide its territory and profit at its expense."[98] He pointed at Japan as a potential enemy in Asia, but in Europe he preferred not to be specific.[99] The result of such a war against the Soviet Union would be disastrous for bourgeois politicians. Stalin asserted, to a thunder of applause, that

one could hardly doubt that this war would be extremely dangerous for the bourgeoisie. It would be the most dangerous not only because the peoples of the USSR would fight to the last for the achievements of the revolution. It would be dangerous for the bourgeoisie also because the war would be waged not only on fronts but at the enemy's rear. The bourgeoisie has every reason not to doubt that the numerous friends of the USSR among the working class in Europe and Asia would try their best to strike at the rears of their suppressors. . . . And let these gentlemen not blame us if the day after the war ends they cannot find some governments close to them now being safely ruled "by the grace of God."[100]

---

96. *Voprosy strategii i operativnogo iskusstva*, p. 636.

97. *XVII s'ezd Vserossiiskoi Kommunisticheskoi partii (b)*, pp. 10, 11.

98. Ibid., p. 12.

99. In his speech at the congress, Voroshilov was quite definite about Japan's being the most probable enemy of the Soviet Union. At the same time, he emphasized the good relations between the Soviet Union and Turkey, Persia, and Afghanistan. Ibid., pp. 234–235.

100. Ibid., p. 12.

V.K. Blukher, commander of the special Far Eastern Division of the Red Army, did not fail to agree with Stalin. "Our tanks and aviation are the offspring of our first five-year plan. I think these offspring of the five-year plan will be able to fulfill their socialist mission for the Soviet Union not only on our borders, not only at the front, but also somewhere in the rear of our imperialist adversaries," he said to applause.[101] Despite the growth of nationalism in the countries that were considered military threats to the Soviet Union, general political approaches like the one put forward by Stalin at the 17th Party Congress remained central to the Soviet ideological stance and propaganda in the second half of the 1930s.

In 1935, Tukhachevsky wrote an influential article on threat assessment titled "Military Plans of Contemporary Germany." This article was a landmark in the public appraisal of the political-military situation at that time. The importance of this article is demonstrated by the fact that Stalin reviewed it while it was being prepared for publication; a typed copy of the article with Stalin's remarks on it is preserved in the archives of the Soviet Ministry of Defense. Among other things, Stalin changed the original title of the article ("Hitler's Military Plans") and heavily edited several passages. He crossed out almost all of Tukhachevsky's discussion of Germany's ability to wage a war on two fronts based on the experiences of the Franco-Prussian War (1870–71) and World War I.

In the article, Tukhachevsky analyzed in depth the pace of the buildup of Germany's armed forces after Hitler came to power, as well as German approaches to conducting war. He concluded that "Germany is developing huge armed forces, and in the first place, those forces which can form a powerful army of invasion."[102] It was not by chance that Tukhachevsky quoted the French Marshal Pétain: "At the present time it is possible to conceive of a war that starts by surprise and is waged by methods that destroy the first echelon of the enemy's combat forces, disrupt its mobilization and destroy the vital centers of its power."[103] Tukhachevsky also drew the important political-military conclusion that "Hitler's imperialist plans are not only aimed against the Soviets. It is a convenient screen to cover his revanchist plans in the West (Belgium and France) and in the South (Poznan, Czechoslovakia, and the Anschluss)."[104] Moreover, "apart from everything else, one cannot deny that Germany needs French ore. It needs to expand its naval base; the

---

101. Ibid., p. 630.
102. M.N. Tukhachevsky, *Selected Works*, Vol. 2 (Moscow: Voenizdat, 1964), p. 235.
103. Ibid.
104. Ibid., p. 239.

experience of war in 1914–1918 made it perfectly obvious that without firm possession of the ports of Belgium and northern France, Germany's naval power could not be built."[105] It is this passage that Stalin edited substantially to accentuate German schemes of aggression against Western countries using anti-Soviet statements as a screen. About two-thirds of the text about the threat to the Soviet Union and Hitler's plans to win the war in the East on the basis of French and British neutrality he crossed out altogether.

In the second half of the 1930s, international tensions continued to increase, which radically affected Soviet interests. On March 7, 1936, German troops entered the demilitarized Rhineland. In the same year, fascist Italy seized Abyssinia, having used toxic agents in violation of the international convention of June 17, 1925, banning the use of chemical weapons. On July 17–19, 1936, the revolt against the republican government in Spain led by General Francisco Franco, governmental commissar of Morocco, started with the support of the German and Italian intelligence services. Later Germany and Italy began to interfere militarily in the Spanish Civil War.[106] In February 1936, the government of Hiroto came to power in Japan with the support of right-wing officers. Japan established a relationship with Nazi Germany which resulted, among other things, in the signing of the Anti-Comintern Pact on November 25, 1936. In the Soviet Union, this step was seen as obviously anti-Soviet.

One year later, on November 6, 1937, Italy joined the Anti-Comintern Pact. Japanese aggression against China was increasing. After a number of armed clashes with the Chinese, Japanese troops seized Shanghai and Tientsin, two major Chinese ports, and China's capital, Nanking. The Soviet-Chinese Nonaggression Treaty was signed on August 27, 1937.[107]

---

105. Ibid.

106. The Soviet Union provided substantial assistance to the Spanish government by sending armaments. Many Soviet military advisers and volunteers were involved in military operations against the rebels; later many of them held important positions in the Soviet armed forces. Three thousand volunteers from the Soviet Union joined the 39,000 volunteers from other countries, and 200 Soviets were killed in action in Spain. The number of German and Italian personnel operating in Spain reached a peak of about 300,000. See A.A. Gromyko and B.I. Ponomarev, ed., *Istoriya vneshnei politiki SSSR 1917–1945* (A history of the foreign policy of the USSR 1917–1945), Vol. 1 (Moscow: Nauka, 1975), p. 332.

107. In 1930, the Soviet Union provided China with credits amounting to U.S. $50 million. In 1938 and 1939, the Soviet Union supplied China with 600 airplanes, 100 guns and howitzers, more than 8,000 machine guns, means of transport, projectiles, and cartridges. In mid-February 1939, 3,665 Soviet military specialists were in China to participate in the fight against Japan. One of them was Hero of the Soviet Union

In October 1938, a Soviet-Japanese armed conflict took place at Lake Khasan, involving rather large forces on both sides.

In 1937, Nazi diplomacy succeeded in establishing closer relations between Germany and Poland, which caused great anxiety in the Soviet Union, Great Britain, and France. (Polish Foreign Minister Colonel Joseph Beck concluded a treaty on "moral nonaggression" and a treaty on national minorities with Germany.) On March 18, 1938, Hitler's troops marched into Austria without any resistance, and in September 1938, the fate of Czechoslovakia was decided by Chamberlain and Hitler in Munich.

All of these developments were reflected in Stalin's report to the 18th Party Congress (March 10–21, 1939). The title of the political-military part of his report was most significant: "The Aggravation of the International Political Situation, the Collapse of the Post-War System of Peace Treaties, the Beginning of a New Imperialist War." One of the important conceptual elements of Stalin's speech was the division of the capitalist states into two groups: aggressive fascist states, and "nonaggressive democratic states," among which he included Great Britain, France, and the United States.[108] Stalin condemned the "nonaggressive states," particularly France and Britain, for refusing to organize a collective retaliation against the aggressors or to follow a policy of collective security, and for maintaining "neutrality." Stalin explained their systematic concessions to the aggressors in traditional ideological terms of class struggle: "It could be explained, for example, by a fear of the revolution which could erupt if the nonaggressive states entered the war and the war acquired a global character."[109] This interpretation dominated Soviet analyses for many years.

There was an obvious hint in Stalin's speech that, being unhappy with the conduct of the "nonaggressive democratic countries," the Soviet Union might ally with other forces: "We stand for peace and strengthening

---

P.V. Rychagov, who had just returned from fighting against Franco in Spain. He carried out several very successful air operations in China; for example, on February 23, 1938, when twenty-eight Chinese bombers destroyed a large Japanese airbase on Taiwan. Later Rychagov served as chief of the main department of the Soviet air forces. See V. Pinchuk, "General Rychagov," *Aviatsiya i kosmonavtika*, No. 8 (1988), p. 47. More than 200 Soviet volunteers were killed in China. See Gromyko and Ponomarev, ed., *Istoriya vneshnei politiki SSSR 1917–1945*, Vol. 1, p. 336.

108. I.V. Stalin, *Otchetnyi doklad na XVIII s'ezde partii o rabote TsK VKP (b) 10 marta 1939 g.* (Report on the Work of the Central Committee of the VKP (b) at the 18th Congress of the Party, March 10, 1939) (Moscow: Gospolitizdat, 1949), pp. 23, 28–29.

109. Ibid., pp. 29, 30.

meaningful contacts with all states." He outlined the Party goals as follows:

- To pursue a policy of peace and strengthening meaningful contacts with all states;
- To be cautious, guarded, and not let our country be dragged into conflicts by provokers of war who have become accustomed to making others do their dirty work for them;
- To strengthen the military power of the Red Army and the Red Fleet in every possible way; and
- To strengthen international ties of friendship with working people of all countries interested in peace and friendship between peoples.[110]

This sequence of priorities was rather significant, particularly since the relationship with "working people of all countries" was at the very end of the list. Stalin seemed to be giving preference to inter-state relations over solidarity with the working people of the world.

On March 17, 1939, German troops occupied Czechoslovakia despite the fact that its new borders had been guaranteed by Great Britain, France, Germany, and Italy at the Munich conference in September 1938. Berlin immediately established the Protectorate of Bohemia and Moravia, which meant the end of Czechoslovakia's sovereignty. A week later, Germany forced Lithuania to sign over to Germany the district of Memel (Klaipeda). At the same time, Hitler began to demand the annexation of Danzig and the creation of extraterritorial rail and road communications across the Polish Corridor for the Germans.

On September 1, 1939, German troops invaded Poland and World War II broke out. A month later, when Poland was defeated and the Third Reich continued the war against Poland's allies, Soviet troops from the Leningrad military district crossed the border into Finland, which started the Soviet-Finnish War. This step had been preceded by complex and tense diplomatic negotiations in which the Soviet Union had sought to change the Soviet-Finnish border to provide greater security to Leningrad. On December 1, 1939, in the Soviet-occupied town of Terijoki, a puppet government was set up with Otto Kuusinen, a Finnish Communist and a secretary of the Comintern, at its head. This alternative government called itself the Provisional People's Government of the Finnish Democratic Republic (FDR) and declared its goals to the people of Finland. The Soviet press reported that information about the developments in Finland

---

110. Ibid., pp. 40, 42–43.

came from wireless interceptions. These reports were completely fake, however. In the archives of the Soviet Ministry of Foreign Affairs there are drafts of the address of the Central Committee of the Finnish Communist Party, the declarations of Kuusinen's government, and the treaty on mutual understanding and friendship written in Russian and edited by Vyacheslav Molotov.[111] The new Finnish government was recognized by the Soviet Union the very day it was established, and a treaty on mutual assistance and friendship was concluded between the Soviet Union and the FDR the following day.[112] A corps of the "Finnish People's Army" was set up in the Leningrad military district, and by early December it comprised 13,500 troops. However, according to documents in the State Archives of the USSR, the corps did not take part in the armed struggle.[113]

The Kuusinen government was established to show that the Soviet Union was not waging a war against Finland but was in fact rendering assistance to the government it had recognized to liberate the country from the "anti-popular clique." This line was upheld in Soviet domestic propaganda as well. A leaflet distributed to Soviet troops in the Leningrad military district on the day of the invasion read: "We are coming as friends of the Finnish people, not as conquerors. . . . The Red Army will support the Finnish people, who stand for friendship with the Soviet Union and wish to have their own Finnish, truly popular government."[114] But the Stalinist leadership missed the target. The Soviet actions made the Finnish resistance even more determined and strengthened the power of the government in Helsinki.

A historian could not fail to notice the similarities between Soviet tactics in Finland and Soviet tactics in Poland during the Soviet-Polish War. A Polish revolutionary committee was established on Polish territory controlled by the Red Army and units of Polish Red volunteers began to be formed. Moscow subsequently took the same line during the liberation of Eastern Europe from the Nazi occupation, in Hungary in 1956, in Czechoslovakia in 1968, and finally in Afghanistan in 1979.

Important aspects of the Red Army's strategic planning and some basic evaluations of military, political, and strategic situations became

---

111. *Vestnik MID SSSR*, No. 22 (1989).

112. See A.G. Dongarov, "*Voina, kotoroi moglo ne byt'*" (A war which could not have taken place), *Voprosy istorii*, No. 5 (1990), pp. 38–39.

113. Central State Archives of the Soviet Army, collection 33987, inventory 3, file 1380, p. 3; and collection 25888, inventory 13, file 75, p. 1.

114. Central State Archives of the Soviet Army, collection 25888, inventory 14, file 2, p. 20.

available to researchers and readers, thanks to the process of lifting the veil of secrecy in the Soviet Union that began in the late 1980s. Thus, M.V. Zakharov, chief of the General Staff in 1967–1971, cited Shaposhnikov's memorandum to Voroshilov on strategic deployment in his 1989 book, *The General Staff in the Prewar Years,* as one of the key assessments of the threat to Soviet security. On November 13, 1938, major points of Shaposhnikov's memorandum concerning the western and eastern theaters of war were discussed and generally approved by the Main Military Council. The main topics of the memorandum included the Soviet Union's most likely adversaries, their armaments, probable plans for campaign tactics, and principles of the strategic deployment of the Red Army in the East and West.

In short, the major conclusions of Shaposhnikov's memorandum were as follows. The main and most dangerous enemy was the fascist bloc—Germany and Italy supported by imperialist Japan. The policies of these countries were oriented toward aggravating relations with the Soviet Union up to the point of armed confrontation. However, these foes lacked the physical resources, foreign policy advantages, and the superiority over the Soviet Union needed to launch an aggressive action against it. The wait-and-see policies of Britain and France were encouraging the fascist bloc to unleash aggression in the East, in the first place against the Soviet Union, and it affected the conduct of Romania, Bulgaria, and Turkey as well as Finland, Estonia, Latvia, and Lithuania. Those states were under pressure from Germany and Poland, and increasingly tended to side with them. Iran and Afghanistan would most probably keep to armed neutrality. The second major source of war could emerge in the Far East. Japan, although it was bogged down in the war in China, had enough forces to attack the Soviet Union, relying on the Manchurian bridgehead, at the same time as the other members of the fascist bloc struck. Thus the Soviet Union had to be prepared to fight on two fronts: in the West, against fascist Germany, Italy, and Poland, on the one hand, and against Romania, Finland, Estonia, Latvia, and Lithuania, all gravitating toward them, on the other; and in the East, against Japan.[115] In case of a conflict, Lithuania might be occupied by Germany and Poland. It was concluded that the most serious threats were coming from

---

115. According to General Staff estimates, in the event of war on two fronts the enemy could concentrate from 194 to 210 infantry divisions, 4 motorized divisions, 15 cavalry divisions, 13,077 guns, 7,980 tanks, and 5,775 aircraft on the Soviet borders. It was assumed that 130 or 140 infantry divisions, 4 motorized and 12 cavalry divisions, 8,500 guns, 6,380 tanks, and 4,136 aircraft could be concentrated in the western theater. See M.V. Zakharov, *General'nyi shtab v predvoennye gody* (The general staff in the pre-war years) (Moscow: Voenizdat, 1989), pp. 125–126.

the West; therefore the West European theater of war was named the main one, and thus the bulk of Soviet forces should be concentrated there.[116] Shaposhnikov argued that the German military experience, traditions, and methods of campaign tactics suggested that Germany and its satellites would concentrate their main forces either north or south of Polesye to avoid the marshes around the Pripyat River. The final decision on this issue would depend on the domestic situations in the East European countries and their attitude toward Ukraine. Germany would use the armies of the Baltic states and Finland to encircle Leningrad and cut it off from the rest of the Soviet Union. Meanwhile, the enemy's naval forces would use cruisers and submarine raids in the Barents and White Seas to blockade Murmansk and Arkhangelsk. In the Baltic Sea, they would try to achieve supremacy and oust the Soviet fleet east of Gotland. In the Black Sea Basin, Italian military ships and German submarines could be expected.[117] In many ways Shaposhnikov's forecast turned out to be correct. However, Poland did not become a German ally; instead it became the first victim of Nazi aggression.

The initial phase of war continued to be of interest to Soviet military scholars and commanders in the second half of the 1930s. They based their work on the earlier research and analysis of Ventsov, Lapchinsky, Svechin, Shaposhnikov, and others. A.I. Yegorov, Red Army chief of staff, did a lot of work on this topic in the late 1930s, which was reported to the Revolutionary Military Council of the USSR. One of his major ideas was that, in peacetime, both parties to a future war would try to form very mobile and maneuverable forces and means (aviation, motorized and mechanized units, and cavalry) as quickly as possible in order to invade the territory of the enemy and to disrupt its mobilization and the concentration of its troops in the border regions. The concentration of forces would be dramatically affected by two major factors: (1) the qualitative and quantitative status of aviation of the belligerents; and (2) the availability of motorized and mechanized shock formations with substantial firepower and mobility. How would these factors affect the concentration of the Red Army? According to Yegorov, enemy ground forces would face great water obstacles and fortified regions on the Soviet Union's western borders, and therefore they could not significantly impede rail transport or the concentration of Soviet troops.[118] The greatest danger would be the enemy's air forces; air attacks and the landing of

---

116. Ibid., p. 127.

117. Ibid.

118. This conclusion was not groundless, since at that time the frontier of the Soviet Union had not yet been affected by the military events of 1939.

airborne troops could seriously upset Soviet transport to a depth of 600–800 kilometers.[119]

In Yegorov's view, future military operations would be vast in scope and fraught with tension. Air forces would assume overriding importance. All available combat aviation (including naval and army aviation) would be used to gain air supremacy, to disrupt the enemy's rear, to wreck its mobilization and concentration of forces, and to destroy its naval forces. After these missions were carried out, heavy aviation would remain in the hands of the High Command for actions against the operational rear of the enemy, while the rest of the air force would switch to supporting the ground forces.

Motorized and mechanized units (which Yegorov called invasion groups) would open a joint offensive with cavalry and aviation forces on enemy territory during the first hours of war in the border regions. The invasion groups would attempt to destroy the enemy's camouflage units, frustrate mobilization in the border regions, and compel the enemy to move the line of deployment into the rear and seize and control areas in the rear. "However," Yegorov wrote, "it is important to recognize that invasion groups can only create a series of crises and inflict some defeats on the camouflage forces of the enemy, but they cannot end the war or decisively defeat . . . the main forces. These are the missions of the next period of operations, when the operational concentration has been completed."[120]

In mid-1934, Tukhachevsky published a detailed article, "The Character of Border Operations," in which he argued that, in new circumstances, mobilization and strategic concentration were only possible with a new approach to border engagements. At the time, the threat to the Soviet Union emanating from Nazi Germany was a popular subject in the Soviet military and political press. Now, Tukhachevsky wrote, "the border fight would not be waged by the main forces of the army as in previous wars, but by special units, a special frontline army stationed on the frontiers."[121] In his view, this frontline army should be a strong, highly mechanized formation, and in addition to ground forces, it should include major air forces stationed not more than 150–200 kilometers from the borders. Even in peacetime, the mechanized corps of this army should be deployed 50–70 kilometers from the border so that they would be able to cross the

---

119. See A.I. Yegorov, "*Taktika i operativnoe iskusstvo na novom etape*" (Tactics and operational art at a new stage), *Voenno-istoricheskii zhurnal*, No. 10 (1963), p. 35.

120. Ibid., p. 35.

121. Tukhachevsky, *Selected Works*, Vol. 2, p. 217.

frontier on the first day of mobilization. Cavalry, whose task would be to consolidate the success of the mechanized formations, should also be stationed near the frontier in a state of near-readiness for war. Ground units would be transported by trucks to strengthen the achievements of the mechanized units and cavalry. The frontline army should include self-propelled artillery, and expeditionary forces would cooperate closely with the army in the initial operations.[122] According to Tukhachevsky, frontline armies would initiate offensive actions immediately after the declaration of war or on the first day of mobilization by inflicting an air attack using assault aviation and bombers against the enemy's system of airports and runways, rail and road centers within a range of 150–200 kilometers from the frontier. Meanwhile, raiding parties would land 250 kilometers behind enemy lines to disrupt mobilization and create diversions on railroads and highways, and mobile troops would start to invade.

If neither side were able to successfully resist invasion, the transport of troops by rail would be ineffective, since the armies mobilized inside both countries would disembark at great distances from one another in a zone about 500 kilometers wide on both sides of the frontier. According to Tukhachevsky's calculations, the main forces of the belligerents would not face each other for at least two weeks after the war started, because they would first have to contend with clashes with enemy landing parties and mobile troops, and repair damaged bridges and lines of communications en route to the border. If, however, one side managed to foil the enemy's invasion with the help of air forces, the opposing troops would detrain 250 kilometers apart from each other. In that case, the battle between the main forces of the warring parties would take place only a week after the declaration of war on the territory of the country that had suffered greater damage from the first strikes.[123]

Approaches to the Great Patriotic War of 1941–45

Soviet appraisals of the external military threat to the Union's security drastically changed in August and September 1939. The day after the Soviet-German Nonaggression Pact was signed (August 24, 1939), an article appeared in *Pravda* on ending the enmity between the Soviet Union and Germany. Eventually the antifascist theme disappeared from Soviet propaganda altogether. The German ambassador to Moscow described these developments in a dispatch to Berlin dated September 6, 1939: "The

---

122. Ibid., pp. 218–219.
123. Ibid.

sudden turn in Soviet policy after many years of propaganda against German aggressors has not yet been clearly grasped by the population. Particular doubts are being raised by statements by official agitators that Germany is no longer an aggressor."[124]

Only in 1941 did the Soviet evaluation of German policy change. Thus in a Kremlin speech to the graduating classes of the military academies on May 5, 1941 (according to notes taken by some participants), Stalin discussed the feasibility of destroying German troops, which he asserted were not omnipotent and, because of Germany's expansionist policy, could not enjoy popular support. In late 1940 and early 1941, the Red Army's political bodies started to show signs of anxiety about the prospect of war.

The experience of the Soviet-Finnish War definitively demonstrated the futility of Soviet hopes of gaining the full support of the working people of the capitalist countries in the event of war. In January 1941, A.I. Zaporozhets, chief of the department of political propaganda of the Red Army, in his classified memorandum to A.A. Zhdanov, Secretary of the Central Committee, pointed out that "a harmful delusion has taken root that in the case of war the population of the countries waging war against us would come out to a man against their bourgeoisie and the only thing the Red Army would have to do would be to triumphantly march around the country and establish Soviet power."[125]

Zaporozhets described the character of a war in which the Soviet Union might be involved in this way:

The Red Army fulfills its international obligations in any war, but not in all cases carrying out these duties is the main task. In any war in which the Soviet Union takes part, the main task of the Red Army will be the defense of the Soviet Union—the homeland of the world proletariat. Wherever and under whatever conditions the Red Army wages war, it will proceed from the interests of the motherland, the goals of strengthening the force and power of the Soviet Union. And only to the extent that this main task is carried out will the Red Army fulfill its international obligations.[126]

The active interference of fascist Italy and Nazi Germany in the Spanish Civil War, the armed conflict with Japan at Lake Khasan and the

---

124. A. Chubariyan, *August 1939 goda* (August 1939), *Izvestiya*, July 1, 1989.

125. *Iz arkhivov partii. Osostoyanii voennoi propagandy sredi naseleniya* (From the party archives. On the state of military propaganda among the population), *Izvestiya TsK KPSS*, No. 5 (1990), p. 192.

126. Ibid., p. 191.

Khalkhin-Gol, and the operations in 1939 and 1940 that started World War II provided Soviet military specialists who were working on the problems of a future war with plenty of material for analysis. The Soviet-Finnish War of 1939–40, which did not proceed as had been foreseen by the top Soviet leadership and inflicted great losses on the Red Army, offered some rather complicated lessons.

Analyzing wars in progress or recently ended wars is always rather difficult. As a rule, the analyst does not have all the needed data. The most important documents are usually classified for reasons of national security. However, Soviet scholars were able to discuss the armed conflicts and wars mentioned above while the trail was still fresh, in part because of Stalin's instruction "not to make a cult of the experience of the Civil War."[127] L. Mekhlis, chief of the political department *(Politupravleniye)* of the Red Army, wrote a memorandum (declassified in 1990) to Andrei Zhadanov on the deficiencies of military scholarship in both the army and the country as a whole. He noted that the experience of the tsarist army and tsarist military theory were being ignored while the experience of the Civil War was overrated.[128] Mekhlis's observation was absolutely correct, albeit late.

In works on the Spanish Civil War, contemporary Soviet analysts usually focused on campaign tactics and evaluated the roles of various weapons. They duly noted the increasing role of tanks and aviation, but also pointed out that the role of artillery did not diminish and may even have increased, and that bombers could not substitute for artillery. Many of their conclusions were rather trivial. However, some authors did emphasize the limited significance and specific character of the Spanish Civil War experience because of the infrequent use of aircraft (1,200–1,500 planes) and tanks (500–600); the absence of expeditionary troops, large cavalries, and mechanized formations; and the inability to transport substantial reserve forces by road or rail.[129] Nevertheless, critical decisions about the structure of the Red Army tank forces were based on the warfare in Spain. The Red Army's mechanized corps were disbanded, which turned out to be a mistake since mechanized corps were a decisive force in the Wehrmacht operations in Poland in 1939 and in France in

---

127. *Iz archivov partii. O rabote Politicheskogo Upravleniya Krasnoi Armii* (From the party archives. On the work of the Political Department of the Red Army), *Izvestiya TsK KPSS*, No. 3 (1990), p. 198.

128. Ibid., p. 199.

129. See *Istoriya voennogo iskusstva* (The history of military art), 4th ed., Vol. 2 (Moscow: Voenizdat, 1952), pp. 276–277, 278.

1940.[130] Only in June 1940 were mechanized corps restored to the Red Army.[131]

Serious mistakes were also made about antitank weapons not long before the war. G.I. Kulik, marshal of the Soviet Union and deputy people's commissar for defense responsible for armaments, demanded a drastic retargeting of the industries producing anti-tank artillery and tank guns to increase the caliber of these weapons. He substantiated this demand with intelligence reports that allegedly stated that the German army was being equipped with tanks of higher quality with heavier armor and armed with guns with a caliber of 100 millimeters. Despite the reasonable arguments of the People's Commissariat for Armaments that it was impossible for the Wehrmacht to re-arm with new technology in such a short period of time, and that the Red Army might in fact be dangerously disarmed during the transition to new artillery systems, Kulik, with the active support of Zhdanov, got his way. As a result, shortly before the German invasion of the Soviet Union, production of the most needed 45 and 76 millimeter guns was halted and production of the new weapons had not yet begun. The Germans advanced without first-rate weaponry: they had numerous obsolete Panzer I and Panzer II light tanks—similiar to the Czechoslovak Skoda and the French Renault. Soviet 45 and 76 millimeter artillery was effective not only against these models but also against newer ones like the Panzer III and Panzer IV.[132]

The most interesting Soviet work summarizing the lessons of warfare in the late 1930s was G.S. Isserson's *New Forms of Fighting*, which was published in 1940. "In terms of putting new forms of military art into practice, the war in Spain could be called the prologue to the tragedy, the German-Polish War was its buildup, the war in Western Europe its development.... The finale of this drama remains hidden in future history,"[133] he rather shrewdly observed. The political context of the mass purges and Stalin's German policy, particularly after the signing of the treaty "on friendship and frontiers," did not permit Isserson to dwell on the questions of who was the Soviet Union's most likely enemy and what the main line of its advance would be. Thus there are very few political or military

---

130. G.K. Zhukov, *Vospominaniya i razmyshleniya* (Reminiscences and reflections) (Moscow: Novosti Press, 1969), p. 205.

131. A.I. Radzievskii, *Tankovyi udar* (Tank strike) (Moscow: Voenizdat, 1977), p. 8.

132. B.L. Vannikov, "*Zapiski narkoma*" (Notes of a people's commissar), *Znamya* (Banner) (January 1988), pp. 139–141.

133. G.S. Isserson, *Novye formy bor'by* (New forms of fighting) (Moscow: Voenizdat, 1940), p. 9.

predictions in his book (as well as in other books on the subject). Rather, it was almost entirely devoted to strategic and tactical issues:

Decisive operations aimed at encirclement and destruction now have new possibilities. The strategy of destruction has new prerequisites for its full realization. The significance of the German-Polish War is that it has demonstrated that . . . the strategy of destruction was realized in forms which were in essence deeply different from everything that the history of war had previously known.[134]

Furthermore, "by the end of the campaign, the depth of the front was greater than its breadth. That was an absolutely new phenomenon in military conflict, vividly expressing its new, profound nature."[135] Isserson underscored that, in the past, as a rule the front moved forward relatively evenly by advancing the general line of infantry and clearing all enemy troops from the territory behind them as they advanced. The only exceptions were fortresses abandoned under siege. He wrote:

Now the front jutted out in various directions as a result of strikes by mobile formations, which left behind scattered hotbeds of fighting. In this respect, the end of the tremendous battle in Poland presented a totally unusual scenario of deep and multilayered fighting. On September 16, the battle was being waged on an enormous territory of about 185,000 square kilometers. Its hotbeds were echeloned to a depth of 500 kilometers and formed at least five lines or five layers.[136]

The features Isserson described were also characteristic of the tragedy that broke out later on the battlefields in the Baltics, Belorussia, and Ukraine.

Isserson's evaluation of the opening stage of the German-Polish War was also insightful. He observed that, despite the obvious growth of tension in the relationship between Poland and Germany, which started in 1938 and developed into mutual threats in 1939, the German assault was an unprecedented strategic surprise:

On September 1, when the German army, fully deployed, opened hostilities by violating the frontier of former Poland all along the Polish-German border, its descent in that particular form was an incredible strategic surprise. No one knows when the Germans mobilized, concentrated, and deployed their

---

134. Ibid., p. 72.
135. Ibid., p. 73.
136. Ibid.

forces, actions which had had quite definite time limits in past wars, particularly in World War I.[137]

"History faces a new phenomenon,"[138] Isserson concluded. In his view, everything that military historians had surmised about an "invasion army" comprising the first echelon followed by the main forces proved to be inadequate. In reality, Germany's main forces had been put into action immediately.[139]

Isserson did not analyze hypothetical options for defensive operations by the Poles and their allies, which is unfortunate because they could have posed a genuine obstacle to the German strategy of destruction, and could have improved the prospects of defense as compared to those of offense.[140] In his earlier book, *The Cannae of the World War: The Destruction of Samsonov's Army*, Isserson provided thought-provoking, sharp analyses that illustrated his ability to hypothesize. For example, he demonstrated how in August 1914 the Russian army under Samsonov's command could have defeated the Germans instead of being crushed by them in East Prussia.[141]

It is quite difficult to determine the extent to which the analyses and predictions of Soviet military specialists were integrated into the development of strategic and tactical documents or helped to form a common approach to future wars among the supreme command and senior military staff. Declassified documents, including the minutes of a meeting of the Main Military Council that started on December 23, 1940, provide some insights. By the time this meeting took place, enough time had passed to summarize and discuss the lessons of the German invasion of Poland in 1939 and of its allies in May 1940. In opening the session, People's Commissar for Defense S.K. Timoshenko underlined the main goal of the meeting: "to encourage bold and inquiring thinking" to strengthen the Red Army. It was also necessary, he said, to find out the

---

137. Ibid., p. 29.

138. Ibid.

139. As Isserson noted, that approach to starting the war had been mentioned in the German press.

140. These alternatives were singled out and analyzed in a fundamental book by D.M. Proektor, *Agressiya i katastropha. Vysshee voennoye rukovodstvo fashistskoi Germanii vo vtoroi mirovoi voine 1939–1945* (Aggression and catastrophe. The Supreme Military Command of fascist Germany in World War II 1939–1945) (Moscow: Nauka, 1972).

141. See G. Isserson, *Kanny mirovoi voiny: gibel' armii Samsonova* (The Cannae of the world war: The destruction of Samsonov's army) (Moscow: Gosvoennizdat, 1926), pp. 55–59.

views of the military leadership on offensive and defensive operations, the use of motorized forces and aviation, and methods of organizing their actions.[142]

As Zhukov, Vasilevsky, and Zakharov later recalled, the participants based their projections on the analysis of local wars and combat actions like the Spanish Civil War, the Soviet-Japanese conflict at Lake Khasan, the rebuff of Japanese aggression by Soviet and Mongolian troops at the Khalkhin-Gol, and particularly the Soviet-Finnish War. In other words, the lessons of the war in the West in 1939–40 were not incorporated into the Soviet analysis at that time. According to Zakharov, the war in Finland demonstrated that some types of combat actions were overrated, like breaching the enemy's fortified defense lines, building up defenses, and preparing the theaters of combat.[143] In training troops, far more attention was paid to overcoming fortified lines of defense than to other kinds of combat actions and maneuvers in the complicated conditions of war.[144]

Most of the speakers at the meeting focused on campaign tactics. Only Timoshenko touched upon issues of strategy. Based on the experience of previous wars and the current war in the West, he said that advances in military technologies and their applications had caused major shifts in the art of war. But the war in Europe offered nothing new to strategic thinking. As far as campaign tactics were concerned, Timoshenko said, some changes had resulted from the massive use of tanks, bombers, and motorized, motorcycle, and airborne troops. His conclusions were based on studies of German operations in the West, particularly in Poland.

A slight reappraisal of the war with Finland was evident in Timoshenko's remarks: "Previously combat actions usually started with a mutual attack, but now that is not always possible. Now the frontiers of the great states, especially in the most important sectors, are encircled by reinforced concrete fortified lines."[145] This conclusion, however, does not seem to be substantiated by the facts. In the West, reinforced concrete defense lines were erected only in rather narrow frontier sectors, mainly in France and parts of Germany.[146] The other countries did not have them.

---

142. See Zakharov, *General'nyi shtab v predvoennye gody*, p. 193.

143. On this issue, also see the noteworthy collection of articles *Voina na Karel'skom peresheike* (The war on the Karelian isthmus) (Moscow: Gospolitizdat, 1941), particularly the article by Major General of the Engineer Corps A. Khrenov entitled "*Liniya Mannergeima*" (The Mannerheim line).

144. Zakharov, *General'nyi shtab v predvoennye gody*, p. 195.

145. Ibid., p. 204.

146. Ibid.

As a result of the 1939 Soviet-German agreement and the subsequent Soviet annexation of Western Belorussia and Western Ukraine, the western border of the Soviet Union was shifted to the West by a few hundred kilometers. Meanwhile, the Red Army was increasingly modernizing. Therefore the Soviet plan of strategic deployment that had been developed in 1938 needed to be reconsidered. In the fall of 1939, the Soviet General Staff began to develop a new plan, and its first draft was ready in late July 1940.[147]

The plan's general evaluation of the contemporary military, political, strategic, and tactical situation can be summarized as follows. Although an enemy attack was most likely to be carried out against the western part of the Soviet Union, the possibility of a simultaneous attack by Japan in the Far East could not be excluded. Germany was considered the most probable adversary in a future war. Italy might also participate in the war, mainly in the Balkan region. Finland, Romania, and Hungary might also fight on the side of Germany. Iran and Afghanistan would adopt "armed neutrality." Turkey would probably openly fight the Soviet Union under German pressure. Thus the Soviet Union had to be ready to fight on two fronts, in the East and the West.[148] In preparing for an assault on the Soviet Union, the Nazi-fascist bloc would probably deploy its main forces north of the mouth of the San River, with the main grouping of troops in East Prussia. From there the main strike could be expected against Riga, Kovno (Kaunas), and then Dvinsk (Daugavpils) and Polotsk, or against Kovno, Vilno (Vilnius), and Minsk. A simultaneous advance might also be carried out in the direction of Baranovichi by another army grouping deployed along the Lomzh-Brest line. The landing of marines in the Libau (Liepaja) region and on the Estonian coast could also be expected. If Finland sided with Germany, Finnish forces supported by German troops would attack Leningrad from the northwest. At the same time, German troops could take the offensive in southern Poland, from the area of Chełm-Tomaszów-Jarosław against Dubno and Brody, in order to capture

---

147. Ibid.

148. It was assumed that Germany, Finland, Romania, and Hungary could together deploy 233 divisions, 10,550 tanks, 13,900 airplanes, and up to 18,000 pieces of field artillery along the Soviet frontiers. In fact, Nazi Germany had concentrated along the western frontiers of the Soviet Union 190 divisions (including 39 tank and motorized divisions), 47,200 guns and mortars, about 4,300 tank and assault guns, and 4,980 aircraft. Germany also had 24 divisions in the reserve of the main command, half of which were assigned to enhance the army groups. See Zakharov, *General'nyi shtab v predvoennye gody*, p. 214; and M.M. Kozlov, V.A. Matsulenko, et al., *Voennoye iskusstvo vo vtoroi mirovoi voine i poslevoennyi period* (The art of war in World War II and the post-war period) (Moscow: Academy of the General Staff Publishers, 1985), p. 19.

the rear of the Soviet Lvov grouping and then to take western Ukraine. Romanian and German divisions could advance toward Zhmerinka at the same time.[149] According to General Staff estimates, Japan could allocate up to 39 infantry divisions, 2,500 airplanes, 1,200 tanks, and 4,000 guns to fighting the Soviet Union and the Mongolian People's Republic. The bulk of Japanese ground forces could be targeted at the Soviet maritime region.

Based on these assumptions, the authors of the plan came to the following conclusion: "Now if there is a necessity for the strategic deployment of the Soviet armed forces on both fronts, the western front should be considered the primary one, and our main forces should be concentrated there." Considering the potential resources of Japan, the draft plan stated that it was necessary to deploy enough troops in the East to guarantee stability there. The plan was to allocate minimum forces to cover and protect the Soviet Union's northern and southern coasts and the frontiers in Transcaucasia and Central Asia.[150]

In August 1940, when K.A. Meretskov became chief of the General Staff, the draft plan was reevaluated. The Operational Department of the General Staff and specifically Major General A.M. Vasilevsky were put in charge of the reevaluation.[151] On September 18, 1940, a report on the basic principles of strategic deployment of the Soviet armed forces signed by People's Commissar Timoshenko and Meretskov was submitted in the Central Committee to Stalin and Molotov for approval.[152]

In both this report and the final draft of the plan, it was pointed out that the Soviet Union should be ready to fight on two fronts: in the West against Germany, which would be supported by Italy, Hungary, Romania, and Finland; and in the East against Japan, which had so far maintained armed neutrality but could at any time initiate hostilities against the Soviet Union. The western front would be the primary one, and the main forces should be deployed there. The General Staff continued to assert that the Soviet Union's most powerful and dangerous enemy was Germany.[153] The western front, from the Barents Sea to the Black Sea, should

---

149. Ibid., p. 214.

150. Ibid., p. 216.

151. See K.A. Meretskov, *Na sluzhbe narodu. Stranitsy vospominanii* (At the service of the people. Pages of memories) (Moscow: Politizdat, 1968), pp. 191–196; and A.M. Vasilevsky, *Delo vsei zhizni* (The business of an entire life) (Moscow: Politizdat, 1974), p. 117.

152. Zakharov, *General'nyi shtab v predvoennye gody*, p. 217.

153. The Soviet military leadership thought that the forces of the fascist bloc and

be the main focus, the report stated. No changes were made to the evaluations of the enemy, or of Soviet troops, their deployment, missions, and combat means. However, the report's approach to the cardinal issue of defense on the western front was radically different.

The draft plan had suggested that the main body of the Red Army ought to be deployed in two sectors either north or south of Brest-Litovsk, depending on the political and military situation on the eve of the war.[154] Thus the plan's authors thought it was necessary to have both options thoroughly developed in peacetime. The report, however, stated that deploying the main forces of the Red Army south of Brest-Litovsk was the primary option.

On October 5, 1940, the Soviet leadership again discussed the plan for strategic deployment. They agreed that it was important to demonstrate more explicitly that the western theater was the primary one, and that the main Soviet forces would be deployed in its southwestern sector. Furthermore, they suggested an accelerated reinforcement of the troops on the southwestern front. The second deployment option (north of the Pripyat River) was not openly rejected, but it did not receive much support. After taking into consideration the comments it had received, the plan was submitted for final approval by the government and the Central Committee on October 14, 1940. Thus the main efforts of the Soviet forces in a future war were completely reoriented from the northwestern (as Shaposhnikov had suggested) to the southwestern sector.[155]

However, that was not the final variant of the plan. After Marshal Zhukov was appointed chief of the General Staff, the plan for strategic deployment once again was the subject of discussion. Additional corrections and more precise definitions were introduced, and the plan was finalized in May and early June 1941. The document was drafted by Vasilevsky and corrected by Lieutenant General N.F. Vatutin. As a result, the southwestern sector was supposed to be strengthened by twenty-five divisions.

What was the reason for such drastic changes in the evaluation of the main strike sector? As Zhukov wrote in his memoirs:

Japan, which could have attacked the Soviet Union simultaneously, were much stronger than they actually were. It was assumed that these potential adversaries had 280–290 divisions, 11,750 tanks, 30,000 pieces of field artillery, and 18,000 aircraft. The General Staff arrived at these figures by analytical calculations. Ibid., p. 218.

154. Ibid.
155. Ibid., p. 219.

Stalin was convinced that the Hitlerites, in the case of war with the Soviet Union, would first of all strive to annex Ukraine and the Donetsk Basin to deprive our country of its most important economic regions and seize Ukrainian grain, Donetsk coal, and later Caucasian oil. While considering the operational plan in the spring of 1941, Stalin said, "Without these most important, vital resources fascist Germany will not be able to wage a lengthy, large-scale war." I.V. Stalin had the greatest authority for all of us. No one then even thought to doubt his judgments and appraisals of the situation.[156]

Zhukov went on to state that Stalin's assumption, "although it was not unfounded, did not take into account the enemy's plans for a blitzkrieg against the USSR."[157]

Zakharov offered a psychological explanation for the focus on the southwestern sector. He pointed out that the key positions in the General Staff, starting with Timoshenko, former commander of the Kiev special military district who had been appointed people's commissar of defense in 1940, were occupied by specialists on the southwestern sector.[158] Those who came from the Kiev military district continued to attach great importance to the southwestern line of advance. When they evaluated the general military strategic situation in the western theater of war, their attention was automatically attracted to what was most familiar to them, what they had studied and had long preoccupied them. Of course, that relegated to the background new, less familiar facts, even if they were essential to a realistic perception of the coming war.[159]

It is important to know that at one time the Germans had considered an attack in the southwest as a viable option and could have carried it out. It was later discovered that in discussing plans of the attack on the Soviet Union on December 7, 1940, the German High Command had reviewed a possible advance along the southwestern line that had been

---

156. G.K. Zhukov, *Vospominaniya i razmyshleniya* (Reminiscences and reflections) (Moscow: Novosti Press, 1969), p. 220.

157. Ibid.

158. In July 1940, the following military leaders came from the Kiev special military district (KOVO): Lieutenant General N.F. Vatutin (chief of the district staff), first as chief of the Operational Department, and then as first deputy chief of the General Staff; Major General N.L. Nikitin as chief of the Mobilization Department; and Corps Commissar S.K. Kozhevnikov as military commissar of the General Staff. In February 1941, KOVO Commander Zhukov became chief of the General Staff. In March, Major General G.K. Malandin, deputy chief of the KOVO staff, was made chief of the Operational Department of the General Staff, and S.I. Shiryaev, chief of the department that administered the KOVO fortified regions, was appointed to the General Staff to again deal with fortified regions.

159. Zakharov, *General'nyi shtab v predvoennyie gody*, p. 221.

developed and presented by General von Zodenstern.[160] (At the beginning of the war, Zodenstern had been appointed chief of staff of the southern group of armies.[161])

It is a well-known fact that Stalin and his closest associates ignored all the warnings from the Soviet military and political intelligence services, not to mention the warnings coming from the U.S. and British governments, about German preparations for war against the Soviet Union. Stalin's thoughts about the character of the war that Germany had unleashed by invading the Soviet Union are less clear. According to some witnesses, when the war started, Stalin hoped that it would be a limited war targeted at gaining some advantages for Germany at the expense of the Soviet Union, and that it could be peacefully settled.[162] That view probably prompted the rather cautious Directive No. 1 sent to the border military districts and to the people's commissar of the navy. By Stalin's instruction, it was signed by military officials only—People's Commissar of Defense Timoshenko and Chief of the General Staff Zhukov. Subsequent directives were also signed by a representative of the political leadership.[163]

There were other shortcomings and even blunders in the Soviet preparations for war. When the operational plans were revised in spring 1941, as Zhukov honestly recognized, new methods of warfare were almost entirely ignored: "The People's Commissariat of Defense and the General Staff were of the opinion that a war between such great powers as Germany and the Soviet Union was likely to start according to the old pattern: the main forces would join the battle after a few days of frontier warfare."[164] These ideas were largely (if not entirely) rooted in Soviet theoretical concepts of the opening phase of war that had been framed in

---

160. Zodenstern's plan was not supported by the German High Command, primarily because the southern theater of military operations, bounded by the Carpathian Mountains and the Pripyat marshes, had only minor operational capacity. The state of communications in Hungary and Romania did not allow a concentration of troops powerful enough and sufficiently well equipped either to advance or to carry out a surprise attack against the Soviet Union. Hitler worried about the unreliable Balkan rear and disliked the need to cross the region's numerous rivers, which flowed from the northwest to the southeast. For all of these reasons, the German leadership adhered to the northern option for attacking the Soviet Union.

161. A. Filippi, *Pripyatskaya problema* (The Pripyat problem) (Moscow: Voenizdat, 1959), pp. 40–41.

162. Zhukov, *Vospominaniya i razmyshleniya*, p. 243.

163. Archive of the Ministry of Defense of the USSR, collection 48-A, inventory 1554, pp. 257–259.

164. Zhukov, *Vospominaniya i razmyshleniya*, p. 224.

the 1920s. Studies by Svechin, Shaposhnikov, Yegorov, and Tukhachevsky from the interwar period went in the right direction, but they did not provide solutions to the challenges that arose on June 22, 1941, when Germany invaded the Soviet Union. Isserson's analysis was closer to reality, but he was not a highly placed official in the Red Army like the others, and while his work was quite profound and original, it did not attract the attention it merited.

Recently it was discovered that rather accurate predictions about the opening stage of war were made by the Intelligence Department of the Soviet General Staff. V.A. Novobranets, in those days acting chief of the Intelligence Department, recalled that the department prepared a report entitled "Notes on the Mobilization in Germany," which concluded that Germany would attempt a surprise strategic attack on the Soviet Union to destroy the enemy with a powerful first strike using all its forces. Referring to Zhukov's view mentioned above, Novobranets assumed that his boss F.I. Golikov, chief of the Intelligence Department, had not even sent this material to the General Staff leadership and that no further actions had been taken.[165]

The Nazi military command was able to activate the Wehrmacht's main forces in June 1941, and during the first days of war, it launched a large-scale offensive against the Soviet Union along three lines of advance. The attack was sustained by the Wehrmacht's high level of operational art and the quality of its leadership, which were grounded in the experience the Germans had gained in Poland and Western Europe. The level of German strategy was obviously underestimated by the Soviet military command, which led to miscalculations by the Soviet General Staff. One of the reasons for this gross misperception was that during the political purges of 1937–38, the Soviet armed forces lost many of their most highly educated military leaders, who had had deep insights into the German military machine and had known the German generals personally. (It might be added that Soviet military analysts still underestimate German strategy and campaign tactics in World War II.) One of the Soviet leadership's most serious mistakes was to ignore the warnings of the intelligence services that Hitler would violate the Molotov-Ribbentrop Pact. As a result, the Soviet armed forces (with the exception of the navy) were not ready for combat at the beginning of the war.[166]

---

165. G. Novobranets, "*Nakanune voiny*" (On the eve of war), *Znamya*, No. 6 (1990), p. 176.

166. See M. Milshtein, "*Po dannym razvedki . . . Yeshche raz o 22 iyunya 1941 goda*" (By secret information . . . Again on June 22, 1941), *Novoe vremya*, No. 26 (1990), pp. 31–32.

Zhukov made another important observation about the miscalculations of the Soviet supreme command: "The timing of concentration and deployment of troops by fascist Germany and the Soviet Union were considered to be similar. In reality, their conditions were far from equal."[167] Zhukov and several other Soviet and foreign experts noted that, on the eve of the German attack on the Soviet Union, German industry had been mobilized to a greater degree than that of the Soviet Union, the Germans had better prepared the theater of military actions, and German troops and those of Germany's satellites (in particular, Hungary and Finland) had been better trained than Soviet troops. There were also radical geostrategic and demographic differences between the two countries, which played an important role in both World War I and World War II. Indeed it is these differences that define the character of the opening phase of war, as A. Neznamov very convincingly demonstrated in his 1909 book, *Defensive War*: "States with vast territories, long land borders, and diverse populations, in addition to having to station their armed forces on various fronts, *due to their very size* are unable to mobilize and transport their troops to the points of strategic deployment as rapidly as states with smaller territories and more homogeneous populations."[168]

Threats to Soviet Security in the Late 1940s and Early 1950s

After the end of World War II, during the early stages of the Cold War, the Soviet Union unquestionably considered U.S. and British imperialism to be its most probable adversary in a future war. That appraisal became the core element of assessments of the threat to Soviet security for almost four decades, until the end of the 1980s. In the late 1940s, in both propaganda and professional military publications, "American-British imperialism" was described as having similarities with German fascism, and thus the United States was proclaimed the successor of German fascism in the quest for world domination. No other interpretation was tolerated. Debates like those of the 1920s on the class and national dimensions of future war were absolutely out of the question.

The most important international event of that period was the Korean War (1950–53), which involved the forces of North and South Korea, U.S. troops, troops of some U.S. allies (under the flag of the United Nations),

---

167. Zhukov, *Vospominaniya i razhmyshleniya*, p. 224.

168. A. Neznamov, "Strategy," Part I, *Oboronitel'naya voina (Teoriya voprosa)* (Defensive war [Theory of the question]) (St. Petersburg: Nikolaevskaya Academy of the General Staff, 1909), p. 9. Emphasis in original.

and a contingent of volunteers from the People's Republic of China that was actively supported by the Soviet Union.[169] Blame for the war was placed entirely on the United States and its "South Korean puppets." This position was maintained in Soviet propaganda until 1990, when the first weak attempts were made to describe more accurately the beginnings of the war. A 1951 editorial in *Voennaya mysl'* was typical of the Soviet line:

Having neglected the lessons of history, the bandits of American imperialism are following the same path on which German fascism met with disaster not long ago in an attempt to establish world domination by force. Having embarked upon the path of overt aggression, the ruling circles of the USA have imposed a "state of emergency" to accelerate the arms race, to facilitate the conversion of the country to fascism, and to intensify the exploitation of the working people.[170]

Soviet experts began to believe that a future war would be an armed clash between two powerful coalitions—the imperialist states headed by the United States and Great Britain, and the states of the socialist community led by the Soviet Union and China. A future war was expected to be global, although local conflicts were thought to be quite probable. It was presumed that the war would be protracted and would require forces of millions to achieve victory. The war aims would be achieved through the united efforts of all the armed services, with the ground forces playing the leading role and the other services supporting them.[171]

These ideas about the character of future war were largely determined by Stalin's concept of "permanently operating factors" of war, which he announced in Order No. 55 issued on February 23, 1942. According to this concept, the outcome of war is not determined by transitory factors like surprise, but by permanently operating factors, including: (1) stability of the rear; (2) morale of the troops; (3) quantity and quality of divisions; (4) weapons that the army has; and (5) organizational ability

---

169. In the critical days of warfare, the Soviet government, at the request of the Chinese government, sent nineteen aviation divisions to the northeastern provinces of China, which protected the northeastern part of China against air attack by U.S. planes. Soviet pilots brought down dozens of U.S. planes in air battles. See Gromyko and Ponomarev, eds., *Istoriya vneshnei politiki SSSR* (History of the foreign policy of the USSR), Vol. 2, 1945–75 (Moscow: Nauka, 1976), p. 165; and V.T. Login, ed., *Opyt voiny v zashchitu sotsialisticheskogo otechestva* (The experience of war in defense of the socialist fatherland) (Moscow: Nauka, 1985), p. 180.

170. "*Vernyi zashchitnik interesov strany sotsializma*" (Faithful defender of the interests of the socialist country), *Voennaya mysl'*, No. 2 (1951), p. 20.

171. See Kozlov, Matsulenko, et al., *Voennoye iskusstvo vo vtoroi mirovoi voine i poslevoennyi period*, p. 448.

of the military command personnel.[172] Stalin's concept was ranked as an official military theory. After the war, during the emerging confrontation with the United States, which now possessed atomic weapons, Moscow's first priority was maintaining the stability of the rear and the troop morale, which would determine the quality of commanders and divisions, as well as the skillful use of available weapons.[173] The Soviet victory in World War II was thought to have proven the theory completely and to have provided a pattern for future victory in the "final" war if the imperialists were to unleash it.

One of the leading Soviet military theorists of that period, Major General N. Talensky, wrote the following incantation in a piece in *Voennaya mysl'*: "Victory is won in modern war by the decisive destruction of the enemy in the course of armed struggle through a series of consecutive, increasingly powerful strikes based on superiority in the permanently operating factors that decide the war, and the unified and comprehensive employment of economic, moral, political, and military resources."[174] That the United States might resort to atomic weapons as it had in the bombing of Hiroshima and Nagasaki was interpreted as reliance on surprise, and was compared to Nazi Germany's use of the blitzkrieg. Soviet writings of the late 1940s and early 1950s (including after the test of the first Soviet atomic bomb in 1949) mocked the defective bourgeois strategy, based on the German strategy of World War II, of an "atomic blitzkrieg," asserting that it had fewer chances of success than the strategy of Hitler's invaders.[175] Stalin himself said that a nuclear war might kill tens or even hundreds of thousands of civilians.[176]

Declassified reports from the Soviet Embassy in Japan on the aftermath of the bombing of Hiroshima and Nagasaki offer an explanation for Stalin's and other top Soviet officials' judgments on the matter. In

---

172. I. Stalin, *O Velikoi Otechestvennoi voine Sovetskogo Soyuza* (On the Great Patriotic War of the Soviet Union), 5th ed. (Moscow: Voenizdat, 1948), pp. 43–44.

173. See K.E. Voroshilov, "*Genial'nyi polkovedets Velikoi Otechestvennoi Voiny*" (The military genius of the Great Patriotic War), *Bol'shevik*, No. 24 (1949), pp. 39–45.

174. N. Talenskii, "*K voprosu o kharaktere zakonov voennoi nauki*" (On the question of the nature of military science), *Voennaya mysl'*, No. 9 (1953), p. 31.

175. F. Isayev, "*Voennyi genii Stalina*" (The military genius of Stalin), *Novoe vremya*, No. 52 (1949), p. 26; and M.V. Taranchuk, *Postoyanno deistvuyushchie factory reshayushchie sud'bu voiny* (The permanently operating factors defining the outcome of war), 2d ed. (Moscow: Voenizdat, 1954), p. 32.

176. "*Otvet tovarishcha I.V. Stalina korrespondentu 'Pravdy' naschet atomnogo oruzhiya*" (Comrade Stalin's answer to a correspondent from *Pravda* on atomic weapons), *Voennaya mysl'*, No. 10 (1951), p. 4.

September 1945, Ambassador Ya. Malik sent Moscow a number of materials under the heading "The Atomic Bomb," including articles on the aftermath of the bombing, descriptions of the events by Soviet witnesses, and damage assessments from the Japanese press. On November 22, 1945, Soviet Foreign Minister Vyacheslav Molotov assigned the materials to "comrades Stalin, Beria, Malenkov, Mikoyan + myself." The number of dead and wounded in Hiroshima—about 120,000 people—cited in these papers had been taken from the Japanese press. In Nagasaki, 15,000 were said to have been killed, 20,000 wounded, with about 90,000 other victims. A detailed description of the effect of the shock wave and radiation was also provided, although obviously underestimated, in part because the information had been provided by U.S. military men (according to a doctor in the Fifth Fleet, "the harmful effect of the atomic bomb lasts only 24 hours"[177]). According to the Soviet embassy, the aftereffects of the atomic bombing were deliberately overstated by the Japanese press to justify Japan's surrender:

The atomic bomb and the destruction it caused shocked the Japanese population. It is being referred to in the imperial rescript and official statements of the Japanese government as one of the reasons for Japan's capitulation. Since it is said to be the immediate reason for Japan's defeat, its destructive power and the duration of the effects after the explosion are being exaggerated in every possible way. Popular rumors pick up on the press reports, distort them, and carry them to the point of absurdity. It has even been rumored that it is now dangerous to be in the area of the explosion. The Americans and the Japanese have stated more than once that women are unable to bear children and men become impotent after visiting the affected area.[178]

Soviet Embassy staff sent to Hiroshima and Nagasaki did not present any specific findings or conclusions, but their attached background materials confirmed the opinion that the Japanese press had exaggerated the consequences of the bombing.

Soviet predictions about a future war in that period were unvarying. They merely projected the previous war into the future. The possibility of the enemy profiting in the short term was perceived as a threat, but it would be overcome by a strategy based on long-term sources of power. An attempt to repeat the 1941 German invasion of the Soviet Union

---

177. "*Tragediya Hirosimy i Nagasaki. Documenty*" (The tragedy of Hiroshima and Nagasaki. Documents), *Mezhdunarodnaya zhizn'*, No. 7 (1990), pp. 142, 144.

178. Ibid.

would definitely end in another Soviet victory and the complete collapse and destruction of imperialism. Atomic and later thermonuclear weapons scarcely affected Soviet political and military thinking in the early postwar years, and continued to be overshadowed by ideology and propaganda.[179]

In 1947, the Soviet government announced that the atomic bomb was no longer a secret, and in 1949, the first Soviet atomic weapon was tested. Three years later, the explosion of the first Soviet hydrogen bomb was publicly reported. In 1948, the first Soviet guidelines on the combat use of nuclear weapons were published, and both the theoretical aspects of the new weapon's combat efficiency and new features of combat if it were used began to be elaborated.[180] The nuclear factor was first mentioned by General Douglas MacArthur, commander of U.S. forces in the Far East, when he proposed using nuclear weapons if defeat at the hands of North Korean troops and Chinese volunteers emerged as a real risk.[181] As some participants in the Soviet decision-making process at the time have noted, the Soviet leadership knew about MacArthur's ideas. However, neither the emergence of a U.S. nuclear threat nor Soviet efforts to construct its own nuclear weapon affected traditional Soviet military theory. Even when a nuclear weapon was used in military exercises in the Totskoe region in 1954, no changes were introduced.[182] There is evidence that some Soviet officials tried not to "exaggerate" the role of nuclear weapons in a future war in order to preserve the morale of the army and of the general public. At the same time, the thesis that a new war would end in the defeat of imperialism was accepted unquestioningly. Georgy Malenkov, chairman of the Council of Ministers, declared in his speech at the 20th Party Congress in 1956 that a third world war would "lead to the complete collapse of the capitalist system."[183]

---

179. V. Tsymburskii, *Nekotorye voprosy evolutsii ponyatiya "voennoi opasnosti" v sovetskoi voennoi doktrine* (Some issues in the evolution of the understanding of the "military danger" in Soviet military doctrine) (Moscow: Institute for USA and Canada Studies [ISKAN], 1989), pp. 14–15.

180. M.M. Kiryan, A.I. Babin, I.M. Kravchenko, et al., *Istoriya voennogo iskusstva* (History of military art) (Moscow: Voenizdat, 1986), p. 394.

181. Richard K. Betts, *Nuclear Blackmail and Nuclear Balance* (Washington, D.C.: Brookings, 1987), p. 36.

182. Kozlov, Matsulenko, et al., *Voennoe iskusstvo vo vtoroi mirovoi voine i v poslevoennyi period*, p. 466.

183. *XX s'ezd Kommunisticheskoi Partii Sovetskogo Soyuza* (20th Congress of the Communist Party of the Soviet Union), stenographic notes (Moscow: Politizdat, 1956), p. 432.

Political-Military Conditions in the Second Half of the 1950s

On August 21, 1957, the Soviet Union launched its first two-stage ballistic missile, which had been built by the experimental design office headed by Sergei Pavlovich Korolev.[184] At the end of the 1950s, the first atomic submarines carrying ballistic missiles appeared. In 1959, the Soviet government decided to turn the strategic rocket forces (SRF) into a separate branch of military service. All existing formations armed with intercontinental ballistic missiles (ICBMs) and medium-range missiles were transferred to the SRF, as well as several educational institutions and offices. M.N. Nedelin, chief marshal of the artillery, was appointed the first commander in chief of the strategic rocket forces. The SRF soon began to vie for primacy with the other armed services, pushing aside the ground forces, the traditional leader.

There was no agreement within the Soviet leadership on the appropriate role of the SRF. Some military leaders suggested that all nuclear weapons should be allocated proportionately among the ground forces, the navy, the air forces, and the anti-air defense. Others argued that it would be more effective to transfer them to the air force and the navy. Instead, the SRF became the fifth branch of the Soviet armed forces. Contrary to what some Soviet historians say, that decision was partially a compromise because a considerable part of the Soviet strategic nuclear arsenal remained in the possession of the air force (long-range bombers) and the navy (strategic nuclear submarines).

The ideological function of Stalin's concept of "permanently operating factors," which played down the significance of nuclear weapons, was increasingly irrelevant. In the late 1950s, a potential third world war was depicted as an extremely destructive nuclear war of unprecedented scope. Many Soviet analysts predicted that it would be a short war, while others forecasted a protracted war.

A detailed exposition of the Soviet military leadership's views on a

---

184. Sergei Pavlovich Korolev and Valentin Petrovich Glushko, pioneers in the creation of powerful Soviet missiles, had been imprisoned for a long time as a result of the purges in the late 1930s. They worked at one of the special research centers set up by the NKVD, the internal security organ, in its prisons and labor camps. Before being sent to one of these centers, Korolev had been imprisoned in a camp in Kolyma and had nearly perished several times. Two indictments of Korolev, dated 1938 and 1940, were declassified during *perestroika*. According to the second one, he was found guilty of being a member of a "Trotskyite sabotage organization operating in Scientific Research Institute No. 3." Like all other similar indictments, Korolev's were entirely falsified. See Ya. Golovanov, *"Katastrofa"* (Catastrophe), *Znamya* (Banner), No. 2 (1990), pp. 111–113.

future war and a future adversary can be found in a 1962 book by Minister of Defense Rodion Malinovsky, *Vigilantly Safeguarding Peace*. Malinovsky viewed the political dimension of the threat as follows: "In the United States, France, West Germany, and some other capitalist countries, the militarization of the economy and the fascistization of social life are increasing. Imperialism is preparing its next adventures and plotting aggression."[185] Neither the wording nor the substance of his definition differed much from what had been stated in the 1940s and 1950s. The United States was still considered the main military threat to the Soviet Union: "All the plots against peace converge in the United States. It has tied up more than 40 bourgeois states in military alliances and is persistently rebuilding the military potential of West Germany and Japan, spreading its military bases all over the world, increasing its military outlays annually, testing new kinds of nuclear bombs and stockpiling various means of war."[186] Relying on the basic principles of the Communist Party program, Malinovsky noted that "recent changes in the political part of the military doctrine reflect the fact that military conflicts will not be inevitable after the world system of socialism has been created."[187] He underscored the Soviet Union's adherence to the concepts of peaceful coexistence and comprehensive disarmament under strict international control.[188]

Nikita Khrushchev expounded his vision of future war in a number of statements, including a speech at the fourth session of the Supreme Soviet in January 1960 in which he emphasized that nuclear weapons were the main means of conducting modern warfare, and many types of conventional weapons were rapidly becoming obsolete.[189] According to Khrushchev, the initial phase of war would be critical, which, many concluded, meant that the Soviet leadership did not expect a future war

---

185. R.Ya. Malinovsky, *Bditel'no stoyat' na strazhe mira* (Vigilantly safeguarding peace) (Moscow: Voenizdat, 1962), p. 12.

186. Ibid., p. 13.

187. Ibid., p. 19.

188. Ibid.

189. In the late 1950s, the Soviet leadership started to take this approach. A decision was made to exclude from the navy not only most of the obsolete artillery ships, but also bombardment, torpedo, and fighter aviation; a great part of the coastal artillery; and the navy's entire anti-aircraft defense. An instruction was issued to scrap nearly completed warships like the *Admiral Kornilov*, which had already passed tests. The new commander in chief of the navy, S.G. Groshkov, who succeeded Kuznetsov, tried to save the ships. However, the minister of defense did not support him. See V.N. Chernavin, "*Yego zhizn'—vernost' dolgu*" (His life—loyalty to duty), *Morskoi sbornik*, No. 3 (1990), p. 88.

to be protracted. Khrushchev went on to say that the Soviet Union, being a huge country, could survive a nuclear first strike and even retaliate. He was confident that Soviet military power deterred the "imperialist camp," and therefore the Soviet Union was in a good position. Khrushchev concluded by declaring that the number of Soviet troops would be reduced by approximately one third from about 3.6 million to 2.4 million. The combat effectiveness of Soviet troops, Khrushchev asserted, would improve after the reduction, since the increase in firepower would make up for the decrease in personnel.[190] He emphasized the special role of missiles and nuclear weapons, which put into question the future of large surface ships, a significant part of aviation, and even tanks.[191]

During his official visit to the United States in September 1959, Khrushchev visited San Francisco, where his schedule included a pleasure trip around the bay in a motorboat. When the boat passed by an aircraft carrier, Khrushchev remarked:

Warships are only good for making state visits. From a military point of view, they have become obsolete. Obsolete! Now they are just good targets for rockets. We have dismantled all our completed aircraft carriers. They had been almost 95 percent completed. Today, using aircraft carriers would scarcely be effective. . . . Earlier a submarine had to approach within five kilometers of an aircraft carrier to sink it. Now they can be sent to the bottom by strikes carried out from a distance of hundreds of kilometers. The development of flying torpedoes and missiles has entirely changed the situation at sea.[192]

Khrushchev's remarks were never subsequently cited in Soviet military circles.

Soon after Khrushchev announced his political program in January 1960, views began to appear in the Soviet military press that could be

---

190. N.S. Khrushchev, "*Razoruzhenie—put' k nadezhnomu miru i druzhbe mezhdu narodami*" (Disarmament—the way to a sure peace and friendship between peoples) (Moscow: Gospolitizdat, 1960), p. 46.

191. Witnesses have described how Khrushchev reacted to a test of the fighting capabilities of anti-tank guided missiles against the newest tanks. After observing the successful demonstration, Khrushchev asked whether the other side possessed the same weapon, and received an affirmative reply. "If that is the case, why do we need tanks at all?" he remarked. Khrushchev's comment was taken quite seriously by the military and by military industrialists, since they knew how decisively the earlier directive on surface warships had been carried out.

192. A. Adzhubei, N. Gribachev, G. Zhukov, et al., *Litsom k litsu s Amerikoi* (Face to face with America) (Moscow: Gospolitizdat, 1956), pp. 307–308.

interpreted as disguised disapproval of Khrushchev's line. Most often they emphasized problems that Khrushchev had not addressed.[193] Malinovsky's speech on Soviet military doctrine at the 22nd Party Congress was illustrative. He reiterated many items from Khrushchev's program about the character of war in new conditions, but also added some important points. For example, Malinovsky stressed the significance of the traditional armed forces; in his view, in any future war massive, million-strong armies would be required to achieve victory.[194] Although he avoided specifying whether a future war would be short or protracted, the very mention of million-strong armies suggested that a war might be protracted, at least comparatively. Malinovsky agreed with Khrushchev's arguments that it was necessary to have enough military power to deter the United States and its allies. However, he also reflected the military's concern that the levels of forces and the means that Khrushchev considered adequate in peacetime might turn out to be inadequate in the event of war. Some military leaders fought to preserve the role of the ground forces, which had traditionally been the core of the armed forces in both the tsarist and Soviet periods. A central issue was the future of tanks, tank formations, and tank units. General S.M. Shtemenko admitted that the armor penetration of modern anti-tank weapons had increased, and that further increasing the armor of military vehicles was useless. However, he also stated that armor plating should provide maximum protection to the crew against radioactivity and reliable protection against artillery strikes. Shtemenko further concluded that "the large-scale introduction of nuclear weapons into the forces has upgraded the role of tanks in future warfare. They are better equipped to resist a nuclear attack by the enemy than other weapons, they can rapidly take advantage of their own nuclear strikes, they can operate in zones of high radioactivity, and they can seize and hold enemy territory."[195]

After Khrushchev was forced out of his Party and state positions, the military continued to promote the role of the ground forces, although the

---

193. The Soviet media began to mention (not groundlessly) that adjusting to civilian life would be a problem for many military officers. This raised the question of whether a reduction in the number of troops would damage military morale.

194. R.Ya. Malinovsky, speech, *XXII s'ezd Kommunistichskoi Partii Sovetskogo Soyuza* (22nd Congress of the Communist Party of the Soviet Union), stenographic notes, Vol. 2 (Moscow: Gospolitizdat, 1962), pp. 111–113.

195. S. Shtemenko, "*Nauchno-tekhnologicheskii progress i yego vliyanie na razvitie voennogo dela*" (Scientific and technological progress and its impact on the development of military affairs), *Kommunist Vooruzhennykh Sil*, No. 3 (1963), p. 25.

immediate danger to the service had passed. The issues now at stake were budget allocations and prestige. As General I. Pavlovsky wrote in *Voennaya mysl'* in 1967, the emergence of missile weapons and strategic forces did not obviate the role of ground forces, which still had an important role to play in nuclear war. His conclusion concurred with that of Shtemenko: "Tank forces . . . are highly capable of efficiently capitalizing on the results of our nuclear strikes, resisting nuclear strikes by the enemy, and overcoming zones contaminated by radiation and areas of destruction."[196]

In the 1960s, the role of the Soviet navy, and particularly submarines armed with missiles, increased by a certain degree. Serial production of nuclear submarines carrying cruise and ballistic missiles and surface ships armed with missiles was started. Long-range marine aircraft for battling enemy aircraft carriers were actively developed.[197] The necessity to develop a Soviet oceanic fleet was substantiated by the military because of the growing strategic threat to the Soviet Union and its allies that was posed by U.S. nuclear-armed aircraft carriers and Polaris submarines. Thus the key mission of the Soviet navy was to destroy the enemy's naval strike force and ground installations.[198] The more traditional mission of breaking up U.S. sea lines of communication, particularly those that connected the United States with its European allies, remained on the navy's agenda.

At the 21st Party Congress, Malinovsky followed the habitual line of praising and exaggerating the potential of the Soviet armed forces:

Our navy has become quite a modern fleet fit to carry out any strategic mission in its field. Across the ocean, they often say that the U.S. fleet can inflict strikes and land troops at any point on our coast. But as the saying goes, "it is easy to boast, but it is easy to fail." It seems to me that some people across the ocean should think about the future of their own shoreline and rather extenuated communications, whose vulnerability is incredibly exposed.[199]

---

196. I. Pavlovsky, "*Sukhoputnye voiska Sovetskikh Vooruzhennykh Sil*" (The ground forces of the Soviet armed forces), *Voennaya mysl'*, No. 11 (1967), p. 37.

197. V. Dotsenko, "*Sovetskoe voenno-morskoe iskusstvo v poslevoennyi period*" (Soviet naval art in the post-war period), *Morskoi sbornik*, No. 7 (1989), p. 21.

198. Ibid., p. 23.

199. "*Rech tovarishcha Malinovskogo*" (Speech of Comrade Malinovsky), *Vneocherednoi XXI s'ezd Kommunisticheskoi Partii Sovetskogo Soyuza* (Extraordinary 21st Congress of the Communist Party of the Soviet Union), stenographic notes, Vol. 2 (Moscow: Politizdat, 1959), p. 126.

As a final verdict, he added: "The traditional invulnerability of the United States has been liquidated forever."[200]

Despite the fact that the 20th Party Congress was followed by liberalization (the "thaw") and the revitalization of social and political thinking in the Soviet Union, the level of threat assessment and Soviet analysis of a future war was rather low, as had also been the case in the late 1930s. The pronouncements by Malinovsky and other top military leaders were not as profound as the writings of military intellectuals of the 1920s like Svechin, Tukhachevsky, and Shaposhnikov. Even some of Voroshilov's evaluations surpassed them. Critical issues such as, for example, the rifts between the United States and France and between France and Britain were not investigated, while NATO's approach to the Federal Republic of Germany was interpreted quite one-sidedly. Nothing was said about the alignment of forces within the leadership of these countries—not even the simplest schemes like the "party of war" versus the "party of peace." Strange though it may seem, the Soviet military utterly ignored the rather acute contradictions between Britain, France, and Israel, on the one hand, and the United States, on the other, during the Suez crisis in 1956. The belief that the Soviet armed forces were superior to all other armed forces in the world and that this superiority would guarantee victory in any war was stated simply and straightforwardly by the Soviet Minister of Defense:

Most characteristic of the present stage of development of Soviet military doctrine is that it is supported by the superiority of the Soviet armed forces over the armies of the most powerful capitalist countries in terms of military-technical means, morale, and combat abilities. This superiority and the just aims of our armed forces give us full confidence that in a future war unleashed by imperialism, however widespread it might be, victory will be ours, the defenders of the achievements of socialism, the defenders of the great cause of communism.[201]

Malinovsky did not express the slightest doubt that Soviet "superiority" could be maintained in the future; in fact, he asserted that it would increase: "In the competition in the quality of weapons imposed on us by aggressive forces, we are not only as strong as they are but in many respects we are stronger. In the future, if the arms race does not end, our superiority will be even greater: we are keen, persistent, and

---

200. Ibid.
201. Ibid., p. 22.

determined people who toil selflessly for the good of our country and the world."[202]

Malinovsky's associates were of the same opinion. For example, Marshal of the Soviet Union S. Biryuzov wrote the following in 1964:

In the past few years there has been a decisive leap in Soviet military development, which has stunned the bourgeois politicians and generals. The socialist structure, the achievements of the Soviet economy, science, and technology have not only allowed us to surpass the United States and the major capitalist countries in the production of nuclear weapons during the past few years, but have also enabled us to be the first in the world to develop large-scale designs and production of principally new means of delivering these missiles for various purposes.[203]

He viewed the decisive advantages of ICBMs as a major factor contributing to victory in a future war. "Intercontinental ballistic missiles have been built which immeasurably surpass strategic bombers in terms of combat abilities. Everybody has seen that the real key to victory on the battlefield is in the hands of the one who not only possesses new weapons but leads in the production of missiles."[204]

Now, however, both Soviet and foreign experts almost unanimously agree that the Soviet Union in no way enjoyed general superiority over the United States and its allies in the 1960s.

The Initial Phase of War and Fighting a Surprise Attack

In the late 1950s and early 1960s, Soviet military thought began to focus more on analyzing the initial phase of war, which was considered to have a decisive impact on the course of fighting and the outcome of the war.

Colonel General N.A. Lomov considered concepts on the initial phase of war to be central to Soviet military doctrine: "During the initial phase of a future world war, the armed forces of the adversary, first and foremost the strategic means of nuclear attack, and the most important government and economic centers of the enemy will be the main targets of the armed strike."[205] Lomov was referring to Malinovsky's argument that

---

202. Ibid., p. 23.

203. S. Biryuzov, "*Novyi etap v razvitii Vooruzhennykh Sil i zadachi obucheniya i vospitaniya voisk*" (A new stage in the development of the armed forces and the tasks of training and developing troops), *Kommunist Vooruzhennykh Sil*, No. 4 (1964), p. 16.

204. Ibid., p. 18.

205. N. Lomov, "*Sovetskaya voennaya doktrina*" (Soviet military doctrine), *Voennaya mysl'*, No. 1 (1963), p. 21.

the first massed nuclear strikes could entirely predetermine the subsequent development of the war. Thus, "frustrating a nuclear surprise attack by the enemy and taking the strategic lead at the very beginning of war" became the most important principle of Soviet military doctrine.[206] Three editions of *Voennaya strategiya* (*Military Strategy*), edited by Marshal Sokolovsky, contained the same idea. The key mission of the initial phase, according to him, "is to work out to the last detail reliable ways to repel the surprise nuclear attack and to frustrate the enemy's aggressive schemes by inflicting a shattering blow at the right moment."[207] The details of how to frustrate "aggressive schemes" were not provided, however. Eight years earlier, in 1955, Marshal of armored tank forces P. Rotmistrov had published an article in *Voennaya mysl'* on the role of surprise in modern warfare, which was well known to the staff of the Soviet command. Rotmistrov pointed out that "the duty of the Soviet armed forces is not to allow a surprise attack against our country, and, in case of such an attempt, not only to repel the attack but to inflict a counterattack or even a preemptive attack of terrible destructive power." Rotmistrov believed that the Soviet army and navy had everything they needed to carry out this mission.[208]

In the second half of the 1960s, Soviet perceptions of the initial phase of war began to change. This shift was caused by the growth of the Soviet nuclear arsenal, the qualitative improvement of Soviet nuclear strategic forces, and the increased stability of the strategic nuclear forces as a result of stationing nuclear missiles in silos. The commander-in-chief of the strategic rocket forces, N. Krylov, wrote in 1967 that

having in service launchers and missiles entirely prepared for operation, an early-warning system for detecting the launch of enemy missiles, and other means of reconnaissance prevents the aggressor from hitting the missiles on the opponent's territory before they can be launched. Even in the most unfavorable case when some of the missiles fail to launch before the aggressor's attack, they will still survive thanks to the high protection of the launchers against a nuclear explosion, and they will still be able to carry out their combat mission.[209]

---

206. Ibid., p. 25.

207. See V.D. Sokolovsky, ed., *Voennaya strategiya* (Military strategy), 3rd ed. (Moscow: Voenizdat, 1968), p. 225.

208. P. Rotmistrov, "*O roli vnezapnosti v sovremennoi voine*" (On the role of surprise in modern war), *Voennaya mysl'*, No. 2 (1955), p. 21.

209. N. Krylov, "*Raketno-yadernyi shchit Sovetskogo gosudarstva*" (The nuclear-missile shield of the Soviet state), *Voennaya mysl'*, No. 11 (1967), p. 20.

That argument was meant to justify the Soviet reliance on a purely retaliatory strike rather than counterstrikes or preemptive strikes as had been suggested explicitly by Rotmistrov and implicitly by Lomov, Sokolovsky, and others.

In the early 1960s, the view prevailed in Soviet military literature that war would begin with a surprise massive nuclear attack, possibly during an international crisis. In the second half of the 1960s, following changes in U.S. and NATO military strategy (a shift from "massive retaliation" to a policy of "flexible response"), multiple scenarios of future war emerged in Soviet military circles. In an article commemorating the 50th anniversary of the Soviet armed forces, Marshal of the Soviet Union I. Yakubovsky emphasized that, in accordance with the strategy of "flexible response," NATO was taking "practical measures to increase the fighting capabilities of its forces to wage a protracted war in Europe without using nuclear weapons."[210] As General Colonel M. Povaly, deputy chief of the General Staff, noted, one should envisage a variety of scenarios for the beginning of war. "War could begin immediately, with unlimited use by both sides of all combat means, including nuclear strategic forces. In this case, the war would be short and would end in an exchange of massive nuclear strikes by the belligerents. It is also possible that war could start, and be waged for some time, strictly with conventional weapons."[211] The latter suggestion was rather important—it highlighted the growing emphasis that Soviet military doctrine placed on conventional war. This trend was more fully developed in the 1970s and 1980s.

Local and Limited Wars

The importance of local and limited wars within the context of a third world war increased in the 1960s. Soviet military thinkers gave special attention to wars of national liberation, which were classified as "just wars." Most of the major Soviet experts of that period were inclined to believe that local wars could trigger a world war, and thus should be avoided. Nevertheless, the Soviet political leadership and military command continually declared their support for national liberation movements. For example, Khrushchev stated in 1961 that national liberation wars must not be identified as either wars between states or local wars. He stressed: "Under contemporary conditions, three following categories

---

210. I. Yakubovsky, "50 let Vooruzhennykh Sil SSSR" (50 years of the USSR armed forces), *Voennaya mysl'*, No. 2 (1968), p. 29.

211. M. Povaly, "*Razvitie sovetskoi voennoi strategii*" (The development of Soviet military strategy), *Voennaya mysl'*, No. 2 (1967), p. 74.

of war should be distinguished: world wars, local wars, liberation wars, i.e., people uprisings. This is important for working out the right tactics as regards these wars."[212] One must remember that a distinctive feature of that era was the breakdown in relations between the Soviet Union and China, which developed into an acute ideological and political struggle in large part over national liberation movements. The Sino-Soviet split pushed the Soviet Union to take a more active stand on the process of national liberation.

Opportunities to contain local wars and prevent them from turning into world war had narrowed, according to Rotmistrov. In his view, a "small" war could grow into a world war regardless of who started it. Yet like many other Soviet military theorists, Rotmistrov differentiated between local wars and wars of national liberation. While firmly struggling against aggressive imperialist wars, he said, Communists completely supported just wars of national liberation since they are a means to free people from oppression and enslavement.[213]

In the late 1960s, probably as a direct result of the flexible response strategy, there were some indications that Soviet military experts, though with some reservations, considered the restricted use of nuclear weapons to be a feasible possibility in the event of war. "Along with conventional war and instantaneous nuclear war of incredible magnitude and devastation, war involving the restricted use of nuclear weapons in one or more theaters of military operations should not be excluded,"[214] Marshal Sokolovsky and Major General M. Cherednichenko wrote in 1968. A few months later, General of the Army S. Ivanov interpreted the prospect of the restricted use of nuclear weapons somewhat differently: "Theoretically one might allow that the two sides might limit themselves to inflicting several selective strikes against secondary objectives in order to deter each other but would not pursue an enlargement of the nuclear conflict."[215] In his opinion, such an exchange of single strikes would not characterize the war as nuclear. Therefore, two types of war are possible:

---

212. N.S. Khrushchev, *"Za novye pobedy mirovogo kommunisticheskogo dvizheniya"* (For new victories of the world communist movement), *Kommunist*, No. 1 (January 1961), p. 20.

213. P. Rotmistrov, *"Prichiny sovremennykh voin i ikh osobennosti"* (Reasons for modern wars and their specific features), *Kommunist Vooruzhennykh Sil*, No. 2 (1963), p. 27.

214. V. Sokolovsky and M. Cherednichenko, *"Voennaya strategiya i yeye problemy"* (Military strategy and its problems), *Voennaya mysl'*, No. 10 (1968), p. 36. The article was published after Sokolovsky's death.

215. S. Ivanov, *"Sovetskaya voennaya doktrina i strategiya"* (Soviet military doctrine and strategy), *Voennaya mysl'*, No. 5 (1969), p. 48.

nuclear and nonnuclear in terms of means of warfare, and global and local in terms of scale.[216]

To summarize the evolution of Soviet military thinking in the 1950s and 1960s, a turbulent period of development and deployment of nuclear weapons by the United States and the Soviet Union, as well as advances in conventional weapons, five types of war, as conceived by Soviet military leaders and theoreticians, can be identified:

- an instantaneous, full-scale nuclear war in which strategic nuclear forces play the principal role;
- a protracted nuclear war involving all the armed forces;
- a major war in one or several theaters of military operations involving the restricted use of nuclear weapons;
- a major conventional war; and
- a local war involving conventional weapons.

The Political-Military Situation during the Era of Détente and Stagnation

In the early 1970s, during the period of political détente between the United States and the Soviet Union, the language and the spirit of most Soviet evaluations of the political and military situation noticeably changed. That imperialism was the main threat to peace, and that the United States and other leading capitalist states were continuing their military buildup, continued to be emphasized, however. It was noted that the forces of imperialism had used military force in Vietnam and the Middle East. For example, in 1973, General V. Kulikov, chief of the Soviet General Staff, wrote the following:

In recent times, thanks to the active, peace-oriented foreign policy of the Communist Party, the Soviet government, and other socialist states, a certain easing of tensions in international relations has been achieved. But imperialism has not lost its aggressive nature.... This is convincingly illustrated by the banditry of the American aggressors in Vietnam, the incessant scheming of Israel against the Arab peoples, and the growth of militarization and revanchism in several European and Asian countries.[217]

---

216. Ibid.

217. V. Kulikov, "*Novyi uchebnyi god v Armii i na Flote*" (The new academic year in the army and the navy), *Voennaya mysl'*, No. 1 (1973), p. 25.

A new feature of the Soviet political and military assessment in the 1970s was that the People's Republic of China was included among the Soviet Union's potential adversaries, and was thus considered an ally of the United States and NATO. Usually this view was expressed in articles in open and semi-restricted military publications written by middle-ranking officers rather than top military leaders. It was assumed that, as in the case of a war between the Soviet Union and its Warsaw Pact allies, on the one side, and the United States and NATO, on the other, a war between the Soviet Union and China would involve nuclear weapons, since China was by now also a nuclear power and the "Peking leadership," like the forces of imperialism, was preparing for nuclear war.[218]

Despite détente and some progress in arms reductions, most Soviet military leaders and theoreticians emphasized the significance of military means rather than political and diplomatic ones in preventing war. According to Kulikov, "the most effective way to curb the aggressor is to strengthen the defensive power of the country and to increase the combat efficiency of the army and the navy and their ability to safeguard Soviet security."[219] Achieving military superiority was no longer on the agenda. Only the first edition of A.A. Grechko's book *The Armed Forces of the Soviet State* (1974) mentioned that aim. Because of the negative response the book received in the West, however, the second edition (1975) did not mention it.

At the same time, in some important works by military authors, the easing of U.S.-Soviet tensions was interpreted as a more or less stable process, and "a radical turn toward détente" was presented as a *fait accompli*—which quite understandably Soviet civilian analysts were careful not to mention. In combination with the ongoing arms race, détente imbued international relations with a "peculiar contradiction," as several Soviet military writers phrased it. The military buildup in the West was attributed to the efforts of the "most aggressive forces of imperialism" rather than the governments and ruling elites. Moreover, in contrast to earlier years, it is hard to find any analogies between American imperialism and German fascism in Soviet military literature from the 1970s. Nevertheless, the general conclusion remained the same: strengthening the defense of the Soviet Union and the socialist community and increasing

---

218. See, for example, L.I. Voloshin, "*Teoriya glubokoi operatsii i tendentsii yeye razvitiya*" (The theory of deep operation and trends in its development), *Voennaya mysl'*, No. 8 (1978), p. 25.

219. V. Kulikov, "*Novyi uchebnyi god v Armii i na Flote*," p. 25.

their capacity to repel aggression were indispensable.[220] The military and strategic dimensions of future world war continued to be envisioned as they had been by Malinovsky, Sokolovsky, and Biryuzov in the 1960s. The following features were highlighted: (1) decisive political and military-strategic goals; (2) the coalitional character of military confrontation; (3) the massive scale of warfare; (4) the disappearance of differences between the front and the rear; and (5) the maneuverability of warfare.[221]

By that time, some Western assessments of the aftereffects of nuclear war and the high number of casualties had become known in the Soviet Union.[222] However, no Soviet military expert questioned the argument of the minister of defense that the nuclear factor should not be exaggerated despite its huge destructive power. The voice of Soviet civilian experts was scarcely heard, particularly in the context of military, political, strategic, and tactical planning. "Unlike bourgeois military science," Grechko stated, "Soviet military science, despite the enormous power of the nuclear weapon, does not consider it absolute; it does not give preference to any particular type of military force as some of the bourgeois military theories now in vogue do." Moreover, "Soviet military science holds that if an imperialist reaction were to unleash nuclear war, it would be active and decisive warfare involving all types of armed forces acting in concert in terms of their mission, time and place."[223] Thus it was concluded that a future war would most likely be protracted.[224]

The concepts and specific plans for the Soviet armed forces and the mobilization of industry and agriculture in wartime were mapped out on this basis. The massive scale of warfare, the vulnerability of the rear, and the enormous casualties and losses were presented as the reasons for increasing the mobilization readiness of industry, huge reserve capacities,

---

220. See, for example, the editorial, "*Vooruzhennye Sily Sovetskogo gosudarstva*" (The armed forces of the Soviet state), in *Voennaya mysl'*, No. 7 (1974), p. 3. The article was written to commemorate the publication of Grechko's book of the same title.

221. See, for example, V. Zemskov, "*Kharakternye strategicheskie cherty mirovykh voin*" (Characteristic strategic features of world wars), *Voennaya mysl'*, No. 7, 8 (1974).

222. For example, the American scientist Linus Pauling estimated that about 500–700 million people would be killed in the area of a nuclear attack during the sixty days after it, while the British scholar John Bernal projected that from 1.5 to 2.2 billion people would be killed as a result of nuclear war. See V. Zemskov, "*Kharakternye strategicheskie cherty mirovykh voin*," *Voennaya mysl'*, No. 7 (1974), p. 32.

223. A.A. Grechko, *Vooruzhennyie Sily Sovetskogo gosudarstva* (The armed forces of the Soviet state) (Moscow: Voennizdat, 1974), pp. 176–177.

224. Zemskov, "*Kharakternye strategicheskie cherty mirovykh voin*," p. 33.

and stockpiles of food, fuel, raw materials, etc. This undoubtedly created an unbearable burden for the Soviet economy and hindered Leonid Brezhnev's economic reforms, which were targeted at loosening the Soviet Union's highly centralized administrative system—the very existence of which had been entirely justified by the requirements of national mobilization in the event of a major war. At the same time, Grechko's thesis about active and decisive warfare involving all types of armed forces implied the necessity of maintaining major ground forces equipped with modern armaments and the buildup of strategic rocket forces and other branches of the Soviet armed forces, including the navy. Moreover, Soviet military analysts often emphasized that tanks had a special role to play in both nuclear and nonnuclear warfare, stressing the necessity to introduce other types of armed vehicles like infantry combat vehicles, self-propelled armored field artillery (artillery combat vehicles), and light, multipurpose tanks (which had not been used since the end of World War I).[225] Only after the Arab-Israeli War of October 1973, with its high tank losses largely resulting from anti-tank guided weapons, did Soviet experts begin to reconsider the role of tanks in modern warfare. A book published by the General Staff Academy (though with the usual references to foreign specialists) pointed out that the sharp increase in the infantry's capacity to fight against tanks and the continuing development of guided missiles had diminished the significance of the tank-bomber-fighter combination, which had been the prevailing tactic in World War I.[226] However, these conclusions were not followed by practical steps, and they did not affect the role of tanks in the Soviet armed forces.

The New Role of the Soviet Navy

In the late 1960s, the Soviet navy had attained higher status within the armed forces, and many have even called this period the apogee of the navy's development not only in the Soviet era, but in all of Russian history. Certainly the fleet was very important in some periods of Russian history, such as in the first decades of the eighteenth century under Peter the Great and in the late eighteenth century under Catherine the Great. However, with some rare exceptions, the Russian navy was not an ocean-going fleet despite the achievements of Russian navigators like V. Bering,

---

225. O. Losik, "*Vremya i tanky*" (Time and tanks), *Voennaya mysl'*, No. 1 (1973), pp. 88–89.
226. I.G. Shavrov, ed., *Lokal'nye voiny. Istoriya i sovremennost'* (Local wars. History and the present) (Moscow: General Staff Academy Publishing House, 1975), p. 292.

F. Bellingshausen, I. Krusenstern, M. Lazarev, Yu. Lisyansky, and others. Nevertheless, the effective performance of Russian squadrons in the Mediterranean in the eighteenth and nineteenth centuries, including victories over the Turkish fleet far from Russian shores in the battles at Chesma in 1770 and Navarino in 1827 (as part of a Russo-Franco-British squadron), should not be underestimated.[227] There was a major development in the 1860s, when two Russian squadrons took to the high seas during a period of rising tensions between Russia and Britain caused by the Polish uprising of 1863. This coincided with the U.S. Civil War, in which Russia sided with the North and sent one squadron to New York and the other to San Francisco.[228] Russia's historical experience and its continuing aspiration for the expanse of the ocean were repeatedly touted by advocates of the navy both in the media and at meetings of the Council of Defense and the Politburo.[229]

The Soviet naval exercise called *Okean* (Ocean), conducted almost globally from April 14 through May 6, 1970, was a significant event for the Soviet navy. Surface warships and submarines of various types, naval aircraft, and naval infantry all took part in the exercise. The chief of the navy's political department, V. Grishanov, proudly described *Okean* in these words: "The very name of the maneuver *Okean* is symbolic. Now we call our navy an ocean-going fleet, and this is correct. There are no areas on the map of the world's oceans where Soviet warships do not sail."[230] Zverev's 1978 book *V.I. Lenin and the Fleet* reported that the main forces of the four Soviet fleets had put out to sea in various regions of the

---

227. See, for example, B.A. Zolotariev and I.A. Kozlov, *Rossiiskii voennyi flot na Chernom more i v Vostochnom Sredizemnomorie* (The Russian navy on the Black Sea and in the Eastern Mediterranean) (Moscow: Nauka, 1988), pp. 26–29, 48.

228. This period followed Russia's defeat in the Crimean War of 1853–56, as a result of which Russia lost the right to have a navy on the Black Sea. Russia had also entered a period of reforms and did not have the resources and capacities to build an armored fleet that could challenge the supremacy of the British and French navies. That is why Russia focused on two major types of naval forces: purely defensive warships able to closely interract with ground forces and coastal artillery in coastal areas; and light cruiser forces for actions on the sea lines of communication of the enemy, which depended on sea trade. Warships of the latter type had been combined into two squadrons that had been put out to high sea in 1863 before the armed conflict had begun.

229. For details, see Andrei A. Kokoshin, *SShA v sisteme mezhdunarodnykh otnoshenii 1980-kh godov* (The USA in the system of international relations in the 1980s) (Moscow: Mezhdunarodnye otnosheniya, 1984), p. 69.

230. M.N. Zakharov, ed., *Na manevrakh "Okean"* (At "Ocean" maneuvers) (Vladivostok: Publishing House of the Political Department of the Red Banner Pacific Fleet, 1970), p. 10.

Atlantic, Pacific, and Arctic Oceans according to a unified plan.[231] Grishanov also pointed out that the exercise was unique not only in Russian but also in world maritime history in terms of both its mission and the forces that took part in it. The maneuvers of the Pacific Fleet took place "in the immediate vicinity of the hotbeds of U.S. military aggression in Southeast Asia, in the zone of war activity of the U.S. Navy."[232] The *Okean* maneuvers ended with a tour by Soviet warships of about a dozen foreign ports on four continents.[233]

These naval exercises are associated with Admiral Sergei Gorshkov, who became head of the navy in 1956 and held that post for more than thirty years. During World War II, Gorshkov commanded the Azov Flotilla and the Danube Flotilla, and was Deputy Commander of the Novorossiisk region. Only in January 1945 was he named to the more impressive post of commander of the Black Sea Squadron. After the war, Gorshkov rose first to chief of staff and then commander of the Black Sea Fleet. For some time he served as first deputy commander of the navy. Gorshkov was distinguished by a strong sense of purpose and a gift for winning over both military and political officers. He was an ardent advocate of a strong Soviet navy, and openly disagreed with the message of *Voennaya strategiya* that the navy's role was merely to assist the Soviet army. His successor, Admiral V.N. Chernavin, complained in 1990, "unfortunately there are still advocates of this point of view."[234]

Although Gorshkov persistently fought for an upgrading of the navy's role, he had to admit that there were no reasons to claim a special naval-military strategy. However, he also noted that the navy called for a "specific aspect of military strategy." An analysis of the strategic concepts of the two world wars and specific aspects of the interaction of fleets and ground forces in past wars led him to believe that "the objective development of events has increasingly reduced the universality of naval strategy and placed it within the framework of a specific area of military strategy."[235] Gorshkov underlined the importance of the navy not only in

---

231. B.I. Zverev, *V.I. Lenin i Flot (1918–1920)* (V.I. Lenin and the fleet [1918–1920]) (Moscow: Voenizdat, 1978), p. 291.

232. Zakharov, *Na manevrakh "Okean,"* pp. 27–28.

233. S.G. Gorshkov, *Morskaya moshch gosudarstva* (The seapower of the state) (Moscow: Voenizdat, 1976), p. 411.

234. V.N. Chernavin, "*Ego zhizn'—vernost' dolgu i flotu*" (His life—loyalty to duty and fleet), *Morskoi sbornik*, No. 3 (1990), p. 89.

235. S. Gorshkov, "*K voprosu o strategii vooruzhennoi bor'by na okeanskikh teatrakh*" (On the issue of the strategy of armed struggle in oceanic theaters), *Voennaya mysl'*, No. 7 (1974), p. 47.

time of war, but in peacetime as well. In his opinion, the Soviet navy could be a deterrent in crisis situations in various parts of the world: "The Soviet navy is an instrument . . . for deterring military adventures and firmly counteracting threats to security from the imperialist states."[236] By gaining access to the high seas, he said, the Soviet Union had new and better opportunities to use the ocean to protect its interests.[237]

Continuity and Revolution in the 1980s

By the early 1980s, U.S.-Soviet détente had become a thing of the past. A new round of international tensions developed, which many in both the West and the Soviet Union began to call a "second Cold War." This could not help but influence the Soviet analysis of the political and military situation. Nevertheless, in that period many new concepts appeared in the Soviet appraisal of a future war, which were integrated into the military and political theories of the late 1980s in the era of *perestroika* and "new thinking." The experience of détente and the awareness of the effects of nuclear war played a very important role in these developments.

Marshal Nikolai Ogarkov's book *History Teaches Vigilance*, which he wrote during the early 1980s, described a future war in a way that echoed the ideas of the 1960s:

Soviet military doctrine assumes that modern nuclear war, if imperialists still unleash it, will have an unparalleled territorial impact, will affect all the continents and oceans, and inevitably will engage most countries of the world. Its destructiveness will be unprecedented. Military actions will be conducted simultaneously across vast areas, and they will be distinguished by their bitterness as well as their high degree of maneuverability and dynamism.[238]

Moreover, "this war will continue until the final victory over the enemy."[239] The views of Army General I.G. Pavlovsky, former commander of the ground forces, were almost identical. He wrote in a new edition of *Ground Forces of the USSR* that "a new war, if the imperialists unleash it, will be a decisive confrontation of the two social systems. It will be

---

236. Gorshkov, *Morskaya moshch grosudarstva*, p. 409.

237. Ibid., p. 410.

238. N.V. Ogarkov, *Istoriya uchit bditel'nosti* (History teaches vigilance) (Moscow: Voenizdat, 1985), p. 10.

239. Ibid.

coalitional, and nuclear weapons will be its main means of warfare."[240] Like Ogarkov, Pavlovsky was convinced that victory in a future war would ultimately be gained by traditional methods, known since the Napoleonic wars. "Victory over the aggressor in such a war can be achieved only through joint coordinated efforts by all forces and means of warfare. That is why, in this sharply divided class war, using missile strikes to destroy the enemy's means of nuclear attack and its main forces will not be enough to secure victory. It will be necessary to completely destroy its armed forces."[241] It is worth noting that victory in a future war was mentioned in statements by many top military men even after Defense Minister Dmitry Ustinov had withdrawn the idea in 1982 by stating that "the USSR does not count on achieving victory in a nuclear war."[242] However, although they continued to mention victory, the Soviet military stopped arguing for military supremacy. Instead, the necessity of maintaining the general military strategic balance was emphasized in many Soviet military statements and writings. Attempts to achieve superiority, if not quantitatively then qualitatively, were ascribed to the other side.[243]

Following the line of the political leadership, Dmitry Yazov, then former Minister of Defense, wrote in 1988 that "the Soviet Union does not strive for superiority, does not claim more security, but it will not agree to less security and will not permit any other power to gain military superiority over it."[244] Some Soviet military analysts went even further; one argued that Soviet military theory had started to take into consideration "the fact that in the context of the established global military-strategic balance and the accumulated stockpiles of nuclear weapons, the very notion of 'military superiority' is useless."[245] Although this idea was not publicly supported by the Soviet military, it was explored in internal discussions.

In the 1980s, the concept of limited nuclear war began to be portrayed

---

240. I.G. Pavlovsky, *Sukhoputnye voiska SSSR. Zarozhdeniie. Razvitie. Sovremennost'* (Ground forces of the USSR. Origin. Development. The present) (Moscow: Voenizdat, 1985), p. 217.

241. Ibid.

242. D.F. Ustinov, *Otvesti ugrozy yadernoi voiny* (To avert the threat of nuclear war) (Moscow: Politizdat, 1982), p. 7.

243. See, for example, N.V. Ogarkov, "*Podvig, ravnogo kotoromu ne znala istoriya*" (A deed unparalleled in history), *Zarubezhnoe voennoe obozrenie*, No. 4 (1989), p. 7.

244. D.T. Yazov, "*O voennom balanse sil i raketno-yadernom paritete*" (On the military balance of forces and nuclear-missile parity), *Pravda*, February 8, 1988.

245. A.A. Babanov, *Vooruzhennye sily posle voiny* (The armed forces after the war) (Moscow: Voenizdat, 1987), p. 257.

quite negatively in Soviet military literature. This issue was of great interest to Soviet analysts since it had become quite topical in the United States. As in the past, the Soviet discussion criticized the relevant U.S. and NATO concepts. This is illustrated in a statement by Sergei Akhromeyev, chief of the General Staff:

Under the present conditions and considering the existence of thousands of nuclear weapons, it is impossible to conduct a limited war. If war breaks out, it will inevitably become total, with all the accompanying consequences. The theory of "limited" nuclear war proceeds from the erroneous conception of the crux of the matter, the willingness to make the idea of nuclear war acceptable to public opinion and to make people believe that nuclear conflict could be developed according to some preestablished "rules."[246]

Ogarkov asserted that "transatlantic strategists" who counted on the possibility of waging a limited nuclear war had no grounds for their confidence under the present conditions. This was a utopia, he said; the "restricted use" of nuclear weapons would inevitably and immediately lead to the use of the entire nuclear stockpiles of the warring parties. "This is the tough logic of war," he said.[247]

The 1983 edition of the Soviet *Military Encyclopedic Dictionary* noted that the concept of limited nuclear war was considered groundless in Soviet military theory since it is practically impossible to contain nuclear war within predetermined bounds.[248]

Soviet "civilian strategists" also contributed to the criticism. Professor Vitaly Zhurkin observed that Western officials and specialists contemplating the idea of limited nuclear exchange and controlled escalation frequently conceived of the first strike as a single, almost symbolic act, after which the warring parties would begin to resolve the conflict and seek a mutually acceptable compromise. Nothing was more dangerous than these misconceptions, Zhurkin warned.[249] The use of nuclear weapons

---

246. S.F. Akhromeyev, Address at the Conference of Scientists for saving humanity from the danger of nuclear war, for disarmament and peace, *Vestnik Akademii Nauk SSSR*, No. 9 (1983), p. 48.

247. N. Ogarkov, "*Zashchita sotsializma: opyt istorii i sovremennost'*" (The defense of socialism: Historic experience and the present), *Krasnaya zvezda*, May 9, 1984.

248. *Voennyi entsiklopedicheskii slovar'* (Military encyclopedic dictionary) (Moscow: Sovetskaya entsiklopediya, 1983), p. 842.

249. V.V. Zhurkin, "*Nyet—kontseptsiyam yadernoi voiny*" (No to concepts of nuclear war), in *Novyi mirovoi poryadok i politicheskaya obshchnost'* (The new world order and the political community) (Moscow: Nauka, 1983), p. 12.

could not be seen as a demarche in a crisis situation; rather, it would be crossing the Rubicon, and would trigger a chain of irreversible developments, he said. Using nuclear weapons would endanger the vital interests of the other side and would provoke a retaliatory strike designed to inflict maximum damage. Nuclear war is not a "joint venture," not a game with known rules and restrictions; based on its physical features and consequences, a nuclear war would be the most serious catastrophe in human history, Zhurkin concluded.

Academician E.P. Velikhov pointed out that a "limited" nuclear war posed a serious danger to the theater of battle, since it would be a total war in that region. A "limited" nuclear war in Europe, from the perspective of the United States, would be a "total" war for Europe, and would mean the destruction of European civilization.[250]

At the same time, the Soviet military leadership maintained that although the concept of "limited" nuclear warfare could not be accepted by the Soviet side, they still had to address the actions of the other side. Thus the Soviet art of war, including strategy, operational art, and tactics, prescribed relevant nuclear means to deter the other side from using force, particularly nuclear force. In some military texts, one can also find passages analyzing the role of nuclear weapons in conventional forces and ways to use them not only strategically but also operationally and tactically. The ambiguity of thinking in the field was obvious.

In the mid-1980s, Ogarkov implicitly questioned the general validity of nuclear weapons. He wrote that, in the 1950s and 1960s, when nuclear weapons were few, they were considered a means of increasing firepower, and they were adapted in various ways to existing methods of warfare, above all carrying out strategic missions. In the 1970s and 1980s, Ogarkov continued, the qualitative growth of nuclear weapons with various yields, the development of various long-range, precise means of delivery, and their integration into forces (including naval forces) shattered the old perceptions of warfare and challenged the feasibility of using nuclear weapons in warfare at all.[251]

Soviet military theorists lagged behind Soviet scientists in their analysis of nuclear war. As far back as 1972, Pyotr Kapitsa, the Nobel Prize–winning physicist, disavowed his own views from the 1950s, when he had compared the consequences of an atomic war to those of an epidemic

---

250. E.P. Velikhov, "Nauka i aktual'nye problemy bor'by protiv ugrozy yadernoi voiny" (Science and urgent problems of struggle against the threat of nuclear war), *Vestnik Akademii Nauk SSSR*, No. 9 (1983), pp. 24–25.

251. N.V. Ogarkov, *Istoriia uchit bditel'nosti*, p. 51.

of the plague in the Middle Ages. He reached the rather radical conclusion that "such a war, wherever it breaks out, could poison the entire globe and end all human life within a few hours."[252]

In the first half of the 1980s, the findings of U.S. and Soviet physicians on the aftermath of nuclear war and the "nuclear winter" theory noticeably influenced the Soviet leadership. An international movement of physicians headed by cardiologists Bernard Lown and Yevgeny Chazov focused on the catastrophic and irrelevant nature of nuclear war and was supported by Brezhnev despite the negative attitude of some highly placed Soviet military men.[253] Those military critics held that the doctors' arguments undermined the morale and fighting spirit of the armed forces.

The "nuclear winter" theory was suggested by several U.S. scientists, and was developed in parallel by a number of Soviet scientists, including, first of all, V.V. Aleksandrov, as well as G.L. Stenchikov, G.S. Golitsyn, A.S. Ginzburg, Iu.A. Izrael, N.N. Moiseyev, and others.[254] The theory argued that the dust and smoke sent into the atmosphere by a nuclear war would block sunlight and reduce global temperatures.

Having begun to acknowledge the irrelevance of nuclear war, Soviet military theorists sought an alternative in a large-scale conventional war, which had already been the subject of study by several analysts back in the 1960s. For example, a 1985 book entitled *Military-Technical Progress and the Armed Forces of the USSR* stated that "future war could be unleashed by both conventional and nuclear weapons; started by conventional weapons, it could develop into a nuclear war at a certain stage; in the case of an attack by an aggressor, the military power of the nation, its armed forces, and various means of warfare should be used to crush it."[255]

---

252. Quoted in *Oktyabr'*, No. 12 (1985), pp. 157–158.

253. The findings of several Soviet medical doctors who based their work on research by their U.S. colleagues were published in Y.I. Chazov, L.A. Il'in, and A.K. Gus'kova, eds., *Yadernaya voina: mediko-biologicheskie posledstviya* (Nuclear war: The medical and biological effects) (Moscow: Novosti Press, 1984), p. 239.

254. The findings of their research can be found in E.P. Velikhov, ed., *Klimaticheskie i biologicheskie posledstviya yadernoi voiny* (The climatic and biological consequences of nuclear war) (Moscow: Mir, 1986). V.V. Aleksandrov, head of the laboratory at the Computer Center of the USSR Academy of Sciences, who developed an original three-dimensional hydrodynamic model of climate changes resulting from nuclear war, disappeared mysteriously in Spain in 1985.

255. M.M. Kir'yan, ed., *Voenno-technicheskii progress i Vooruzhennye Sily SSSR* (Military-technical progress and the armed forces of the USSR) (Moscow: Voenizdat, 1982), p. 312.

Thus "Soviet military thinking developed ways to wage war both with and without nuclear weapons."[256]

Deputy Chief of the General Staff M.A. Gareyev linked conventional weapons primarily with the opening phase of war. However, his view could be interpreted as supporting the feasibility of conducting a war by conventional means only. "World war could start with the use of conventional weapons only, but the expansion of military operations might lead it to develop into a nuclear war."[257] Lieutenant General A.I. Yevseyev also suggested that large-scale conventional war was possible: "In terms of the scope of military operations, the opening phase of a future war would differ substantially from the initial stages of past wars. This does not apply only to nuclear war."[258]

Akhromeyev, who replaced Ogarkov as chief of the General Staff in 1984, wrote the following:

In recent years our probable adversaries, aware of the inevitability of a retaliatory nuclear strike and its catastrophic effects, have paid special attention to the development of a conventional weapons system with improved yield, range, and precision. At the same time, they are improving the methods of initiating military operations with conventional means of destruction, first of all with new kinds of automatically guided, highly precise weapons.

Akhromeyev concluded: "All these actions by the adversary are within the field of vision of Soviet military science. We take these trends into consideration in the training of our troops (forces)."[259]

A monograph published by the Voroshilov Military Academy of the General Staff further developed these ideas, stating that, at the new stage in the development of Soviet military strategy, operations using conventional weapons were again considered relevant, and the traditional categories and principles of operational art had been restored to their rightful

---

256. Ibid., p. 313.

257. Gareyev, *Frunze—voennyi teoretik*, p. 237.

258. A.I. Yevseyev, "*O nekotorykh tendentsiyakh v izmenenii soderzhaniya i kharaktera nachal'nogo perioda voiny*" (On some trends in the changing context and character of the initial phase of war), *Voenno-istoricheskii zhurnal*, No. 11 (1985), p. 18.

259. S. Akhromeyev, "*Prevoskhodstvo sovetskoi voennoi nauki i sovetskogo voennogo iskusstua—odin iz vazhneishikh faktorov pobedy v Velikoi Otechestvennoi voine*" (The superiority of Soviet military science and the Soviet art of war—One of the most important factors in the victory in the Great Patriotic War), *Kommunist*, No. 3 (1985), p. 62.

position.[260] The thesis was repeated using the same wording by General of the Army Salmanov, chief of the academy, in a 1988 article in *Voennaya mysl'*.[261]

In internal discussions on questions of military theory in this period, the thesis developed that military operations during a confrontation between the two major political-military blocs could be waged exclusively by conventional means, since the warring parties were aware of the consequences and would not cross the "nuclear threshold." This argument was substantiated by a reference to Hitler, who had decided not to use chemical weapons allegedly because he feared a retaliatory chemical attack.[262]

Increasing attention was given to highly precise conventional weapons—anti-tank, anti-aircraft, anti-warship, anti-radar, etc. This was prompted by the Arab-Israeli conflict in the Bekaa Valley in 1982 and the British-Argentine war over the Falkland/Malvinas Islands in 1982. Advocates of radioelectronic means, primarily from the navy, promoted these systems in the 1980s. Their importance had increased as a result of a sudden leap in the development of various information technologies. They emphasized that disturbances in the steady rhythm of information reception or defects in a single component of monitoring equipment would negatively affect the combat efficiency of the forces at large. Disruptions in several components could do as much harm as the direct use of force.[263] The effects of radioelectronic methods of struggle against combat control, communications, and reconnaissance systems are comparable to the effects of firepower. Radioelectronic conflict was transcending the limits of combat support functions and becoming an integral part of combat operations.

In evaluating the new, highly precise conventional weapons, Ogarkov questioned the necessity of tanks, aircraft, and warships.[264] I.G. Pavlovsky, who had been commander of the Soviet ground forces for many years, held the opposite view, which differed little from those of marshals

---

260. Kozlov, Matsulenko, et al., *Voennoe iskusstvo vo vtoroi mirovoi voine i v poslevoennyi period*, p. 478.

261. G.I. Salmanov, "*Sovetskoe voennoe iskusstvo za 70 let*" (The Soviet art of war over the past 70 years), *Voennaya mysl'*, No. 2 (1988), p. 36.

262. M.P. V'yunenko, B.N. Makeyev, and V.D. Skugarev, *Voenno-morskoi flot: rol', perspectivy razvitiya, ispol'sovanie* (The navy: Its role, perspectives on its development, and its use) (Moscow: Voenizdat, 1988), p. 33.

263. See V.S. Pirumov and R.A. Chervinskii, *Radioelektronnaya bor'ba na more* (The radioelectronic struggle on the sea) (Moscow: Voenizdat, 1987), pp. 5–13.

264. Ogarkov, *Istoriya uchit bditel'nosti*, p. 54.

of tank forces Rotmistrov, Babadzhanyan, Losik, and many others in the 1950s and 1960s. In Pavlovsky's words,

tank forces are the main shock force of the ground forces and a powerful means of war assigned to carry out important missions in various kinds of military operations. They are a modern and rather prospective branch used mainly on the decisive lines of advance to inflict powerful and penetrating blows against the enemy.[265]

The authors of *Military-Technical Progress and the Armed Forces of the USSR* expressed a similar opinion:

The main force of the ground forces, as before, is the tank forces. High mobility, major firepower and shock power, massive armored protection all make this branch of forces extremely effective . . . the role of tank forces is extremely important in conventional military operations. All of this has predetermined their special position in the ground forces and has decisively affected their organizational development.[266]

In the latter half of the 1980s, radically new Soviet appraisals of the effects of conventional warfare, in the event of a major war in Europe, were made public. The most precise description was provided by V.M. Shabanov, deputy minister of defense, who asserted that the qualitative leap forward in the development of conventional weapons entailed changes in preparations for and the conduct of military operations. This in turn predetermined the possibility of fundamentally new and much more destructive forms of conventional warfare. Shabanov said that the use of automated command and control systems for troops and weaponry, the emergence of global systems of reconnaissance, "strike-reconnaissance" complexes, the complete mechanization and high mobility of troops, and the use of military robotics all contributed to the transfer of an increasing number of functions from people to machines. The rapid development and changes in tactical and operational conditions; the huge territory of Europe; the seriousness of any, no matter how slight, deliberate violation of communications by the enemy; and the ability to conduct military operations twenty-four hours a day in any weather conditions would not allow the top political and military leadership to control the military decision-making process. Under extreme conditions, this could lead to an irreversible escalation of warfare culminating in the use of tactical nuclear weapons. Moreover, combat involving weapons of mass

---

265. Pavlovsky, *Sukhoputnye voiska Sovetskikh Vooruzhennykh Sil*, p. 288.
266. Kir'yan, *Voenno-tekhnicheskii progress*, pp. 301, 302.

destruction might be sudden and unpredictable, which would prompt the need to maintain nuclear forces at increased levels of combat readiness, which in turn would upgrade the danger of nuclear war and its escalation. With the massive use of conventional weapons, Shabanov warned, a deliberate or accidental attack on the enemy's nuclear or chemical stockpiles, launchers, transport vehicles, etc., could not be excluded. The consequences could be similar to those of weapons of mass destruction, and could violate the balance in tactical and nuclear forces and provoke unpredictable retaliatory actions. Furthermore, conventional strikes could destroy numerous European nuclear power stations and power installations. The effect, he said, could be similar to that of a nuclear attack, and the aftereffects could be more serious than those of the Chernobyl nuclear disaster.[267]

The Soviet leadership's acknowledgment that there could be no victory in a nuclear war was momentous. This only occurred after Mikhail Gorbachev came to power in 1985. "It is impossible to win not only nuclear war but also the arms race. Socialist countries will not permit military-strategic parity, ensuring their security and peace in the world, to be violated," Soviet Minister of Defense Sokolov stated in 1986.[268] His successor, Dmitry Yazov, wrote in *Pravda* in July 1987: "At the present time, when huge stockpiles of nuclear weapons exist, endangering the fate of humanity, nuclear war cannot be an instrument for achieving political goals."[269]

It is worth mentioning that in the past, statements by the Soviet military about victory being the ultimate goal of war were ritualized, and targeted first of all at raising the morale of the troops. However, they missed the point that the notion of victory could be applied not only at the strategic level but also at the tactical level.

Soviet analysts could not fail to notice that in the early 1980s, U.S. Department of Defense policies advocated more explicitly than during the Carter administration the mission of ensuring U.S. dominance (i.e., victory) in various armed conflicts, and restoring peace under terms that would be advantageous to the United States.[270]

---

267. See V. Shabanov, "'*Obychnaya' voina: novye opasnosti*" ("Conventional" war: New dangers) *Novoe Vremya*, January 14, 1986, p. 8.

268. S.L. Sokolov, "*Pobeda, obrashchennaya v nastoyashcheye i budushcheye*" (The victory that appeals to the present and future), *Pravda*, May 9, 1986.

269. D.T. Yazov, "*Voennaya doktrina Varshavskogo Dogovora—doktrina zashchity mira i sotsializma*" (The military doctrine of the Warsaw Pact is a doctrine in defense of peace and socialism), *Pravda*, July 27, 1987.

270. See, for example, Statement of U.S. Secretary of Defense in the Senate Foreign

This formula was included in President Ronald Reagan's January 1987 report, *National Security Strategy of the United States*, in which he stated that the United States, in cooperation with its allies, should deter any aggression threatening their security, and if the deterrence fails, the United States should be ready to rebuff a military attack and end the conflict under terms that were favorable for the United States and its allies. A similar statement was included in Reagan's report of 1988.[271] In the view of many Soviets, this was a disguised appeal for military superiority over the Soviet Union and a continued reliance on the concept of victory in war. In the 1980s, Soviet military thinking continued to officially reject the idea of a limited nuclear war, and even expanded this negative opinion. Soviet military leaders, military theorists, and civilian analysts were of the same opinion on this point.

Strategic stability was a central issue in the Soviet evaluation of political and military conditions in the 1980s. It was recognized as a major precondition for averting war. A number of Soviet works published in the 1980s differentiated between military-strategic parity and strategic stability. In his political report at the 27th Party Congress in 1986, Gorbachev noted that the present level of the nuclear balance was too high and posed an equal danger to both sides. The continuation of the nuclear arms race, he asserted, would inevitably increase this mutual danger, to the point that it would no longer be a deterrent.[272] Soviet military leaders soon followed suit. For example, in 1988, Marshal of the Soviet Union D.G. Kulikov wrote that "further raising the level of parity would not increase the security of either side. Instead it would lead directly to the opposite result."[273]

Ronald Reagan's Strategic Defense Initiative (SDI), announced on March 23, 1983, triggered the Soviet debate on strategic stability. The first unclassified literature on the subject was a report of the Committee of Soviet Scientists for Peace and Against the Nuclear Threat entitled

---

Relations Committee, in *U.S. Strategic Doctrine*, Hearings of the 97th Congress, 2d Session, U.S. Senate, December 19, 1982, p. 12.

271. *National Security Strategy of the United States* (Washington, D.C.: The White House, January 1987), p. 4.

272. *Materialy XXVII s'yezda KPSS* (Materials of the 27th Congress of the CPSU) (Moscow: Politizdat, 1986), p. 65.

273. Kulikov also noted that an extremely high level of parity in both nuclear and conventional weapons would make it difficult to avert or reduce the destructive consequences of a military clash. V.G. Kulikov, "*O voenno-strategicheskom paritete i dostatochnosti dlya oborony*" (On military-strategic parity and defense sufficiency), *Voennaya mysl'*, No. 5 (1985), p. 7.

"Strategic Stability in the Context of a Radical Reduction in Nuclear Weapons," published in 1989. In the late 1980s, many Soviet analysts began to remark on an improvement in the international situation and a decrease in tensions. Ogarkov presented the most detailed analysis, in which he concluded that international tensions had noticeably diminished.[274] At the same time, Soviet experts recognized that the danger of war and military conflicts still existed, and in some respects continued to increase. The buildup of the counterforce capacities of U.S. strategic forces, the development of highly precise conventional weapons, and the buildup of the naval forces of the United States and other states were all areas of special concern. Dmitry Yazov stated the following in February 1989:

It is clear that NATO, with the assistance of specially selected and prepared "factors," is attempting to revive the false thesis of the "Soviet military threat" . . . and at the same time to justify the expansion of NATO's long-term military programs to equip the bloc's armed forces with new, highly precise conventional weapons systems as well as automatic command and control systems, and systems of communications, reconnaissance and radioelectronic combat. Only by strengthening these systems is it possible to plan, for example, to increase the combat potential of NATO's ground forces by 40 percent.[275]

In the estimation of General of the Army M.A. Moiseyev, then chief of the General Staff, NATO military doctrine continued to threaten the Soviet Union and its allies.[276] In 1983, he wrote in *Pravda* that "NATO military doctrine, despite public assurances of its 'defensive' character, has provided for and continues to provide for the use of nuclear weapons to threaten, to conduct combat actions, and to achieve victory in a nuclear war. All U.S. plans are based on waging military operations on foreign territories, and allow preemptive strikes 'on suspicion' and massive strikes to overcome any resistance in the 'opening phase of war'."[277]

The Soviet military command focused on U.S. activity in the Far East in its analysis of the global military and political situation. According to

---

274. Ogarkov, "*Podvig, ravnogo kotoromu ne znala istoriya*," p. 7.

275. D. Yazov, "*Na nachalakh realizma i balansa interesov*" (On the basis of realism and a balance of interests), *Pravda*, February 9, 1989.

276. M. Moiseyev, "*Sovetskaya voennaya doktrina: realizatsiya yeye oboronitel'noi napravlennosti*" (Soviet military doctrine: Implementation of its defense mission), *Pravda*, March 13, 1989.

277. M. Moiseyev, "*Istoki napryazhennosti*" (Sources of tension), *Pravda*, May 4, 1983.

Marshal Akhromeyev, "U.S. activity in the Far East and in Southeast Asia is oriented toward a further deformation of the regional balance of forces, a buildup in military potential, the aggravation of conflicts, and the pursuit of an obstructionist policy regarding the issues of a peace settlement." In September 1988, he stated that "the naval forces of the United States have gone beyond the limits necessary for defense."[278] Soon after Gorbachev announced a unilateral reduction of the Soviet armed forces by 500,000 troops in a speech at the United Nations on December 7, 1988, Main Commander of the Navy V. Chernavin wrote the following:

Representatives of the NATO countries could not fail to see the changes that have taken place in the theory and practice of Soviet military development under the influence of *perestroika* and the new political thinking. However, NATO's leadership prefers to pretend that nothing important has happened, and an adequate response has not been forthcoming from their side. They continue to hold large-scale exercises in the spirit of offensive strategy, often near the frontiers of the Soviet Union. And lately the intensity and extent [of these exercises] have increased.[279]

Chernavin's sharp criticism of the naval strategy of the United States was not unfounded:

According to the "New Maritime Strategy" adopted by the Pentagon in 1986, gaining advantages through preventive measures, taking initiatives when a conflict begins, and inflicting strikes against objectives located deep within Soviet territory are the U.S. Navy's missions. The naval arms race initiated by the United States and several other NATO countries and the sharp increase in their maritime activity have increased the military threat, particularly in the world's oceans, where the possibility of a conflict involving the use of weapons has become likely.[280]

Chernavin also charged that the West was unwilling to enter into negotiations on the limitation and reduction of naval forces and weaponry as the Soviet Union had proposed. "Our proposals are being ignored. This reality has to be taken into consideration."[281] He also warned that reactionary forces in the West were attempting to destabilize positive devel-

---

278. S.F. Akhromeyev, "*Voenno-morskie sily i vseobshchaya bezopasnost'*" (The navy and comprehensive security), *Pravda*, September 5, 1988.

279. V. Chernavin, "*Gotov' sebya k sovremennomu boyu*" (Prepare yourself for modern battle), *Morskoi sbornik*, No. 1 (1989), p. 3.

280. Ibid.

281. Ibid.

opments in the world and demanding a buildup in sea-based weapons. "The American leadership is trying to violate the military-strategic parity between the USSR and the United States and ensure their military superiority."[282] Chernavin's conclusion was completely in line with the philosophy of the preceding decades of Cold War hostility: "The nature of imperialism is such that it is unable to abandon its hopes to change the course of historic development by military force."[283]

In the late 1980s, Soviet civilian specialists, who were now more engaged in the political-military field, made a substantial contribution to the critical analysis and revision of the deep-seated Marxist theory that militarism is an inherent feature of imperialism and capitalism. A distinguished Soviet economist, Professor I.D. Ivanov, argued that it was incorrect to evaluate militarism as an inevitable and fatal stage in the genesis of capitalism. In his view, militarism is economically reversible and can be dismantled by economic means. Ivanov pointed out that a model of a demilitarized capitalist economy existed and had been applied in several countries.[284]

According to academician Georgy Arbatov, there was a noticeable trend toward a shrinkage of the social basis for militarization; it was becoming increasingly clear that war no longer met the class interests of the bourgeoisie. One reason for that, in his view, was that capitalism had to pay for wars with social upheavals. Another reason was rooted in scientific and technological progress, which made waging war both reckless and suicidal. At the same time, scientific and technological progress presented new opportunities for solving problems peacefully rather than through the use of force.[285]

According to A.N. Yakovlev, director of the Institute of World Economy and International Relations (and later a member of the Politburo and of the Presidential Council), the logic and facts of political struggle demonstrated that the expanding influence of the military-industrial complex is neither automatic nor predetermined. "The degree of its influence on sociopolitical life can be a variable quantity."[286]

---

282. Ibid.

283. Ibid., p. 8.

284. I.D. Ivanov, "*Amerikanskie korporatsii i militarizm*" (American corporations and militarism), *SShA: Ekonomika, politika, ideologiya*, No. 2 (1986), pp. 22–23.

285. G. Arbatov, "*Militarizm i sovremennoe obshchestvo*" (Militarism and modern society), *Kommunist*, No. 2 (1987), pp. 113–114.

286. A.N. Yakovlev, *Ot Trumena do Reigana. Doktriny i real'nosti yadernogo veka* (From Truman to Reagan. Doctrines and realities of the nuclear age) (Moscow: Institute of World Economy and International Relations [IMEMO], 1984), p. 129.

The views of Soviet civilian experts on the feasibility of war were based on an analysis of the goals and resources of the countries involved. Vitaly Zhurkin, Sergei Karaganov, and Andrei Kortunov, all analysts at the Institute of USA and Canada Studies (ISKAN), concluded that there were no conflicts in the East-West relationship that could lure the two sides into a war to resolve them.[287] A similar observation was made by Andrei Kokoshin and General of the Army Vladamir Lobov in their joint contribution to *Znamya* in 1990.[288] Among other things, Kokoshin and Lobov pointed out that for many decades, Soviet military and political predictions did not adequately appreciate the differences between democratic regimes and radical right-wing regimes of the Nazi type within the capitalist world. Something else that had been ignored, they wrote, was the change in public consciousness in the developed capitalist countries as a result of World War II, which posed an important obstacle to major wars.

Thus, in the late 1980s, Soviet defense needs began to be reassessed in conformity with the existing threat. The weakness of the Soviet economy also pushed the Soviet leadership in that direction. S. Blagovolin, a department head of IMEMO, wrote that "an analysis of the events of recent years leads to the conclusion that the scale of our military preparations, whether one likes it or not, has exceeded all reasonable parameters."[289] His colleague Alexei Arbatov raised strong doubts in a number of his writings about several directions in the development of the Soviet armed forces, including the necessity of anti-aircraft defense.[290] Arbatov's article on this issue, which was published in the main Soviet military theoretical magazine, *Voennaya mysl'*, launched a useful discussion.[291] It was not surprising that much of the above-mentioned literature received a critical or negative response from the military. The debates between civilian scholars, on the one hand, and some military experts and leaders,

---

287. Vitaly Zhurkin, Sergei Karaganov, and Andrei Kortunov, "*Vyzovy bezopasnosti—starye i novye*" (Challenges of security—old and new), *Kommunist*, No. 1 (1988), p. 44.

288. See A.A. Kokoshin and V.N. Lobov, "*Predvidenie (General Svechin ob evolyutsii voennogo iskusstva)*" (Foresight [General Svechin on the Evolution of Military Art]), *Znamya* (Banner), No. 2 (1990), pp. 170–182.

289. S. Blagovolin, "*Geopoliticheskoe aspekty oboronitel'noi dostatochnosti*" (Geopolitical aspects of defense sufficiency), *Kommunist*, No. 4 (1990), p. 115.

290. His ideas are summarized in A.G. Arbatov, *Oboronitel'naya dostatochnost' i bezopasnost'* (Defense sufficiency and security) (Moscow: Znanie, 1990).

291. See A.G. Arbatov, "*K voprosu o dostatochnosti protivovozdushnoi oborony*" (On the issue of the sufficiency of anti-air defense), *Voennaya mysl'*, No. 12 (1989), pp. 41–45.

on the other, were rather bitter, and it is important to point out that the military side made some rather serious political accusations which in the past could have cost the individuals who were targeted their freedom or even their lives.

Chapter 3

Offense and Defense in Soviet Military Strategy

The problem of correlation between offense and defense was an important point in the process of working out Soviet military strategy, operational art, and tactics. In this way, the Soviet Union did not differ much from other states of the world. Although the trends toward offense prevailed in the official attitudes of top political and military leaders of the country, and the offensive character of Soviet military strategy was quite obvious up to the end of 1980, the background debates in the military community were under way. They were very active in the 1920s and the early 1930s, when some noteworthy points of view were expressed by military experts. The intensity of discussion on the subject was brought to zero during the Stalin period and was very low from then on. In the early 1980s, changes took place in the strategic area when the policy of not being the first to use nuclear weapons was discussed and adopted by the leadership. Later the concept of "defense sufficiency" was put forward.

Debates on Offense and Defense in the 1920s

From the Red Army's earliest days, the majority of Soviet military commanders advocated an active offensive strategy and combat operations. Although this policy logically flowed from Marxist-Leninist ideology and the belief in world revolution, it did not contradict pre-revolutionary Russian military traditions, which exclusively relied on offense. (Indeed, most of the great powers had an offensive strategy before World War I, including Germany, Austria-Hungary, and France.)

Mikhail Frunze was an active proponent of an offensive strategy, asserting that it was the only way to achieve victory and that it corresponded to the offensive foreign policy of Soviet Russia. As late as 1921, Frunze wrote that "the very development of the historic revolutionary process will force the working class to take the offensive against capitalism when favorable conditions arise. Thus on this point the requirements of the art of war and general policy completely concur."[1] The economic chaos that the country was experiencing at the time did not alter his approach, since he assumed that "not only Russia but a whole series of other countries could be the basis for our advance."[2] But unlike many other military leaders, Frunze never considered offense to be totally sufficient, recognizing that, under certain circumstances, it might be necessary to conduct defensive operations or to retreat within the offensive framework. "By no means do we reject retreat operations, but we consider retreat to be a part of the offense. Accepting the idea of retreat alone, disconnected from the idea of taking the offensive, in our opinion, must not occur," Frunze stated at a meeting of military delegates to the 11th Party Congress in 1922.[3]

Advocates of offense in the Red Army included political workers and leaders who came from the lower classes, as well as several former tsarist generals like A.M. Zaionchkovsky, who pointed out in his lectures that an indecisive defensive strategy did not correspond to the concept of class war.[4] He did, however, recognize the necessity of defense at the tactical and strategic levels to preserve forces, secure mobilization, and protect economic resources.[5]

Others within the Soviet military in the 1920s favored defense as the preferable kind of warfare for the Red Army. Svechin, Verkhovsky, Neznamov, and Melikov were the most prominent adherents of this view. Svechin's thoughts on offense and defense at the strategic level stemmed from his general political and military assessments of a future war. As discussed in Chapter 2, Svechin was skeptical that a future war involving

---

1. M.V. Frunze, *Izbrannye proizvedeniya* (Selected Works), Vol. 2 (Moscow: Voenizdat, 1957), p. 17.

2. Ibid.

3. *Osnovnaya zadacha momenta. Diskussiya na temu o yedinoi voennoi doktrine* (The fundamental task of the moment. Discussion on the theme of a unified military doctrine), stenographic notes of the second day of the meeting of the military delegates to the 11th Party Congress on April 1, 1922 (Moscow: Supreme Military Editorial Council, 1922), pp. 53–54.

4. See, for example, A.M. Zaionchkovsky, "*Lektsii po strategii chitannye na Voenno-akademicheskikh kursakh vysshego komsostava i v Voennoi akademii RKKA 1922–1923*" (Lectures on strategy delivered in the military academic courses for command personnel and in the Military Academy of the Red Army in 1922–1923), unpublished typewritten manuscript, 1923, p. 47.

5. Ibid., p. 39.

Soviet Russia would be of a revolutionary character. He repeatedly demonstrated the advantages of a defensive strategy as well as dimensions not sufficiently addressed by his contemporaries in both Russia and the West. In *The Evolution of the Art of War*, Svechin wrote the following:

Defense at the strategic level can take advantage of the lines and the depth of a theater, which forces the advancing adversary to expend energy on consolidating the captured territory and to take time to pass over it, but any saving of time is an additional advantage for the defense. The defending side reaps where it has not sown . . . since offense is often stopped by falsified intelligence, fear, and inertia.[6]

The military historian A.I. Verkhovsky (1886–1938), war minister of the Provisional Government from August to October 1917, who then crossed over to the side of the new Soviet power, also considered the choice that the Red Army would face in the case of aggression. Verkhovsky compared two strategies—the "Cannae model" and the "Poltava model"—and concluded that the latter was the preferable alternative for the Red Army. In considering the Cannae model, Verkhovsky did not focus on the famous battle of the Second Punic War, in which the Carthaginian leader Hannibal won a splendid tactical victory over the far stronger Roman troops. Rather, what interested Verkhovsky was the idea of a major offensive operation that would envelop the flanks, and encircle and destroy the main concentration of enemy troops. This idea had been set forth in modern times by Alfred von Schlieffen, former chief of the German General Staff, in his well-known book *Cannae*.

Verkhovsky also considered the Poltava model, though not so much the concrete battle at the town of Poltava in which Peter the Great defeated the Swedish army in 1709. Instead, Verkhovsky analyzed it as an example of a deliberate strategic retreat and deliberate strategic defense that succeeded at the tactical level and led to positive strategic results for the Russian army. As Verkhovsky saw it, the young Russian army, which had been formed not long before this battle and was numerous but not well trained for maneuvers, challenged the best European army of the time: "It was necessary to overcome the enemy by a new method of fighting, to disrupt its excellent maneuvering skills and to attack after it had fallen into disorder."[7] To disrupt the Swedish army's

---

6. A. Svechin, *Evolyutsiya voennogo iskusstva* (The evolution of the art of war), Vol. 2 (Moscow: Gosvoenizdat, 1928), p. 227.

7. A.I. Verkhovsky, *Osnovy nashei taktiki. Ogon', manevr, maskirovka* (The bases of our tactics. Fire, maneuver, concealment) (Moscow: Voennyi Vestnik, 1928), p. 129.

maneuverability, a very serious advantage the Swedes had over the Russians, Peter the Great ordered the installation of a system of field fortifications—redoubts in an original configuration (six frontal redoubts and four perpendicular redoubts)—at the approaches to the Russian garrison town of Poltava. His plan to exhaust the Swedes along the line of redoubts and then decisively defeat them in a battle proved to be effective.

Verkhovsky continued his line of argument by referring to major deliberately defensive operations in World War I and the Russian Civil War. He pointed out the political benefits of defense in the strategic context, wisely highlighting the strong antiwar sentiments prevalent in Europe after the long and agonizing war. In his words:

A defensive battle has many political advantages. The attitude of the popular masses toward war is painfully negative in all the countries of Europe, and anyone who appears to take the offensive, even from a distance, will immediately bring hatred upon himself. The troops of a government waging an offensive war on a foreign territory lose their combat effectiveness. And vice versa, the deeper the defense is conducted inside a country, the better the defensive side performs. Considering our territory, we should not forget this idea. Past defeats do not lower troops' strength to resist if the interests of broad sections of the population are at stake. On the contrary, the strength of their resistance grows.[8]

Verkhovsky followed this with a prophetic phrase: "From this perspective, it is more advantageous for us to surrender Minsk and Kiev in the first engagements than to take Bialystok and Brest."[9] By the irony of fate, in World War II the Red Army occupied Bialystok and Brest immediately after entering Poland in 1939, but was badly defeated by the Germans near Bialystok in June 1941, and subsequently had to surrender Kiev and Minsk, and lost several armies on the southwestern front in the "pocket" the Wehrmacht made east of Kiev.

However, during the campaign against the so-called Svechin school, Verkhovsky's phrase was frequently cited by the persecutors of Svechin, Verkhovsky, and their supporters as proof of their defeatism, their lack of understanding of the "revolutionary spirit" of the Red Army, and even treason, "complicity with the class enemy," and anti-Sovietism.

Tukhachevsky opposed the advocates of defense in strategic and tactical planning and sided with the critics of Svechin and Verkhovsky. His attitudes toward offense and defense were the logical outcome of his

---

8. Ibid.

9. At that time, Bialystok and Brest were part of Poland, which was considered the Soviet Union's most likely Western adversary. Ibid., p. 130.

basic views on the character of a future war. The following passage from one of his speeches illustrates how deeply Tukhachevsky's strategic, political, and ideological concepts were imbued with the offensive spirit. Having seriously criticized the views of Melikov, a young disciple of Svechin, labeling him an "anti-Marxist" and an "opportunist," Tukhachevsky said the following:

Comrade Svechin has an ally in another old specialist, Verkhovsky, who went so far as to say that we had better give up Minsk and Kiev than take Bialystok and Brest . . . . This kind of attitude is not only the lot of old specialists but is also spread among Communists. For example, we disputed one "wise" strategic theory which advocated something more than defense, i.e., an inland retreat, almost like that of 1812, which was mockingly referred to as the "Mozhaisk strategy" by Kliment Yefremovich Voroshilov. These major mistakes certainly are not accidental. We had a big discussion on the issue of policy and strategy at our first All-Union Congress of the VNO [*Voenno-nauchnoe obshchestvo*, Military Science Society]. There, even very serious Marxists maintained that the proletarian state had no right to overthrow by armed force the bourgeois government of another country.[10]

Tukhachevsky put himself forward as an active champion of a decisive offense in the spirit of the "strategy of destruction," which, in his opinion, Clausewitz had preferred in his teachings on war. At the same time Tukhachevsky attacked the German military theoretician Delbrück, who had introduced two concepts—the "strategy of attrition" and the "strategy of destruction"— to which Soviet military theoreticians (in particular, Svechin and Verkhovsky) often referred in the 1920s.

It is important to add that in the uncivilized campaign against the proponents of strategic defense, some sound points were raised. For example, one P. Suslov indicated in his contribution to the anti-Svechin book that both Svechin and Verkhovsky ignored the political importance of Soviet Belorussia and Soviet Ukraine, ranking them as a secondary factor in strategic planning.[11] The geopolitical dimension actually presents

---

10. M.N. Tukhachevsky, "*O kharaktere sovremennykh voin v svete reshenii VI Kongressa Kominterna*" (On the character of modern wars in the light of the decisions of the 6th Comintern Congress), in *Zapiski Kommunisticheskoi Akademii* (Proceedings of the Communist Academy) (Moscow: Komakademiya, 1930), p. 24.

11. P. Suslov, "*O kharaktere budushchei voiny po Svechinu*" (On the character of future war according to Svechin), in *Protiv reaktsionnykh teorii na voenno-nauchnom fronte. Kritika strategicheskikh i voenno-istoricheskikh vzglyadov prof. Svechina* (Against reactionary theories in the military-scientific field. A critique of the strategic and military-historical views of Prof. Svechin) (Moscow: Gosvoenizdat, 1931), p. 67.

a great problem for almost any state or alliance in developing concepts of defense and strategic and tactical plans.

Proponents of strategic defense in the Red Army had predecessors, though not many, in the tsarist military who strongly believed in the advantages of defense over offense. The most prominent were N.P. Mikhnevich, an infantry general, and Lieutenant General A.A. Neznamov. Unlike his Russian and foreign colleagues, Mikhnevich paid attention to the fact that Clausewitz considered "defense to be the strongest form of waging war."[12] In his book *Strategy*, which was published in 1911, Mikhnevich stated that

> defense has strategic advantages: the defensive side is close to its resources. To the extent that it retreats, its forces are increasingly concentrated and its resources are augmented, while the offensive side finds itself in the opposite situation. The defensive side can move faster than the offensive side because the latter must pull along the whole rear, restore railroads, destroyed bridges, etc., whereas the defensive side can move almost without transport if the theater of military actions has been skillfully prepared administratively. Speed of movement is an increase in power. "Like in mechanics, the power of an army is measured by its mass multiplied by its speed," Napoleon said. The side defending itself within its own country suffers fewer hardships than the offensive side, and the morale of the army defending its native hearths is much more serious.[13]

The skillful administrative preparation of the theater of military actions is a noteworthy point in Mikhnevich's reasoning. This requirement still seems to be underestimated by many states, and should be given special attention when carrying out truly defensive strategic and tactical plans.

For all that Mikhnevich said about the advantages of defense, ultimately he was a partisan of offense. He had been educated as a military theorist in tsarist Russia, which had pursued a policy oriented toward territorial conquest. It is also important to bear in mind that Russia's financial and political dependence on France prior to World War I greatly affected its political and military orientation. The French government and General Staff insisted on a Russian offensive against Germany in the event of war with the Central Powers (i.e., the German Empire and the Austro-Hungarian monarchy) in order to divert as many German forces as possible from the western front. Following that line under pressure from France, in conjunction with Russia's own poorly prepared advance in

---

12. N.P. Mikhnevich, *Strategiya* (Strategy) (St. Petersburg: Commissioner of Military Boarding Schools, 1911), p. 147.

13. Ibid., pp. 146–147.

August 1914 (before the complete deployment of armies in the theater), resulted in the terrible defeat of Samsonov's army.

Lieutenant Colonel A.A. Neznamov of the tsarist General Staff singled out three reasons why states like Russia might choose strategic defense in a future European war. First, if such a state is temporarily unprepared for a decisive offensive, it may have to delay its offensive.[14] Second, if the enemy enjoys an overwhelming superiority, then the state cannot afford to put equal forces into action (the reasons may include an inadequate military system, a small population, a struggle with coalitions, etc.).[15] Finally, if the state is defeated in a decisive battle and finds itself weakened and unable to take the offensive for a time, it may turn to a defensive strategy.[16]

Neznamov repeatedly argued that "the ultimate aim of defense is absolutely the same as that of offense—to triumph over the enemy in a decisive battle—and all forms of defensive warfare being developed are nothing but means to ensure success in this decisive battle."[17] He summarized the aim and mission of defense as "postponing the denouement until a suitable time by slowing down the enemy's advance, creating obstacles to the implementation of the enemy's intentions, and protecting the vital centers of one's own country."[18] In Neznamov's view, past wars demonstrated that "the best military leaders, when they had to act on the defensive, always defended actively. They did not confine themselves to merely detaining the enemy's offense but constantly took the offensive, with the best forces attacking various groups of the adversary and defeating them in turn. If the forces of the adversary were concentrated, they split them up and did the same thing."[19]

Svechin concurred with Mikhnevich and reiterated that, according to Clausewitz, defense was the most vigorous form of warfare, and the side with fewer material resources should resort to defense.[20] He drew

---

14. A. Neznamov, "Strategy," Part I, *Oboronitel'naya voina. (Teoriya voprosa)* (Defensive war. [The theory of the question]) (St. Petersburg: Nikolaevskaya Academy of the General Staff, 1909), p. 10.

15. Ibid.

16. Ibid.

17. Ibid.

18. Ibid., p. 12.

19. Ibid.

20. A. Svechin, "*Evolyutsiya strategicheskykh teorii*" (Evolution of strategic theories), in B. Gorev, ed., *Voina i voennoe iskusstvo v svete istoricheskogo materializma* (War and military art in the light of historical materialism) (Moscow and Leningrad: Gosizdat, 1927), p. 73.

attention to the fact that in Clausewitz's *On War*, the section on defense was the longest—257 pages in the 1937 Russian edition, compared to only 67 pages devoted to offense. Moreover, the defense section covered some issues of offense (e.g., "The Interaction between Offense and Defense").[21] Svechin showed that Clausewitz's concept of defense as a more effective method of waging war had been criticized by German and French military critics and academics in the period between the Franco-Prussian War of 1870 and World War I. Mesmerized by the successful offensive undertaken by Clausewitz's follower, Helmuth von Moltke the elder, in 1870, the critics asserted that Clausewitz had been bewildered by Napoleon's failure in Russia in 1812.[22] They even accused Clausewitz of pacifism, and only his preeminent authority kept them from accusing him of decadence and defeatism.[23] Describing the vicissitudes of the German military theorist's life in his 1935 book *Clausewitz*, Svechin had every reason to draw a parallel to himself and the fate of his school of military thought. Addressing his colleagues who advocated a revolutionary offensive strategy, he wrote: "We do not think that recognizing defense as the strongest form of warfare was a mistake, at least in the conditions of a Europe not embraced by a revolutionary movement."[24]

Svechin examined defense and offense together, in their dialectical unity. Contrary to the accusations brought against him, Svechin (like Neznamov) never relied solely on defense, but considered it a means of creating the conditions for launching an effective counteroffensive. "In most cases the efficacy of strategic counterattack surpasses the original strike by the offensive side. . . . Did not we see evidence of the profound correctness of Clausewitz's views throughout World War I? Was not his idea proved entirely correct by Foch's strategic counterattack in July 1918 and by that of the Poles in August 1920?"[25] Aware that the concept of strategic defense was unpopular with his contemporaries just as it had been unpopular with the generals of all the great powers prior to World

---

21. See K. Clausewitz, *O voine* (On war), Vol. 2 (Moscow: Gosvoenizdat, 1937), pp. 51–329.

22. Clausewitz was in the service of Russia at that time. He wrote a book on the 1812 campaign which is probably less known than his other books. It includes an analysis of the war and some reflections on politics, strategy, and tactics. He expanded on some of these ideas in his main work, *On War*. See Clausewitz, *1812 god* (1812) (Moscow: Gosvoenizdat, 1937).

23. A. Svechin, *Klausevits* (Clausewitz) (Moscow: Journal and Newspaper Association, 1935), pp. 258–259.

24. Svechin, *Evolyutsiya strategicheskikh teorii*, p. 74.

25. Ibid.

War I, Svechin attempted to get at the roots of this viewpoint. He turned to such stable categories of the art of war as initiative and activity:

> Quite often the mistakes observed in setting a goal that is inappropriate for the resources available to achieve it can be ascribed to false notions of activity. Defense was given the disrespectful epithet of "base" [podlyi]. All academic courses before the war [World War I] glorified the merits of offense, activity and seizing the initiative. However, true activity primarily lies in a sober look at the conditions of a war; one must see everything as it is and not construct a deceptive future for oneself. Initiative may be interpreted as a narrow concept defined solely by time; beating the enemy to the punch and seizing the initiative . . . . However, we can also make a more profound interpretation of preserving the initiative as the art of carrying out one's will in a struggle with the enemy.[26]

Svechin cited a number of examples from World War I that demonstrated that prominent military leaders, in the name of action, seizing and keeping the initiative, made serious mistakes which ultimately led to defeat.[27] By contrast, he continued, in some cases strategic defense was the only way to defeat the enemy, but it was rejected by the political leadership and military command and was not supported by the public. Moreover, Svechin stated that more than once in the history of warfare the proponents of offensive actions and an immediate decisive battle remained in the rulers' good graces even after their line of action had proved to be completely wrong and resulted in grave defeats. In *Strategy*, Svechin made this point by describing the fate of the two Roman consuls who had led the Roman troops defeated by Hannibal at the battle of Cannae in the Punic Wars.

> Long ago it was observed that of the two Roman counsels [sic] the wise Paul Emilius was killed at the battle of Cannae, while Terrentius, who was responsible for the defeat [by recommending the offensive] and saved himself by fleeing from the battlefield, subsequently recovered and left behind numerous progeny. Any leader who intelligently leads an operation can count on finding one of the ideological heirs of Terrentius in the person of his partner. The breed of such sorry military leaders is ineradicable.[28]

---

26. Aleksandr A. Svechin, *Strategy* (Minneapolis, Minn.: East View Publications, 1992), pp. 319–320.

27. The same mistakes were made during World War II, including by the Red Army command. See G.K. Zhukov, *Vospominaniya i razmyshleniya* (Reminiscences and reflections) (Moscow: Novosti, 1969), p. 264.

28. Svechin, *Strategy*, p. 279, note 6.

Unfortunately, Svechin's forecasts in that area were also prescient: the Great Patriotic War provided a great many similar examples.

It is apropos to recall how painful the strategic retreat of the Russian armies during the war with Napoleon was for the Russian public. During the retreat Russia inflicted a number of blows on the enemy (though none was decisive), and partisan actions were targeted at the aggressor's lines of communications. The military commanders Barclay de Tolly and Kutuzov had to defend their ideas of strategic retreat in sharp debates with Emperor Alexander I, his military advisers, and the majority of generals and officers of the Russian army (including the able military leader P. Bagration, who almost openly accused Barclay of a lack of patriotism). The opponents of retreat demanded engagement in battle with the French invaders at the western frontiers of the Russian Empire and then along various lines of defense.[29] They were unwilling to face the grim realities of the military situation and were guided mainly by emotions rather than by accurate assessments of the correlation of forces or the dynamics of the opportunities available to the Russian army as well as to the French, who were penetrating deep into Russian territory.

Svechin viewed strategic defense as a combination of operations, including counterstrikes, engagements, and battles on various lines prepared in advance. Contrary to what some critics claimed, Svechin never emphasized Russia's huge territory, its cold climate, or lack of roads as the main factor in favor of strategic defense. Rather, as early as 1924 he warned against these illusions: "Soviet power inherited a complicated legacy from the old regime, including the featherbed of notions about the boundless Russian territory providing ample opportunities for retreat, the invulnerability of the political center to a foreign enemy, and the Russian winter's ability to stop any invasion."[30] He convincingly demonstrated that the means of war had drastically changed since Napoleon's failure in Russia, that the telegraph, radio, aviation, and automobiles were "great devourers of space [*prostranstvo*]."[31] He noted that Russia's vast expanse had been a much more dangerous factor for Napoleon, whose offensive was often carried out along a front narrowed to one or two days' march, than for modern armies "sweeping across the whole width of the theater of military actions like a gigantic broom."[32] History, Svechin asserted, had

---

29. See L.G. Beskrovnyi, *Russkoe voennoe iskusstvo XIX veka* (The Russian art of war in the 19th century) (Moscow: Nauka, 1974), pp. 98–105.

30. A. Svechin, "*Opasnye illyuzii*" (Dangerous illusions), *Voennaya mysl' i revolyutsiya* (March 1924), p. 49.

31. Ibid.

32. Ibid., p. 51.

always taught that the strategic significance of the capital city directly depended on "the tension of political passions."[33] Thus in a future war, which Svechin expected to be markedly political in character, primary attention should be paid to the defense of Moscow and "the decisive match should be played here."[34] At the time Svechin was writing, Poland, supported by France, was considered the Soviet Union's most likely adversary, and when he mentioned "the tension of political passions," he was projecting the situation of 1924 into the future.

The General Conference for the Reduction and Limitation of Armaments, 1932–34

In the late 1920s and early 1930s, Soviet views on the relationship between offense and defense dramatically changed as a result of developments in the material means of waging war and in strategic concepts. Advances in military technology reached new levels, including strike aviation and tanks. The navy was equipping itself with aircraft carriers, and submarines were gaining new combat capabilities. Meanwhile, in the sphere of diplomacy, the political leaders of several states were attempting to promote arms reductions. The General Conference for Reduction and Limitation of Armaments, held in Geneva in 1932–34, was an important result of these efforts.

The political background of the Geneva conference was rather complex. The "era of pacifism" had come to an end. The political initiative in the West had been seized by conservative forces that considered negotiations on arms reduction to be utopian and believed that military force was the only reliable means of securing national interests, which ranged from protecting colonial possessions to defending the Versailles system against the "Soviet threat." The Japanese aggression in Manchuria in September 1931 damaged the already fragile foundations of international law, and undermined faith in collective security. Meanwhile, the Nazi threat was growing in Germany, and the fascist regime in Italy was a political factor of no small importance.

Nevertheless, some earlier positive political tendencies had not yet disappeared. At that time, for example, the German government maintained a policy of more or less friendly relations with the Soviet Union, although the issue was the subject of domestic debates. A turn for the

---

33. Ibid., p. 52.
34. Ibid.

better in Franco-Soviet relations in 1932 improved both the Soviet position and the international climate in general.[35]

The most noteworthy aspect of the Geneva conference was the concept of "qualitative disarmament" put forward by several Western leaders and pacifist groups. Among the first to suggest that quantitative reductions did not show much promise was the prominent British military strategist B.H. Liddell Hart, who began to promote a concept of disarmament that could destroy the very basis for carrying out major offensive operations.[36] On the fifth day of the conference, Lord R. Cecil presented theses on qualitative disarmament on behalf of the International Federation of Societies for the League of Nations. The antiwar campaign in Western Europe and the United States gained widespread public support for that approach. The ministers of foreign affairs of Great Britain and Italy, as well as the U.S. representative, supported Cecil's proposals. France and its allies, which advocated establishing an armed force for the League of Nations, opposed these proposals. Some time later, the U.S. representative announced President Herbert Hoover's proposals on arms reductions and disarmament, which provided for increasing the relative power of defense by decreasing the power of offense. Toward this end, the United States suggested that a proposal made earlier at the Geneva conference to abolish all tanks, chemical weapons, and heavy mobile guns should be accepted. Furthermore, it was suggested that all bombarder aircraft should be abolished. However, the U.S. proposal did not cover naval armaments, the field in which the United States seemed to want to preserve a free hand.

In the discussion of qualitative disarmament, the negotiations got stuck on the definition of offensive weapons. Several technical subcommittees were set up to settle the issue; two-thirds of their membership were professional military experts. The meetings were closed, and independent nongovernmental experts and scientists were not invited to participate in the discussions. Ultimately the delegates from Great Britain, France, the United States, Japan, and several other countries succeeded in drowning the issue in numerous details and reservations. Almost every weapon in which a particular state enjoyed superiority was declared by

---

35. As a result, Moscow signed a nonaggression pact with Paris on November 29, 1932. Later the Soviet Union concluded similar pacts with Poland, Finland, Latvia, and Estonia. At that time the Soviet Union had special military and political relations (contacts, information exchange between the general staffs) with Lithuania, a considerable part of which was under Polish control after the wars of the 1920s.

36. See V.M. Zubok and A.A. Kokoshin, "Upushchennye vozmozhnosti 1932 goda?" (Lost opportunities of 1932?), *Mezhdunarodnaya zhizn'*, No. 3 (1989), p. 128.

that state to be absolutely defensive and not a threat to other countries.[37] In the ground forces subcommittee, for example, French and British experts ardently tried to prove that light and medium tanks were defensive weapons. That is why the British suggested banning tanks weighing more than 25 tons. A French general went even further and insisted that tanks weighing 70 tons were not a threat to modern defense.[38] His claim probably can be attributed to the fact that French military thinking lagged behind technological advances. Although at that time France had one of the biggest tank parks in the world, French military theory held that the tank was only a tactical means of accompanying infantry. Moreover, French patriotic circles emphasized the invincibility of the Maginot Line.

But World War II proved all these calculations wrong. Eight years later, in May 1940, German mobile formations armed with light tanks and supported by bombing aviation went around the Maginot Line, invaded France, and drove the Anglo-French forces to the sea at Dunkirk.

In the Geneva conference's naval subcommittees, the British representatives flatly refused to negotiate any reductions in battleships, which for centuries had been the core element of British sea power. Instead, they chiefly sought a reduction in submarines, as the records of several conversations with Soviet representatives show.[39] During World War II, German submarines in fact posed the greatest danger to Great Britain (as they had in World War I), so the British classification of submarines as offensive weapons at the Geneva conference proved to be absolutely justified. But there was something else important that the war demonstrated: the era of battleships had passed, and they no longer played a decisive combat role. A great many British battleships, as well as German, American, Italian, and Japanese ones, were sent to the bottom by torpedoes and bombs.

American experts categorically refused to accept the Japanese approach which classified aircraft carriers as offensive weapons. The war showed the truth of the matter: the attack on Pearl Harbor was carried out by Japanese planes, which had taken off from the decks of aircraft carriers.

The Soviet representatives who worked on the conference subcommittees repeatedly stated their support for the concept of qualitative

---

37. Ibid., p. 132.

38. Foreign Policy Archives of the USSR, collection 423, inventory 1, folder 18, file 81, p. 39.

39. See, for example, a conversation between Soviet military expert S. Ventsov and the British expert Vice-Admiral Pound dated April 28, 1932. Foreign Policy Archives of the USSR, collection 0415, inventory 3, folder 7, file 11, pp. 90, 92.

disarmament. S. Ventsov, A. Yegor'ev, and A. Langovoi advocated the prohibition of light and medium tanks, all military aircraft, large-caliber mobile artillery, aircraft carriers, and submarines.[40]

The Soviet military specialists recognized the offensive capabilities of tanks, mobile artillery, and aviation no less than their foreign counterparts, and may even have had a better grasp of them because of the concept of "deep battle" or "deep operations" that was evolving in the Soviet Union in the late 1920s and early 1930s. The practical aims of this concept were breaking through the enemy's fortified defense and enabling maneuver warfare. Even as they advocated the elimination of the above-mentioned weapons, the Soviet representatives to the Geneva conference played down the importance of "qualitative disarmament" since their main aim was to promote the Soviet proposals for quantitative reductions.

The Soviet Theory of "Deep Battle" or "Deep Operations"

The theory of "deep battle" or "deep operations" merits special consideration, since it underpinned the development of the offensive strategy and tactics of the Soviet military from the 1930s until the 1980s. This theory remains a source of pride for the Soviet military, who still give these new kinds of battle and operations priority because they drastically changed the strategic landscape during World War II and for decades afterward. A number of Russian experts, as well as some from other countries, hold that the U.S. Army's concept of Air Land Battle of the 1980s has something in common with the Soviet theory.

The theory of "deep battle" can be traced back to the late 1920s, to works by Tukhachevsky, N.E. Varfalameyev, A.K. Kalinovsky, I.P. Uborevich, V.K. Triandofilov, and others whose ideas were incorporated in the Field Regulations of 1929.[41] A great deal was contributed to the development of the basic principles of the theory by Red Army members G.S. Isserson, E.A. Shilovsky, S.N. Ammosov, A.N. Lapchinsky, A.I. Sedyakin, S.M. Belitsky, and others who worked under the guidance of A.I. Yegorov, chief of the General Staff, and B.M. Shaposhnikov, who served as chief of

---

40. Foreign Policy Archives of the USSR, collection 423, inventory 1, folder 3, file 10, p. 61.

41. V.A. Semenov, *Kratkii ocherk razvitiya Sovetskogo operativnogo iskusstva* (A brief review of the development of the Soviet art of war) (Moscow: Voenizdat, 1960), pp. 114–122; and I.A. Korotkov, *Istoriya sovetskoi voennoi mysli. Kratkii ocherk. 1917–iyun' 1941* (The history of Soviet military thought. A brief review. 1917–June 1941) (Moscow: Nauka, 1980), pp. 147–161.

the Academy of the General Staff from 1932 to 1935. In the early 1930s, the theory was included in the curriculum of the Frunze Military Academy.[42]

When the first Five-Year Plan for the reconstruction of the Red Army was adopted, the search for new approaches to military development and more efficient, modern methods of fighting intensified. By a special resolution of the Revolutionary Military Council of the USSR, that mission was assigned to the Operational Department of the Red Army General Staff.

By early 1931, the first stage of work had been finalized.[43] A few months before Triandofilov's tragic death in a plane crash in 1931,[44] his report on "The Main Issues of Tactics and Operational Art Related to Reconstruction of the Army"[45] was submitted to the Red Army General Staff. His report outlined the main features of "deep battle" and attempted to find a general line for the development of tactics, operational art, and new methods of warfare. Triandofilov assumed that modern weapons presented new opportunities for a simultaneous attack along the enemy's entire tactical depth, the simultaneous attack on the enemy's defenses by several echelons of tanks supported by infantry, artillery, and assault aviation. Such a powerful blow would make the attack short and swift. The deep tactical effect on the combat order of the enemy's troops would create conditions for waging operations across vast territories. Conducting "deep operations" required a considerable concentration of forces and matériel in the direction of the attack. The operational battle order of the shock forces included the attack and advance attack echelons, as well as aviation and airborne troops.

After a discussion of Triandofilov's report within the Supreme Command, Red Army Chief of Staff Yegorov and the Operational Department headed by I.P. Obysov finalized Triandofilov's work. On April 20 and May 20, 1932, the main parts of the report were forwarded to the Revolutionary

---

42. See G.S. Isserson, *Konspekt lektsii po teorii glubokoi taktiki, chitannykh na operativnom fakul'tete Akademii im. M.V. Frunze v 1932 g.* (Synopsis of lectures on the theory of deep tactics delivered to the campaign tactics department of the academy named for M.V. Frunze in 1932) (Moscow: Frunze Military Academy, 1933).

43. M.V. Zakharov, *General'nyi Shtab v predvoennye gody* (The General Staff in the prewar years) (Moscow: Voenizdat, 1989), p. 88.

44. K.B. Kalinvosky, deputy chief of the Red Army Department of Mechanization and Motorization, M.I. Arkad'ev, assistant to the sector head of the Red Army Staff, and members of the flight crew were also killed in the crash.

45. Zakharov, *General'nyi Shtab v predvoennye gody*, p. 88.

Military Council of the USSR for discussion.[46] Soon afterward "Provisional Instructions for Organizing a Deep Attack" were developed on the basis of Triandofilov's report and incorporating comments from provincial military organizations. In February 1933, the instructions were approved by the People's Commissar for Military and Naval Affairs and distributed to military formations and units as official guidelines.

In the mid-1930s, deep operations were conceived of as actions waged by shock troops in the direction of the main strike. In the second half of the decade, they began to be considered in terms of their utility for front (i.e., groups of armies) operations. Shortly before the outbreak of World War II, it was decided that deep operations could be employed not only on one front, but on a group of fronts.

However, the theory of deep operations and deep battle also had opponents. Among its most highly placed critics was Kliment Voroshilov, then people's commissar for defense and chairman of the Revolutionary Military Council of the USSR. Voroshilov did not object to the concept of a massive offensive per se, but criticized some methods of putting it into action that Tukhachevsky, Triandofilov, and others had suggested. Only after the bloody battles of 1941–43 and the subsequent shift of the strategic initiative to the Red Army did the opportunity to implement the theory arise.

With what did the Soviet Union enter the war? The offensive character of Soviet military strategy was quite obvious. For example, the draft of the Red Army Field Regulations stated that

any attack on the Union of Soviet Socialist Republics will be fended off with all the might of its armed forces. If the adversary inflicts war upon us, the Workers' and Peasants' Army will be the most offensive army of all the armies that have ever taken the offensively oriented. We will wage an offensive war, moving the conflict onto the territory of the adversary. Combat actions will be targeted at destruction, with the aim of total defeat of the enemy.[47]

The Soviet Union's powerful mechanized corps, established shortly before the war, were considered the main means of achieving success in a strategic offensive. According to some sources, Stalin himself gave the order to establish this kind of formation. However, they were large, unwieldy formations. Each mechanized corps was supposed to include

---

46. Ibid., p. 89.
47. Field Regulations of the Workers' and Peasants' Red Army (draft) (Moscow: Voenizdat, 1939), p. 9.

two tank divisions and one motorized division (1,108 tanks and 37,200 personnel).[48] According to plans of the General Staff, the Red Army would require about 32,000 tanks to fully equip these corps.[49] On the eve of the war, the Red Army had a total of 26,000 tanks, and a considerable number of them needed to be repaired or rebuilt.[50] This total included 1,816 of the latest KV ("Kliment Voroshilov") heavy tanks and T-34 medium tanks, which were unrivaled by the tanks of any other country. Of these, 508 KVs and 963 T-34s were stationed in the military districts on the Soviet Union's western border.[51] In comparison with the German tank park, and particularly that portion that was deployed in the East against the Soviet Union, it was a considerable force, which could have been effectively used for both the offensive and defensive. However, that did not turn out to be the case, despite the heroic efforts of Soviet tankmen who did not spare their own lives to repel the attack by the powerful, self-confident, and well-trained German army.

The actual number of Soviet tanks in existence before the war was kept top secret until 1990, when Chief of the General Staff Moiseyev revealed the figure in an interview with Major General Filatov, editor-in-chief of *Voenno-istoricheskii zhurnal*— forty-nine years after the start of the war.[52] In previous years, attempts had been made to calculate the number, and these findings were reported in several Soviet military journals.[53] This effort was undertaken not out of pure historical interest: many Soviet military experts associated the events of the past with the search for the optimal composition of the nation's armed forces.

---

48. A. Ryzhakov, "K vosprosu o stroitel'stol bronetankovykh voisk Krasnoi Armii v 30-kh godakh" (Toward the question on the building of armored troops of the Red Army in the 1930s), *Voenno-istoricheskii zhurnal*, No. 8 (1968), p. 110.

49. Zhukov, *Vospominaniya i razmyshleniya*, p. 205.

50. By June 15, 1941, a week before the German invasion of the Soviet Union, 73 percent of older model Soviet tanks required repair. See Central Archives of the Ministry of Defense, collection 2, inventory 75593, file 13, p. 26. Repairs were behind schedule because of a shortage of spare parts.

51. O.A. Losik, ed., *Stroitel'stvo i boevoe premenenie sovetskikh tankovykh voisk v gody Velikoi Otechestvennoi Voiny* (The development and combat use of the Soviet tank forces in the years of the Great Patriotic War) (Moscow: Voenizdat, 1979), p. 910.

52. See "*Tsena pobedy*" (The price of victory), *Voenno-istoricheskii zhurnal*, No. 3 (1990), p. 15.

53. V.V. Shlykov's article on tank forces before and during the war, "*I tanki nashi bystry*" (Our tanks are fast), in *Mezhdunarodnaya zhizn'*, No. 9 (1988) was most thought-provoking.

The Offense in Stalin's Naval Strategy

Stalin had serious plans to make the Soviet naval strategy offensive. That was the aim of a major shipbuilding program initiated in 1937, which provided for the construction of battleships and heavy cruisers primarily for the fleets of the Black, Baltic, and Barents Seas.[54] As a former naval commissar, Admiral Kuznetsov pointed out in his memoirs that the Spanish Civil War pushed Stalin in that direction: "We could not really participate in the sea control introduced by a decision of the Committee on Noninterference because we did not have enough appropriate ships and floating bases. At the same time it became especially clear how important the sea was for us and how badly we needed a powerful fleet."[55]

Once he had inaugurated the shipbuilding program, Stalin did not find it necessary to define its political-military significance. According to Kuznetsov, Stalin had some plans of his own but he was not willing to share them with others.[56] Meanwhile, the navy leadership, including Kuznetsov, was more inclined toward increasing the production of minesweepers and patrol vessels. On July 15, 1938, the first lead battleship, *Sovetskii Soyuz* (*Soviet Union*), was launched (59,130 tons displacement, nine 406 mm guns, three gun turrets). In 1938 and 1939, three more battleships—*Sovetskaya Ukraina* (*Soviet Ukraine*), *Sovetskaya Rossiya* (*Soviet Russia*), and *Sovetskaya Belorussiya* (*Soviet Belorussia*)—were launched. Altogether fifteen battleships and fifteen heavy cruisers were planned.[57] *Kronshtadt*-class heavy cruisers were in fact designed as battleships with 32,870 tons displacement and carrying nine 305 mm guns (two other ships of that class were the *Sevastopol* and the *Stalingrad*). According to estimations by the Naval Academy and the designers' office, heavy cruisers of this class were capable of inflicting decisive damage on *Scharnhorst*-class German battle cruisers (26,000 tons displacement, eight 280 mm guns) or battling with Italian modernized *Julius Caesar*-class battleships (23,622 tons displacement, ten 320 mm guns).[58]

When the war broke out in Europe and it became clear that it would

---

54. V.I. Achkasov and N.B. Pavlovich, *Sovetskoe voenno-morskoe iskusstvo v Velikoi Otechestvennoi Voine* (Soviet naval art in the Great Patriotic War) (Moscow: Voenizdat, 1973), p. 14.

55. N.G. Kuznetsov, *Nakanune* (On the eve) (Moscow: Voenizdat, 1966), p. 259.

56. Ibid., p. 260.

57. V. Krasnov, "Linkory tipa 'Sovetskii Soyuz'" (Soviet Union-class battleships), *Morskoi sbornik*, No. 5 (1990), pp. 60–61.

58. V. Krasnov, "Kreisery tipa 'Kronshtadt'" (Kronshtadt-class cruisers), *Morskoi sbornik*, No. 8 (1990), pp. 54–55.

not spare the Soviet Union, the construction of big surface warships began to be curtailed, though not abruptly: in summer 1940 this construction was reconsidered for the first time, and in October 1940 there was a drastic reevaluation. Yet work on building two heavy cruisers and three battleships continued in the shipyards of Leningrad, Nikolayev, and Molotovsk. The construction of the *Sovetskaya Belorussiya* was discontinued, and its metal structure was dismantled. Four destroyers were planned instead.[59]

Documents on the operational and combat activities of the Soviet naval force paid particular attention to offensive operations and combat activity. First priority was given to the traditional mission of destroying the enemy's naval forces, an approach that was similar to that of the General Staff of the tsarist navy. Methods of conducting joint defensive operations and joint combat actions with coastal ground forces received far less attention.[60] It was precisely these actions, however, in which the Soviet naval forces had to engage during the Great Patriotic War.

The primary orientation of both the Soviet ground forces and navy toward the offense had a negative impact on Soviet defensive capabilities and lowered the level of military readiness in the theaters of combat.

Pre-war Soviet Concepts of Initial Strategic Operations

On the eve of World War II, the Soviet military's tentative plans for initial strategic operations after the first strikes by the enemy and the completion of mobilization can be briefly described as follows. The main strike was to be inflicted on the enemy on the Krakow line of advance by forces from the southwestern front and the right wing of the western front in order to cut Germany off from the Balkans, its major source of raw materials, food, and, above all, oil. Later, a Soviet attack would be carried out on the northern and northwestern lines of advance to destroy the main German forces and take Poland and East Prussia. The northwestern front and two armies of the right wing of the western front were supposed to go on the defensive, but if conditions were favorable, they were to launch an offensive to take the Suwałki region and then to attack Insterburg (Chernyakhovsk) and Allenstein (Olsztyn) in order to tie down enemy forces operating northwest of Brest and in Western Prussia. In the first stage of advance, the task of the main forces of the southwestern front

---

59. Central State Archives of the Navy, collection R-1877, inventory 9s, file 56, pp. 163–175.

60. Achkasov and Pavlovich, *Sovetskoe voenno-morskoe iskusstvo v velikoi Otechestvennoi Voine*, p. 21.

and the left wing of the western front would be to defeat the Lublin and Sandomierz groupings of the enemy and in five to ten days reach the Vistula River. They were then supposed to attack Krakow and Kielce, reach the Pilica River and the upper waters of the Oder in twenty to thirty days.

The Soviet navy's tasks were to destroy the fleets of the enemy in joint actions with the air force, assist the advance of the ground forces, breach the enemy's lines of communications, block the transport of troops and arms to enemy ports, defend Soviet coasts from marine attack, and assist in landing Soviet troops.

To shorten the time needed to form shock groups, the Soviet command had already deployed its best mobile formations at full strength around Bialystok and Lvov during peacetime. This deployment fully conformed to the offensive conception of the Soviet armed forces, since they had already taken a position surrounding the enemy's formations. However, it seems that even at that time it could have been understood that in the event of successful operations by the enemy (e.g., a preemptive attack, a high concentration of forces, continuity of efforts), those two troop formations would be at risk of envelopment by the enemy. Unfortunately, after the defeat of the Svechin school of military theory, defense was of only marginal importance in both the theory and concrete plans of the Red Army.

Relying on an offensive (counteroffensive) strategy, the Red Army General Staff planned that the armies of the first echelon would deliver a powerful initial strike. The concentration of the main forces in the first echelon of the group of armies was also a key feature of Operation Barbarossa.[61] The deployment of German forces was completely subordinated to the requirements of a decisive offense. In the event of a successful counterattack and a deep breakthrough by Soviet mobile formations, the commanders of the Wehrmacht would not have had sufficient reserves to cope with the threat of defeat.

The Far Eastern and Zabaikals fronts also had offensive missions in the event of a Japanese attack. Enjoying both qualitative and quantitative superiority in tanks and airplanes, they were to destroy the Japanese troops in the border area in the opening period of war, i.e., while the mobilization, concentration, and deployment of troops were still under way. Then the forces of the Zabaikals front were to go around the Da

---

61. "Sovershenno sekretno! Tol'ka dlya komandovaniya!" Strategiya fashistskoi Germanii v voine protiv SSSR. Dokumenty i materialy ("Top Secret! Only for the command!" The strategy of fascist Germany in the war against the USSR. Documents and materials) (Moscow: Nauka, 1967), pp. 149-154.

Hinggan Ling Mountains to Tao'an and Qiqihar, and, together with the troops of the Far Eastern front, take northern Manchuria.

The offensive orientation of the strategic and tactical directives of the Soviet Union's top political and military leadership was most vividly reflected in their first war documents. Most noteworthy was Directive No. 3, dated June 22, 1941, which was issued after it had already become clear that Nazi Germany was carrying out a massive invasion of the Soviet Union along the whole line of confrontation rather than a limited military engagement.[62] According to this directive, the immediate tasks of the forces of the northwestern, western, southwestern, and southern fronts (to be carried out on June 23–24, 1941) were quite decisive: (1) to destroy the concentration of German troops in the Suwałki region and seize the area; and (2) to encircle and destroy the enemy by attacking on the Vladimir-Volynsky and Brody lines and then capture Lublin. The directive was signed by Timoshenko, Malenkov, and Zhukov. The attempts to implement it only aggravated the situation and further disadvantaged the positions of the Soviet forces in these areas.

Zhukov acknowledged in his memoirs that Directive No. 3 was ungrounded and erroneous. It is worth mentioning that one of the main reasons, in his view, for that gross misperception, had been pointed out by Svechin years earlier, i.e., the desire to take action merely for its own sake. Zhukov wrote: "In its decision the Main Command did not proceed on the basis of an analysis of the actual situation and substantiated calculations, but on the basis of intuition and a desire for action without considering the potential of the troops."[63]

When it became obvious that it was impossible to shift the fighting into enemy territory or even to halt it at the border areas, the Soviet command formulated new missions for the military. The main objectives were the following:

- to delay the enemy at the line of defense as long as possible to gain maximum time for mobilizing forces from deep within Soviet territory, to get new reserves, and to transport and deploy them on the most important lines;
- to do maximum damage to the enemy forces in order to exhaust them and thus to improve the correlation of forces in the Soviet Union's favor;

---

62. Central Archives of the Ministry of Defense, collection 48-A, inventory 1554, file 90, pp. 260–262.

63. Zhukov, *Vospominaniya i razmyshleniya*, p. 264.

- to evacuate the population and industrial enterprises from the front to the rear and convert civilian industries to wartime purposes; and
- to concentrate the maximum force and take a counteroffensive to frustrate Hitler's general plan of war.[64]

These were exactly the tasks that Svechin, Verkhovsky, and Neznamov had considered essential for organizing a deliberate strategic defense, but they had been rejected for not conforming to the military doctrine of the "proletarian state."

The potential for strategic defense was neglected not only on the Soviet-German (eastern) front in the summer of 1941; the Wehrmacht also profited from the European countries' emphasis on the offense in their strategic and tactical plans.[65] The Wehrmacht's Polish campaign in September 1939 and the campaign in May 1940 can be seen as the implementation of Schlieffen's idea of a Cannae-type battle in strategic terms, succeeding where Moltke the younger had failed in 1914. As Schlieffen shrewdly remarked in his book *Cannae*, the realization of the Cannae model was quite rare in military history, since it was necessary to have a Hannibal on one side and a Terrentius on the other, with each seeking to achieve his great goal in his own way.[66] In May 1940, the German supreme command played the part of Hannibal, while the political and military leadership of France, Great Britain, Belgium, and the Netherlands assumed the role of Terrentius.

The German command achieved good tactical and strategic results in line with Schlieffen's ideas on the eastern front in the summer of 1941 and also the following summer after recovering from defeat in the battle of Moscow. However, at Stalingrad in the winter of 1942–43, Hitler and his generals had to play the role of Terrentius. One of the Red Army's most important departures from strategic offense was the battle of Kursk, a major engagement in the summer of 1943. In the course of this battle, the deliberate defense by the troops of the Voronezh and central fronts echeloned in depth and supported by the Steppe front proved to be impenetrable even by the Wehrmacht's most powerful tank attacks employing the newest heavy-armored vehicles (e.g., Panther and Tiger tanks and Ferdinand self-propelled guns) and the latest aircraft.

Zhukov and Vasilevsky were among the chief advocates of defense

---

64. Ibid., p. 281.

65. See D.M. Proektor, *Agressiya i katastropha* (Aggression and catastrophe) (Moscow: Nauka, 1972), p. 127.

66. Schlieffen, *Kanny* (Cannae), 2d ed. (Moscow: Gosvoenizdat, 1938), p. 350.

at Kursk, and they succeeded in convincing Stalin as well, although he had originally planned to launch a preemptive attack against the Germans. The battle of Kursk resulted in the decisive defeat of the Germans. From that moment on, the Red Army never lost the initiative in the war, and subsequently carried out a series of victorious offensive operations.

Issues of Offense and Defense Immediately after the War

A well-known toast by Stalin, which he proposed at a Kremlin reception in honor of the commanders of the Red Army on May 24, 1945, was "to the health of the Russian people." In this toast, Stalin said that the Soviet government had made quite a few mistakes and had had moments of despair in 1941–42. "Another people could have said to the government: you have fallen short of our expectations, go away, we shall set up another government which will make peace with Germany and ensure peace for us." But the Russian people did not do that, Stalin said, because it believed in its government and made sacrifices in order to defeat Germany.[67]

That toast was an acknowledgment of mistakes, even self-criticism, since Stalin identified himself with "the government." But there was another message in his toast. By no means was Stalin calling upon other people, including historians, to critically analyze the course of the war. Although it sounded like an appeal to tell the whole truth about the war, in reality his words concealed a firm intention to close the door upon any further discussion. As the highest court of judgment, Stalin had stated his views on the matter, and his word was final. A well-known Soviet fiction writer, Konstantin Simonov, who often wrote on military themes and knew Stalin personally, wrote the following: "It is not difficult to imagine what might happen to a person who, having armed himself with quotations from that famous toast, would try on the basis of concrete historical material to develop Stalin's words about the government having made a lot of mistakes, or as a witness and a participant in the war would try to illustrate those words with his own recollections."[68]

Thus the Soviet experience of retreat and defense in 1941 and 1942 remained unexamined for a long time after the war, since even a purely military analysis would immediately recall Stalin's political and strategic blunders. Besides, as Gareyev noted in his book about Frunze, several

---

67. I.V. Stalin, *O Velikoi Otechestvennoi voine Sovetskogo Soyuza* (On the Great Patriotic War of the Soviet Union), 5th ed. (Moscow: Voenizdat, 1948), pp. 196–197.

68. K. Simonov, *Glazami cheloveka moego pokoleniya* (With the eyes of a person of my generation) (Moscow: *Novosti*, 1989), p. 292.

Soviet commanders had been praising themselves to the skies for their wartime successes for too long, remarking that "life teaches that sometimes it is easier to learn from defeat than from victory."[69] Instead, the focus of study was placed on the Soviet Union's successful counteroffensive and offensive, and particularly "Stalin's ten strikes" in January–October 1944 that drove the fascist troops out of Soviet territory, and the offensive operations that liberated Eastern Europe and crushed the Wehrmacht on German soil. Several attempts were also made to present the actions of the Soviet armed forces in 1941 as luring the enemy into a trap in the depths of Soviet territory (similar to the strategic retreat of the Russians in 1812). Several former students of the Frunze Military Academy recalled that a special documentary film had been shown to them as a part of the curriculum in the first few years after the war. The film was about defense lines that supposedly the Red Army had relied on in order to compress itself like a spring only to leap up and destroy the enemy later, but in fact these defense lines never existed. In 1946, Stalin said that Kutuzov had defeated Napoleon with the help of a well-prepared counteroffensive.[70] This idea was immediately adopted by Soviet military leaders and theorists. For example, General A. Yeremenko wrote:

The most prominent historical example is the counteroffensive of the Russian army in the Patriotic War of 1812 when the great Russian military leader Kutuzov brilliantly used that form of struggle to destroy the army of Napoleon. . . . Only the Soviet army and Stalin's art of war have provided genuine models of a counteroffensive in the modern period.[71]

In the period immediately following the war, official Soviet military theory postulated that strategic offense was the most important type of strategic operation, and that it should be carried out by consecutively achieving intermediate strategic goals. The offensive operations of fronts were still considered the basic form of strategic operations, and all of the armed services should take part in them. Strategic defense was viewed as only a temporary strategic operation. Unlike pre-war Soviet concepts, however, the post-war military concepts implied that defensive operations would be conducted not only on the strategic line but in the entire

---

69. M.A. Gareyev, *M.V. Frunze—voennyi teoretik* (M.V. Frunze—military theorist) (Moscow: Voenizdat, 1985), p. 429.

70. See P. Cherkasov, "*Mifologiya ili istoriya?*" (Mythology or history?), *Novyi mir*, No. 9 (1989), p. 258.

71. A. Yeremenko, "*Nekotorye voprosy kontrnastupleniya po opytu Velikoi Otechestvennoi voine*" (Some questions on the counteroffensive based on the experience of the Great Patriotic War), *Voennaya mysl'*, No. 2 (1951), p. 39.

theater, and would involve the forces of two or three fronts and the participation of several other services.[72]

The principal method of carrying out a strategic offensive operation was encircling and destroying the enemy, dividing its strategic formations, splitting up the strategic front, and subsequently destroying the isolated parts of the enemy's forces. Encirclement, which was considered the most decisive and effective way to crush the enemy in the spirit of 1944–45, was to be implemented by converging on or surrounding and pushing the enemy toward a natural obstacle (like the sea, for example).[73]

In reality, however, Soviet tactical and strategic plans were not totally oriented toward an immediate strategic offensive. For example, the plan for the defense of the German Democratic Republic that was in place in the late 1940s and early 1950s (which was declassified in 1989) provided for defensive operations and a counterattack in the first stage to restore the defense.[74] According to the "Plan of Operational Defense for the Territory of the Soviet Union" that the General Staff presented to the USSR Supreme Military Council in late 1946 and early 1947, the main tasks of the armed forces were the following: relying on fortified regions, the Soviet army must drive back the enemy and destroy its troops at the border zone of defense and prepare to launch an offensive; the air forces and anti-air defense forces must cover the main Soviet forces and be ready to repel the enemy's attack; and the reserve troops of the main command, together with the army, must inflict a crushing defeat on the main forces of the enemy in order to destroy them and to act on the counteroffensive.[75] The documents did not specify the scale and depth of the offensive operations.

Meanwhile, the Soviet navy was still considered a defensive factor in tactical and strategic terms during the first decade after World War II. As in the past, the navy was intended for coastal operations, to carry out the aims of the massive frontal operations.[76] Nevertheless, there are some indications that as early as 1950, when a Soviet Ministry of the Navy

---

72. M.M. Kozlov et al., *Voennoe iskusstvo vo vtoroi mirovoi voine i v poslevoennyi period* (Military art in the second world war and in the post-war period) (Moscow: Academy of the General Staff, 1985), p. 468.

73. B.V. Popov et al., *Istoriya voennogo iskusstva* (The history of military art) (Moscow: Voenizdat, 1984), p. 447.

74. "Omkuda ugrosa" (Where the threat comes from), *Voenno-istoricheskii zhurnal*, No. 2 (1989), pp. 27–31.

75. Ibid., pp. 24–25.

76. S.G. Gorshkov, *Morskaya moshch gosudarstva* (The seapower of the state) (Moscow: Voenizdat, 1977), p. 290.

briefly existed, Stalin was considering building an ocean-going surface and submarine fleet that would have strategic offensive missions. One of the fundamental aims of this plan was to create a threat to the United States on the seas that was analogous to the U.S. naval threat to the Soviet Union.

Only after the 20th Party Congress in 1956 and the subsequent dismantling of Stalin's cult of personality did Soviet historians and military strategists begin to analyze the mistakes of 1941 and 1942. However, they emphasized Stalin's misreading of Hitler's intentions, his refusal to take seriously the warnings of Western statesmen about Hitler's aggressive schemes, and how those miscalculations in fact helped the Nazis to carry out a surprise attack both tactically and strategically, rather than Soviet mistakes in the conduct of the early phases of the Great Patriotic War.

The Enhanced Role of Offensive Operations in the 1960s

One of the standard Soviet military texts of the 1960s, *Military Strategy*, edited by Sokolovsky, stated that strategic theory paid insufficient attention to issues of defense. It stated that "questions of organizing and carrying out defense were not fully developed in our prewar theory. It was believed that defense, playing a subordinate role to offense, would be conducted only on some lines rather than on the whole front of armed conflict."[77] On the role of retreat in a defensive operation, the authors stated that, "in our prewar theory, a forced retreat in some sectors was accepted in principle. Yet the problem of leading the major forces out from the enemy's attack was not developed in either theoretical or practical terms."[78] Meanwhile, this book devoted most of its attention to offensive operations, and above all, offensive strategic operations conducted by groups of fronts. It concluded the following: "The last war confirmed the vitality of the fundamental position of Soviet military doctrine, that only as a result of a decisive offensive is it possible to destroy the armed forces of the enemy, seize its territory, break down its will to resist, and achieve a decisive victory in war."[79]

The authors of *Military Strategy* asserted that debates were under way over whether a future war would be a land war involving nuclear weapons to support the ground forces or a new kind of war in which nuclear

---

77. V.D. Sokolovsky, ed., *Voennaya strategiya* (Military strategy), 2nd ed. (Moscow: Voenizdat, 1963), p. 169.

78. Ibid.

79. Ibid., p. 173.

weapons would be used as the main means of fulfilling strategic missions. The authors disagreed with those specialists who favored defense in the new conditions of the nuclear age, and argued that in ground theaters the missions of the armed struggle would be carried out by taking the offensive. In this context, they emphasized that the main task of the ground forces was not so much to break through the enemy's defenses as to "gnaw" through them. That was not considered the urgent problem that it had been in past wars, and in particular, during the opening phase of the Great Patriotic War. The destruction of any enemy forces in the ground theaters of combat that survived strikes by strategic rocket forces and long-range aviation during the offensive would be accomplished first and foremost by using nuclear strikes to destroy its nuclear weapons and divisions with nuclear strikes and a rapid, deep attack by tank formations and airborne forces against its conventional forces.[80]

Recognizing strategic defense as one of the essential strategic operations in modern warfare, the authors of *Military Strategy* believed, would mean accepting the defensive strategy in general and transplanting the situation in the initial period of the Great Patriotic War into a contemporary setting.[81] That approach did not seem justified to them. They assessed the character of the war preparations of the United States and its allies in the 1960s as follows:

The imperialists are preparing for an offensive war against our country, a war of all-out destruction and the mass annihilation of our people with nuclear weapons. Therefore we must oppose them with decisive, active operations by our armed forces and, in the first place, destructive nuclear strikes by our strategic forces. Only this can curb the imperialist aggressors, frustrate their criminal plans, and rapidly inflict defeat on them.[82]

They reached the fundamental conclusion that "strategic defense followed by a counteroffensive cannot assure the achievement of decisive goals of war in contemporary conditions."[83] Thus the lessons of the battle of Kursk were absolutely rejected. As in the pre-war period, defense was assigned a subordinate, marginal role, and was considered at best a temporary military action and only at the tactical level. "As far as strategic defense and a defensive strategy are concerned, they must be decisively rejected as extremely dangerous for the country," the authors bluntly

---

80. Ibid., p. 370.
81. Ibid.
82. Ibid., p. 371.
83. Ibid.

stated.[84] This view remained unchanged in the Soviet Union until the mid-1980s.

In the 1960s and 1970s, several Soviet analysts attempted to define defense and offense in both tactical and strategical terms. The most detailed analysis can be found in Lieutenant General I. Zav'yalov's article, "The Competition between Offensive and Defensive Means and its Impact on the Means of Conducting Military Operations," published in *Voennaya mysl'* in 1970. The methodology he suggested and his evaluations and findings seem to be relevant today when many states are searching for reliable formulas for "nonoffensive defense." According to Zav'yalov's definition, the modern offensive is "the forward movement of carriers of various types of weapons and means of destruction launched by them, culminating in a strike on the enemy with the devastating firepower and striking force of the weapons."[85]

Since the destructive features of offense are the forward movement and strike, then, according to Zav'yalov, the destructive features of defense should be blocking and preventing them by holding certain positions, and repelling the enemy's strikes. The first task can be accomplished by building various fortifications and artificial barriers, special covers for troops and military equipment, and individual protective devices. These means are purely defensive even if they are used in the course of an offensive. But those are only one component of defensive means, Zav'yalov wrote. Beginning in World War I, in addition to passive protective equipment, active means of defense (anti-tank, anti-aircraft and anti-missile weapons) were developed and put into widespread use. According to Zav'yalov, the weapons are defensive means, since their key mission in both offense and defense is to combat the corresponding offensive weapons of the adversary. Although their mode of operation is forward movement (their own and that of the weapons with which they are armed) and the strike, in his view, this does not change their defensive essence.[86]

It is only possible to launch an offensive or a surprise attack with offensive weapons. Defensive means merely impede the offensive and drive back the enemy. Even active defensive weapons can only be used for retaliatory strikes on the attacking enemy, Zav'yalov theorized. For

---

84. Ibid.

85. I. Zav'yalov, "*Sorevnovanie mezhdu nastupatel'nymi i oboronitel'nymi sredstvami i yego vliyanie na sposoby vedeniya voennykh deistvii*" (The competition between offensive and defensive means and its impact on the means of conducting military operations), *Voennaya mysl'*, No. 7 (1970), p. 22.

86. Ibid.

example, anti-aircraft defense and anti-tank weapons cannot be used until attack aviation or tanks appear. This, according to Zav'yalov, is the basic criterion for classifying means of armed struggle as either offensive or defensive.[87]

Dialectics of Defense and Offense in the Nuclear Sphere

The most optimistic Soviet forecasts about anti-missile defense were made in the early 1960s, when positive results were first achieved in tests of technology for intercepting single ballistic targets. One of the most zealous Soviet proponents of anti-missile defense was Rodion Malinovsky, the Soviet minister of defense, who repeatedly stated that the Soviet Union had in principle resolved the problem of intercepting ballistic missiles. "I should report in particular that the problem of destroying the missiles in flight has been successfully solved," he stated in his address to the 22nd Party Congress, to "tumultuous applause."[88]

By that time, in fact, some tests had proved that intercontinental ballistic missiles (ICBMs) could be intercepted by anti-missile weapons with nonnuclear warheads that had been developed in the design office headed by G. Kisun'ko. The first test took place on March 4, 1961, at the Sary Shagan proving ground (the ICBM was launched from the Kapustin Yar proving ground) and was a success. At one of his press conferences, Khrushchev nonchalantly remarked, "Our missile, one might say, could hit a fly in outer space."[89] Everyone understood his message. However, the goal of establishing a safe anti-missile defense, a complex system to destroy not a single target but a great many targets, had not been achieved. A number of Soviet military professionals were rather cautious, if not skeptical, in their assessments of the capabilities and potential of the anti-missile system. They recommended that attention should be paid not only to developing missile-intercepting weapons, but also to developing capabilities to destroy the enemy's missiles in their launch sites, or to employing methods of passive defense. At the same time, it was stated that establishing an anti-missile defense would require huge allocations

---

87. Ibid., p. 23.

88. *XXII s'yezd Kommunisticheskoi Partii Sovetskogo Soyuza* (22nd Congress of the Communist Party of the Soviet Union), stenographic notes, Vol. 2 (Moscow: Politizdat, 1962), p. 117.

89. See G. Kisun'ko, "*Den'gi na oboronu. Chetyre monologa o sekretakh 'zakrytoi' nauki*" (Money for defense. Four monologues on the secrets of the "hidden" science), *Sovetskaya Rossiya*, August 5, 1990, p. 4.

of resources and thus would only be available to economically developed countries.

But the concept of anti-missile defense penetrated the top Soviet political echelons. A highly detailed explanation was given by A.N. Kosygin, president of the Council of Ministers, at a press conference during his visit to Great Britain in 1967. When he was asked by a British journalist whether the deployment of a Soviet anti-missile system would be a new step forward in the arms race and what the chances were of a U.S.-Soviet agreement on a mutual moratorium on anti-missile defense deployment, Kosygin responded:

That is an important question in the military sphere. I would not like to answer it directly, and in turn I would like to ask the author of this question . . . what kind of weapon—offensive or defensive—should be considered a factor of tension? I think that defensive systems which prevent attack are not the cause of the arms race, but are a factor preventing the death of people. Some people reason like this: which is cheaper—to have an offensive weapon that can destroy cities and entire states, or to have a defensive weapon that can avert this destruction. At present, there is a theory in circulation that the cheaper system should be developed. These "theorists" are debating how much it costs to kill a person—500,000 dollars or 100,000 dollars. Perhaps an antimissile system is more expensive than an offensive one, but its mission is not killing people, but the protection of human lives. I am aware that I am not answering the question that was posed to me, but you yourself can draw the appropriate conclusions. For solving the problem of security, there are other ways, much safer ways, which actually could suit humanity. You know that we support stopping nuclear armament and destroying stockpiles of nuclear weapons.[90]

The U.S.-Soviet Treaty on Anti-Ballistic Missile (ABM) Systems of May 1972 was an important milestone in the development of Soviet approaches to the offense-defense issue. This treaty imposed tough restrictions on anti-missile weapons and, more important, banned anti-missile systems, which reflected an awareness that retaliation in nuclear war was inevitable and hopes for a reliable and secure defense system were futile. That was a radical departure from the prevailing views of the Soviet political and military leadership in the 1960s.

After the ABM Treaty was signed, the Soviet discussion focused on the high cost of an anti-missile defense. It was repeatedly stated that intercepting one missile would require employing at least three interceptors. Much attention was paid to the qualitative dimensions of the

---

90. A.N. Kosygin's address before English and foreign journalists, *Izvestiya*, February 10, 1967.

development of U.S. strategic offensive forces, above all to multiple independently targeted reentry vehicles (MIRVs). It was stressed that although the United States was not planning to increase the number of its launchers, it was dramatically increasing the number of warheads on them. Experts realized that opportunities for interception were drastically narrowing, and acknowledged the limitations of an anti-missile system. Marshal of the Soviet Union P. Batitsky, who was the commander in chief of the nation's anti-missile defense, acknowledged that "within the framework of the achieved agreements on the limitation of anti-missile defenses, this system will probably only change qualitatively, and in terms of its capabilities, it will only be able to cover the capitals . . . against the possibility of nuclear attack."[91]

The Development of the "Deep Battle" Theory in the 1970s

In the 1970s, the development of Soviet offensive operational and strategic concepts continued to follow the principles of the theory of deep operations, or deep battle, that had been formulated in the 1930s. According to Army General Pavlovsky, "the high combat qualities of the Soviet ground forces, armed with powerful, long-range means of destruction, and the dramatic increase in mobility of all troop formations have created favorable conditions for further development of the theory and practice of deep offensive operations."[92] In his view, the ground forces had gained the capability, either independently or jointly with other services, to inflict fire strikes on the entire depth of the enemy's operational order, and to conduct a more intensive offensive at a higher tempo and a greater depth than had been possible at the end of World War II. Army General V.I. Varennikov wrote that battle using operational reserves had acquired greater significance because of the increased maneuverability of the defensive side. As a consequence, the vanguard forces had gained a more important role, and by undertaking decisive actions on a wide front in the enemy's rear, Varennikov noted, they could seize intermediate lines, important objectives, road junctions, and crossing points in order to support the successful development of the operation.[93]

---

91. P. Batitsky, "*Voiska protivovozdushnoi oborony strany*" (The anti-aircraft defense forces of the country), *Voennaya mysl'*, No. 7 (1970), p. 36.

92. I. Pavlovsky, "*Sukhoputnye voiska*" (Ground forces), *Voennaya mysl'*, No. 4 (1973), p. 30.

93. V.I. Varennikov, "*Nekotorye problemy razvitiya uspekha v nastupatel'nykh operastsiyakh*" (Several problems of the development of success in offensive operations), *Voennaya mysl'*, No. 8 (1979), p. 35.

The surprise factor, Soviet analysts underlined, was increasingly important in the success of offensive operations. Employing methods unfamiliar to the enemy in tactical missions was thought to be particularly significant.[94]

In the mid-1970s, a new notion was introduced into the Soviet military debate, the concept of "three-dimensional battle" developed by Lieutenant General I.I. Yurpol'sky. According to his theory, in the present stage of technological advances in weaponry, traditional schemes of offensive operations (e.g., establishing a concentration of forces, penetrating the enemy's defense, building up strength, developing a tactical and operational breakthrough, and completing the destruction of the adversary) could and should be changed. The point was that new means of warfare enabled the defending side, at the outset of the offensive operation, to create conditions to prevent the ground organization of the attacker from operating effectively (by radioactively contaminating large zones, mining the territory, flooding, building fortified regions, deploying powerful anti-tank systems, etc.). To ensure the success of the offensive and to achieve victory more quickly, Yurpol'sky suggested that it would be necessary to transport some ground forces by air (after the nuclear and conventional strikes) over the zones of contamination and defense lines.[95] Major General I.I. Dzhordzhadze supported the idea of a "three-dimensional battle," and noted that its principles were of global relevance to strategy and tactics, and to offense and defense.[96]

Lieutenant General G.I. Demidkov wrote that "detailed analysis of possible ways to resolve problems of modern offensive operations has shown that the most useful approaches should be sought in the fullest possible use of the airspace by ground forces."[97] An offensive conducted by an air echelon instead of episodic operations by airborne forces, according to these analysts, was an important issue for all forces, and a key factor in the defeat of the enemy. Conducting operations in line with this

---

94. See P.G. Lushev, "*K voprosu o dostizhenii operativnoi nevzapnosti*" (On the question of succeeding in operational surprise), *Voennaya mysl'*, No. 2 (1980), p. 30.

95. I.I. Yurpol'sky, "*Evolyutsiya vzglyadov na vedenie nastupatel'nykh operatsii sukhoputnykh voisk*" (The evolution of approaches to offensive operations carried out by the ground forces), *Voennaya mysl'*, No. 6 (1976), p. 48.

96. I.I. Dzhordzhadze, "*Evolyutsiya vzglyadov na vedenie nastupatel'nykh operatsii sukhoputnykh voisk*" (The evolution of approaches to offensive operations carried out by the ground forces), *Voennaya mysl'*, No. 10 (1976), p. 48.

97. G.I. Demidkov, "*Evolyutsiya vzglyadov na vedenie nastupatel'nykh operatsii sukhoputnykh voisk*" (The evolution of approaches to offensive operations carried out by the ground forces), *Voennaya mysl'*, No. 11 (1976), p. 53.

theory "might help achieve more decisive aims with fewer losses and ensure the best possible way of employing new combat means and inflicting a surprise attack."[98] According to Demidkov, developing and introducing the theory into the forces would only take a few years. He also stressed the importance of keeping ahead of the enemy by adopting a theory precisely tailored to the present military and political situation.[99]

Critics in the military objected to the three-dimensional battle theory's focus on ground forces only in offense, underscoring that modern offensive operations were being conducted on a large scale in joint efforts involving all branches of the military, and that within this framework, a number of land, sea, and air operations were being prepared to carry out common missions. Modern operations thus were not only joint but also integrated. In the opinion of General M.V. Smirnov (Ret.), Yurpol'sky based his theory on the extensive use of airborne troops and air cavalry.[100] However, Smirnov continued, the height at which combat operations are carried out had never been used to measure the scope of modern operations, despite the fact that aviation and airborne forces had been widely used for many years. Ground forces, including airborne forces and air cavalry, had always been assigned to carry out combat missions on the ground; transporting them by air is only a short phase of the operation. Thus, Smirnov concluded, calling modern "deep offensive" combat "three-dimensional" was not justified. Moreover, he added, by emphasizing the prime importance of airborne troops and air cavalry, Yuropol'sky was ignoring the fact that powerful, battle-tested mobile formations had not stopped being critical in modern warfare.[101] Judging by the fact that the Soviet military developed and adopted the concept of Operational Mobile Groups (OMG) in the late 1970s, Smirnov's viewpoint prevailed in the debates on three-dimensional battle.

Nevertheless, it would be unfair to conclude that Soviet military theory in the 1970s was not engaged in studying strategic and tactical defense with regard to conventional forces. Military writings of the period never categorically rejected strategic defense as *Military Strategy* had. However, according to my own estimations, Soviet miltitary literature (above all, *Voennaya mysl'*) carried three or four times as many articles on

---

98. Ibid., p. 54.

99. Ibid.

100. M.V. Smirnov, "*Evolyutsiya vzglyadov na vedenie nastupatel'nykh operatsii sukhoputnykh voisk*" (The evolution of approaches to offensive operations carried out by the ground forces), *Voennaya mysl'*, No. 11 (1976), p. 55.

101. Ibid., p. 56.

offense as on defense in that period. Although the range of topics discussed was rather narrow, new ideas occasionally appeared. For example, it was noted that, if a system of strategic defense were damaged, its rapid repair would present a huge problem in a situation when weapons of all kinds were used. Resolving such a problem would require taking advance measures in order to compensate for probable casualties, and several measures that had been suggested by Western military analysts were discussed.[102]

Offense and Defense in Soviet Military Strategy in the Early 1980s

The early 1980s were marked by some changes in Soviet military doctrine and strategy regarding the use of strategic nuclear forces. As far as conventional forces were concerned, these changes remained latent.

In 1982, the Soviet Union adopted the policy of not being the first to use nuclear weapons. This stance was based on the then widely accepted view that no country could win in a nuclear war. Moreover, it was argued that it was not possible to make an effective, preemptive strike on the Soviet Union because of the level of combat readiness of Soviet nuclear forces and the effectiveness of Soviet detection systems. As Soviet Defense Minister Dmitry Ustinov phrased it in 1982:

If the aggressor uses nuclear weapons first, it will bring our peoples countless disasters. However, the aggressor should know that the advantages of preemptive use of nuclear weapons will not lead to victory. . . . With modern detection systems and the level of combat readiness of Soviet nuclear weapons, the United States will not succeed in inflicting a disarming strike on the socialist countries. The aggressor will not escape a crushing retaliatory strike.[103]

To safeguard Soviet defenses under the conditions of the no-first-use pledge, Ustinov considered it necessary to upgrade the combat readiness of Soviet troops and to improve control and communication in order to minimize the negative consequences of a surprise attack and to make preventing an unauthorized Soviet launch as comprehensive as possible.[104] It seems rather strange, however, to see the latter measure on the

---

102. V.V. Gurchenko, "*Tendentsii v razvitii teorii i praktiki strategicheskoi oborny*" (Trends in the development of the theory and practice of strategic defense), *Voennaya mysl'*, No. 8 (1979), p. 24.

103. D.F. Ustinov, *Otvesti ugrozu yadernoi voiny* (Avert the danger of nuclear war) (Moscow: Politizdat, 1982), p. 11.

104. Ibid., p. 7.

list since this kind of control should be exercised even without a no-first-use pledge.

From that point on, all the Soviet literature on military doctrine mentioned the commitment to no first use, and in many cases this policy was presented as the cornerstone of Soviet military doctrine. For example, in his well-known book *History Teaches Vigilance*, Ogarkov stated that "the principle that the Soviet Union will not be the first to use nuclear weapons is at the foundation of Soviet military doctrine."[105] Yet the principle itself was not developed and its strategic operational aspects were not specified. For instance, the kinds of targets that would be hit by a retaliatory strike were not indicated, and the threshold of unacceptable damage was not defined (which had been done by U.S. Secretaries of State Robert McNamara in the 1960s and Harold Brown in the 1970s). A booklet called "Whence the Threat to Peace," published by the Soviet Ministry of Defense in 1984, seemed to be an exception; since it stated that Soviet military doctrine did not embrace the concept of preemptive attack.[106] But no further explanation was given there either, and that made the declaration of no first use less convincing.

Meanwhile, despite the pledge, some Soviet military writings published at the time did not interpret issues of Soviet nuclear strategy in line with the no-first-use commitment—to put it mildly. For example, in these works, among possible targets for Soviet strategic nuclear forces (strategic rocket forces, nuclear submarines, and long-range aviation) the strategic forces of the other side were listed first, followed by military-economic objectives, troop concentrations, and government and military headquarters. They also underscored the special significance of a massive strategic first strike, which could decide the outcome of war.[107]

Ronald Reagan's Strategic Defense Initiative (SDI) posed a great challenge to Soviet perceptions of the defense-offense relationship, triggering major debates among specialists in both the Soviet Union and the Warsaw Treaty countries. Some unclassified Soviet publications bore traces of the debate. Civilian analysts necessarily played the most important role in the debates because their subject was weapons that operated on new physical principles and were based on research in the field of artificial

---

105. N.V. Ogarkov, *Istoriya uchit bditel'nosti* (History teaches vigilance) (Moscow: Voenizdat, 1985), p. 77.

106. *Otkuda iskhodit ugroza miru* (Whence the threat to peace) (Moscow: Novosti, 1984), p. 13.

107. See, for example, M.M. Kirian, ed., *Voenno-tekhnicheskii progress i Vooruzhennye sily SSSR* (Military-technological progress and the armed forces of the USSR) (Moscow: Voenizdat, 1982), p. 14.

intelligence. In May 1983, soon after Reagan's well-known "Star Wars" speech on SDI, Soviet scientists issued a statement which declared that "there are no effective means of defense in nuclear war, and their creation is practically impossible."[108] This statement underscored the threat to international security that the prospect of establishing a national antimissile defense posed.

> In reality, an attempt to create a so-called "defensive weapon" against the nuclear strategic weapons of the other side, which the U.S. president has announced, would inevitably result in the emergence of another element strengthening American "first strike" potential. . . . Such a "defensive weapon" would leave no hope for a country subjected to a massive surprise attack since it [the weapon] is obviously not capable of protecting the vast majority of the population. Antimissile weapons are best suited for use by the attacking side to seek to lessen the power of the retaliatory strike. However, they cannot avert it entirely.[109]

This evaluation was supported by the Soviet Union's top political leadership, as well as many in the military leadership. The scientists' statement seems more significant if one recalls that, in the 1970s and early 1980s, several Soviet scientists had proposed establishing a large-scale anti-missile system including space echelons. For example, in the early 1970s, academician G.I. Budker advocated the idea of a space-based anti-missile system, but his proposal was criticized by academicians L.A. Artsimovich and B.P. Konstantinov and was rejected. Another variant of a space-based, anti-ballistic missile system, using missile interceptors based on orbital platforms in outer space, was suggested by academician V.N. Chelomei. He presented his idea to Brezhnev, and the discussion at the highest levels was rather tense. A commission headed by V.M. Shabanov, deputy minister of defense, was established to study the proposal. Thanks to the responsible attitudes of several military leaders and scientists, Chelomei's proposal was not accepted. As academician E.P. Velikhov noted, these earlier discussions gave Soviet scientists a kind of immunity against "Star Wars" ideas and prepared them for the debates of the 1980s.[110]

As a result, rather than reacting to SDI by launching a similar pro-

---

108. Quoted in *Novoe vremya*, No. 6 (1983), p. 10.
109. Ibid.
110. E.P. Velikhov, "*Nauka rabotaet na bez'yadernyi mir*" (Science works for a nonnuclear world), *Mezhdunarodnaya zhizn'*, No. 10 (1988), pp. 50–51.

gram, the Soviet Union began to formulate a different line of action. In the diplomatic sphere, the Soviet Union inaugurated a campaign to preserve the 1972 ABM Treaty. Meanwhile, the Soviet military introduced a program of asymmetrical response to preserve the capabilities of strategic nuclear forces to make adequate retaliatory strikes (i.e., to maintain the offense-defense ratio, which had been established in the early 1980s). Several Soviet studies on the potential of a national, space-based antimissile system and countermeasures were made public in 1983–86 in a series of reports by the Committee of Soviet Scientists for Peace set up at the initiative of E.P. Velikhov. These reports were summarized in the 1986 book *Space Weapons: The Dilemma of Security*, which was widely circulated within the Soviet military and scientific communities.[111] By Soviet standards, this book was unusually frank. (In fact, both its authors and the Mir publishing house received letters from angry readers who accused the authors of revealing state secrets.)

Of course, the most important statements were those of military professionals. General of the Army V.M. Shabanov wrote in July 1985 that any comparisons that the U.S. media made between SDI and the Manhattan Project or the Apollo Project to land a man on the moon were not justified. The principal difference was that SDI not only challenged nature, but also faced a sophisticated adversary. And while nature is unchangeable and its secrets can be learned, the adversary can also master the secrets of nature to take countermeasures, thus creating the necessity to provide for the possibility of all kinds of counter-countermeasures.[112]

This emphasis on retaliation was reflected in Soviet approaches to the role and mission of the strategic component of the navy, the main mission of which had become increasing the combat stability of nuclear submarines in their combat patrol areas by using various naval forces.[113] The survival capacity of strategic submarines, some naval representatives asserted, would be ensured by, among other means, *Tbilisi*-class heavy aircraft carriers (the Soviet navy launched the first warship of that class in 1989).

---

111. E.P. Velikhov, R.Z. Sagdeev, and A.A. Kokoshin, eds., *Kosmicheskoe oruzhie: dilemma bezopasnosti* (Space weapons: The dilemma of security) (Moscow: Mir, 1986).

112. V. Shabanov, "*Chto stoit za 'tekhnologicheskim ryvkom' v kosmos?*" (What is behind the "technological dash" into space?) *Izvestiya*, July 27, 1985.

113. N.P. V'yunenko, B.N. Makeyev, and V.D. Skugarev, *Voenno-morskoi flot: rol', perspektivy razvitiya, ispol'zovaniie* (The navy: Its role, prospects of development, use) (Moscow: Voenizdat, 1988), p. 237.

"Defense Sufficiency" and the New Relationships between Offense and Defense

At the 27th Party Congress in 1986, the concept of reasonable sufficiency in the military potential of both sides was introduced, which gave impetus to the search for a new relationship between offense and defense in conventional forces in Soviet military doctrine and strategy. The experience of World War II played an important part in this quest. As early as 1985, Deputy Chief of the General Staff Makhmut Gareyev provided an extremely negative retrospective commentary on Soviet strategic defense in the Great Patriotic War. He pointed out that, prior to this most serious of tests a nation had to face, the Soviet military and political leadership had not adequately reviewed the forms and methods of strategic defense and had neglected the practicalities of its tactical dimensions. The idea of immediately shifting the battlefield onto the territory of the enemy, in Gareyev's view, was deeply rooted within the Soviet leadership even though neither theory nor pragmatic considerations nor operational calculations supported it. The prospect of a lengthy struggle on Soviet territory was beyond the leadership's ken. Meanwhile, it was quite obvious that driving back a strategic offensive by an enemy army more numerous than the Red Army could not be achieved without prior preparation. A series of fierce, protracted battles and operations were inevitable, Gareyev wrote. If plans for that contingency had existed, the troops of the Western military districts would have been deployed differently with due regard to their defensive mission.[114]

Gareyev was quite right in noting that, from the Stalin era onward, those issues were not given due consideration in the Soviet literature on military problems.[115] However, Gareyev himself did not project the lessons of 1941–42 into the strategy of the 1980s, and following the post-war line, he wrote a great deal on offensive operations in modern conditions.

In principle, we have developed a clear system of concepts about preparing for and conducting offensive operations. But, like any other theoretical principles, they are constantly evolving. Among other things, it is necessary to continue researching ways to ensure the continuity and speed of a deep offensive. This raises many problems: breaching enemy defenses equipped

---

114. Gareyev, *M.V. Frunze—voennyi teoretik*, p. 230.
115. Ibid., p. 231.

with various antitank weapons; organizing the assured destruction of the enemy, especially its armored objectives in the defense.[116]

Meanwhile, high-ranking Soviet military professionals were growing increasingly skeptical about strategic offense as the predominant approach to armed struggle. Indeed, some began to consider this concept to be dangerous since, if it were successful, it would increase the likelihood of crossing the nuclear threshold through irreversible escalation. However, no one had stated this skepticism publicly yet.

In the mid-1980s, the volume of Soviet military writings literature on the defense in World War II, particularly in 1941–42, began to increase.[117] New editions of military memoirs appeared, and many of them now included passages on the Soviet retreat and Stalin's miscalculations which had not appeared in earlier editions. The most interesting memoirs were those of Rokosovsky and Zhukov. In the 1989 edition of Rokosovsky's memoirs, he discussed the subject of fortification—fortified regions and fortresses—at length. In 1941, Rokosovsky, who had himself begun his military service in the cavalry and later led a mechanized corps (a major mobile formation), carried out painstaking independent research on the Russian plan of strategic deployment that had been mapped out not long before World War I. He discovered that, contrary to what Soviet analysts had said about its "stupidity" after the revolution, the tsarist plan had actually been quite reasonable. It had been drawn up giving great consideration to realistic prospects and actual conditions. A comparative analysis of German and Russian potential, and particularly their respective ability to mobilize and concentrate their main forces in the border regions, supported the suggested line of deployment and its remoteness from the border. The plan's authors visualized the deployment line as a fortified line. "That particular plan I could comprehend," Rokosovsky wrote. It led him to believe that the most logical line of action for the Red Army would be to face the German threat by using the old fortified regions that were somewhat removed from the old Soviet frontier,

---

116. Ibid., p. 244.

117. See, for example, A.P. Maryshev, "*Nekotorye voprosy strategicheskoi oborony v Velikoi Otechestvennoi voine*" (Some issues of strategic defense in the Great Patriotic War), *Voenno-istoricheskii zhurnal*, No. 6 (1986), pp. 9–16; A.N. Batelov, "*Puti povysheniya ustoichivosti operativnoi oborony*" (Ways to increase the stability of defense carried out in operations), *Voenno-istoricheskii zhurnal*, No. 5 (1987), pp. 16–24; and A.A. Gurov, "*Boevye deistviya sovetskikh voisk na yugo-zapadnom napravlenii v nachal'nyi period voiny*" (Combat operations of Soviet troops on the southwestern line of advance of the opening period of war), *Voenno-istoricheskii zhurnal*, No. 8 (1988), pp. 47–54.

without resorting to mobilization until the outbreak of war. It had been a mistake, he wrote, to disarm the old fortified areas and to begin to construct new fortifications at the new Soviet border under the very eyes of the Germans.[118]

The publication of General L.M. Sandalov's *Military Operations of the Fourth Army in the Opening Phase of the Great Patriotic War*, which earlier had been a classified document, was characteristic of the kind of military literature published in the Soviet Union in the late 1980s.[119] Sandalov discussed how shoddily the new fortifications had been constructed before the war and how badly they had functioned after its outbreak. He knew about this from his own wartime experience as the leader of the army stationed on the main line of the attack.

Another characteristic feature of the late 1980s was a growing interest in the Battle of Kursk as an example of deliberate defense. Major General A.P. Maryshev called it a classic example that could serve as a model. However, he also reasonably pointed out that the favorable conditions in which the Red Army found itself at the time of the battle were exceptional, and probably it would be wiser to thoroughly examine the defense experience of the first phase of the war.[120]

A 1987 article coauthored by Andrei Kokoshin and General Valentin Larionov, "The Battle of Kursk in the Light of Contemporary Defensive Doctrine," discussed the battle with reference to new approaches and concepts of the Soviet armed forces in the 1980s.[121] Army General S.I. Postnikov, in his article commemorating the forty-fifth anniversary of the Battle of Kursk, noted that, although numerous changes in the forms and methods of warfare had taken place in the post-war period, they did not eclipse the experience of the Great Patriotic War as the most valuable source of military knowledge. Studying the Battle of Kursk is "of

---

118. See K.K. Rokosovsky, "*Soldatskii dolg*" (A soldier's duty), *Voenno-istoricheskii zhurnal*, No. 5 (1989), p. 61.

119. See L.M. Sandalov, "*Stoyali nasmert'*" (We made our last stand), *Voenno-istoricheskii zhurnal*, Nos. 10, 11, 12 (1988), Nos. 2, 8 (1989). Sandalov began his field service in the war as chief of headquarters of the Fourth Army stationed around Brest. Later he was chief of headquarters of the front. After the war, Sandalov headed the headquarters of the Carpathian military district, and later served as deputy chief of the Main Staff of the ground forces, and then was appointed chief of the headquarters of the Moscow military district.

120. Maryshev, "*Nekotorye voprosy strategicheskoi oborony v Velikoi Otechestvennoi voine*," p. 16.

121. A.A. Kokoshin and V. Larionov, "*Kurskaya bitva v svete sovremennoi oboronitel'noi doktriny*" (The battle of Kursk in the light of contemporary defensive doctrine), *Mirovaya ekonomika i mezhdunarodnye otnosheniya*, No. 6 (1987).

permanent significance to the further development of the art of war on the basis of exclusively defensive socialist military doctrine," he concluded.[122] In a word, the Battle of Kursk was considered a kind of a prototype for a new Soviet defensive strategy in the major theaters of battle.

In a meeting in Berlin on May 9, 1987, the Political Consultative Committee of the Warsaw Treaty States adopted a document "On the Military Doctrine of the Warsaw Treaty States." This statement made quite a few important points; for example, it declared that "the military doctrine of the Warsaw Treaty as well as that of each of its members serves the purpose of averting war—both nuclear and conventional."[123] It also proclaimed that "the military doctrine of the Warsaw Treaty states is strictly defensive and assumes that at the present time attempting to solve any disputable issue by nuclear means is inadmissible."[124]

The evolutionary transition of the military doctrine of the Warsaw Treaty Organization and the Soviet Union toward a more defensive stance was largely related to prior statements about the necessity not only to reduce conventional forces and weapons in Europe but also to change their qualitative features in order to ensure greater stability. The key statement was made at the Budapest meeting of the Political Consultative Committee of the Warsaw Treaty member countries in 1986, and its formula was repeated in the document of the 1987 meeting in Berlin. The Budapest statement proposed to reduce "armed forces and conventional weapons in Europe down to a level at which neither side would have the means to inflict a surprise attack on the other side in order to launch general offensive operations."[125] Meanwhile, an overwhelming majority of Soviet military leaders had argued in the not-so-distant past that a general defensive orientation of Soviet military doctrine did not signify a rejection of the primary emphasis on offense in the event of war. (Incidentally, similar logic characterized political-military thinking in other countries as well, including the United States.) That was probably the reason why the Berlin document said almost nothing about the military (or, in Frunze's terms, the military-technical) side of the doctrine,

---

122. S.I. Postnov, "*Razvitie sovetskogo voennogo iskusstvo v Kurskoi bitve*" (The development of the Soviet art of war in the battle of Kursk), *Voenno-istoricheskii zhurnal*, No. 7 (1988), p. 18.

123. *Soveshchanie Politicheskogo konsul'tativnogo komiteta gosudarstv-uchastnikov Varshavskogo Dogovora, Berlin 28–29 maya, 1987* (Meeting of the Political Consultative Committee of the Warsaw Treaty States, Berlin, May 28–29, 1987) (Moscow: Politizdat, 1987), p. 7.

124. Ibid., p. 8.

125. Ibid., p. 10.

including strategic and operational guidelines and priorities for offensive and defensive military operations. The defensive character of Soviet military doctrine was deduced from two assumptions: (1) the Soviet Union did not have political goals that required it to unleash war on military aggression by its own initiative; and (2) the Soviet armed forces were oriented exclusively toward retaliatory operations.

That conception of the interrelationship between the political and military dimensions of the doctrine was criticized by some Soviet experts, including military professionals, who considered it necessary to bring the two dimensions into full conformity with each other with the unconditional subordination of strategy (and tactics) to political missions. Any dichotomy in that most delicate sphere imperiled national and international security, and, to use Svechin's term, the prospect of the "emancipation" of strategy from policy could have extremely serious repercussions in a crisis situation. If strategy or tactics do not correspond to a state's political-military course, its conceptions and policies of national security, then an offensive orientation could have an almost decisive impact on the behavior of the state leadership in a crisis.

Despite a certain time lag, a number of Soviet military theorists were becoming aware of the abnormality of a situation in which the political dimension of military doctrine was defensive and the military dimension was offensive. Moreover, they had to acknowledge that the political dimension of Soviet doctrine had not always been defensive (the Soviet-Finnish War of 1939–40, which was rather actively discussed in the Soviet media in the late 1980s, was a prime example). In order to smooth over the negative impact of this acknowledgment, it was stressed that in the initial days of the Soviet state, in 1917, the military doctrine of the Bolshevik government had a defensive line and, based on their military policy, the Bolsheviks were in principle *oborontsy* (supporters of defense). Those circumstances demanded a corresponding approach in military affairs. However, although Soviet diplomacy in its early years observed a defensive line, Soviet military policy before World War II and for a long time afterward assigned a secondary role to defensive operations. In some cases this line was justified, according to Colonel General I.N. Rodionov, chief of the Military Academy of the General Staff and Minister of Defense of the Russian Federation in 1996–97, but it was politically damaging and gave credibility to charges that the Soviet Union harbored aggressive intentions.[126]

It is noteworthy that the first statement about changes in Soviet

---

126. I.N. Rodionov, "*Lenin i sovremennaya voennaya mysl'*" (Lenin and modern military thought), *Voennaya mysl'*, No. 4 (1990), p. 16.

military doctrine and its political-military dimension was made in 1987 by a General Staff representative, Makhmut Gareyev, at a joint press conference with Deputy Minister of Foreign Affairs Vladimir Petrovsky. Gareyev stated that, in accordance with the new doctrine of the Soviet Union and the Warsaw Treaty Organization, first priority was given to defensive operations. Another participant in this press conference from the General Staff, Colonel General N.F. Chervov, emphasized that "our country stands for the reduction of its military potential in line with the limits of reasonable sufficiency. By this we mean that the structure and role of the armed forces will allow them to carry out only defensive operations."[127]

Other Soviet military leaders and analysts supported this idea in their writings. However, to the many who were accustomed to the opposite assumption—that victory could be won only through offense—the new pronouncements sounded rather strange. Soviet Minister of Defense Dmitry Yazov tried to reassure this part of the military, and wrote that "it is impossible to break down the enemy only by defensive means. That is why, after driving back an attack, the army and the navy must be ready to launch a decisive offensive."[128]

The sociopolitical changes taking place in the Soviet Union and throughout the socialist bloc in the late 1980s under the banners of Gorbachev's policies of *perestroika* and "new political thinking" also had an impact on the theoretical and practical dimensions of defensive doctrine. "Deep analysis and a realistic appraisal of a new situation in the world" enabled the Central Committee of the Communist Party to set forth a concept of new political thinking, according to Army General G.I. Salmanov. This was reflected, he added, in military strategy: new measures to avert war and to ensure the stability of strategic parity, as well as the interrelationship between defensive doctrine and prospects for military development, had been defined.[129] Salmanov also said that, of all the types of strategic operations, strategic defense and a counteroffensive after driving back the enemy were now at the forefront.[130]

---

127. Press conference of June 22, 1987, *Vestnik MID SSSR*, No. 1 (1987), pp. 52, 56, 57.

128. D.T. Yazov, *Na strazhe mira i sotsializma* (On guard over peace and socialism) (Moscow: Voenizdat, 1987), p. 33.

129. At the time, Salmanov headed the Voroshilov Military Academy of the General Staff, which was the main think tank of the Soviet armed forces.

130. G.I. Salmanov, "*Sovetskoe voennoe iskusstvo za 70 let*" (The Soviet art of war over 70 years), *Voennaya mysl'*, No. 2 (1988), p. 32.

A highly placed strategist on the General Staff, Colonel General V.V. Korobushin, agreed with Salmanov's observation,[131] noting that "Soviet defensive military strategy has created new, higher requirements for the stability and activity of the defense ... first, defensive operations are the main form of warfare during the aggressor's attack, while counteroffensive operations are the main form of offense in the opening phase of war."[132] The goals of the counteroffensive in the opening phase were defined by another author as follows: to frustrate the enemy's offensive; to destroy its main grouping of troops; to prevent the enemy from creating a wedge; to restore earlier positions; to seize the initiative; and to create favorable conditions for subsequent operations.[133] Marshal of the Soviet Union Viktor Kulikov wrote that "it is rather important to learn to organize and carry out an active defense that envisions the effective destruction of the enemy by fire and by carrying out counterattacks and counterstrikes."[134]

The concept of active defensive operations was thoroughly addressed in the Soviet military literature of the late 1980s and early 1990s. Generals A.S. Kulikov and A.D. Nefedov pointed out the necessity to define the optimal combination of maneuverability and positional forms of defense in a 1990 article in *Voennaya mysl'*. In their view, the aim of defense was to drive out the aggressor, destroy it, and regain lost positions. Concentrating military efforts on the most probable lines of the enemy's advance and creating a strong positional defense were the main prerequisites for carrying out these steps.[135] In a lengthy theoretical article on "Strategic Military Parity as a Deterrent Factor," an able theorist of a new generation, Lieutenant Colonel V.F. Andreyev, went further than his colleagues, and stated that the maxim "offense is the best defense" was no longer adequate in contemporary conditions. In his view, a preemptive strike (which

---

131. V.V. Korobushin, "*O povyshenii effektivnosti voenno-nauchnykh issledovanii*" (On the increasing effectiveness of military-scientific research), *Voennaya mysl'*, No. 5 (1988), p. 42.

132. Ibid., pp. 40–41.

133. V.M. Evlakhov, "*Nekotorye voprosy teorii i praktiki kontrnastupleniya*" (Some questions on the theory and practice of counteroffensive), *Voennaya mysl'*, No. 10 (1989), p. 12.

134. V.G. Kulikov, "*O voenno-strategicheskom paritete i dostatochnosti dlya oborony*" (On military-strategic parity and sufficiency for defense), *Voennaya mysl'*, No. 5 (1988), p. 10.

135. A.S. Kulikov and A.D. Nefedov, "*Pozitsionnye i manevrennye deistviya: rol' i mesto v oboronitel'noi operatsii*" (Positional and maneuver warfare: Their role and place in defensive operations), *Voennaya mysl'*, No. 3 (1990), p. 24.

continued to preoccupy many military minds) was not adequate either. In conditions of nuclear parity, Andreyev wrote, to be the first to use the offensive potential (a preemptive offensive), even for the sake of defense, would be suicidal. The safest defense, he asserted, is a nonoffensive defense that excludes preemptive offensive operations.[136]

Soviet naval strategy underwent a similar revision in the late 1980s. A series of publications stated that a new period in Soviet naval development had begun. The reorientation of Soviet military doctrine toward the defensive demanded a revision of many notions and categories of naval strategy, wrote V. Dotsenko in *Morskoi sbornik*. Defensive operations were becoming the navy's principal operations. The current revisions, Dotsenko continued, should include a fundamental reconsideration of the navy's guiding documents and a search for the optimal composition of the Soviet fleet and the optimal organization of its activity.[137] The Soviet naval leadership declared that naval personnel would be reduced, and that the character of naval maneuvers would change and they would be held closer to the Soviet coasts.

All of the above differed greatly from what had been stated in the Soviet Union over the previous fifty years. However, these new principles of Soviet military strategy were not put into practice right away. Like any other major state institution, the armed forces have tremendous momentum of their own, and it takes quite a long time to shift to new guiding principles. Thus in 1988 Colonel General Makhmut Gareyev noticed the substantial insufficiencies that were evident in tactical exercises at the time, and made a series of suggestions on how to make defensive actions more effective.[138]

It is important to note that the changes in the military-technical dimension of Soviet doctrine, particularly in strategy and campaign tactics, were initially overlooked by the West (although some first-rate experts—Raymond Garthoff, Michael MccGwire, David Holloway, and others—were writing about them). As a result, the unilateral reduction of the Soviet armed forces, declared by Mikhail Gorbachev on December 7, 1988, at the United Nations General Assembly, came as quite a surprise for many American Sovietologists. This was probably rooted in the

---

136. V.F. Andreyev, "*Voenno-strategicheskii paritet kak faktor sderzhivaniya*" (Military strategic parity as a factor of deterrence), *Voennaya mysl'*, No. 2 (1989), p. 47.

137. V. Dotsenko, "*Sovetskoe voenno-morskoe iskusstvo v poslevoennyi period*" (Soviet naval art in the post-war period), *Morskoi sbornik*, No. 7 (1989), p. 28.

138. M.A. Gareyev, "*Razvitie form i metodov operativnoi i boevoi podgotovki Sovetskoi Armii*" (The development of forms and methods of operational and combat training of the Soviet army), *Voennaya mysl'*, No. 2 (1986), pp. 49–50.

peculiarities of the Western mentality, especially that of Americans. Whereas in Russia the traditional way of thinking is deductive (i.e., from the general to the specific), in the United States it is the opposite (i.e., from the specific to the general). In a way, these inverse approaches coincide with the decision-making process in these two countries. In the Russian system, the political and even philosophical conceptions of the leadership are essential to the development of practical measures. Only in a few instances did concepts that the top Soviet leadership had proposed not lead to practical steps, and that only happened when the state leadership was weak or when the conditions were not yet ripe. In the mid-1980s, however, favorable conditions for change existed. Moreover, new approaches were not just imposed by the Soviet leadership, but were also developing among military and civilian specialists who perceptively recognized the significance of both past experiences and contemporary trends.

Chapter 4

In Lieu of a Conclusion: Russia's National Security and Military Power

The end of the Cold War has produced neither a new and stable system of international relations nor the "new world order" that so many policymakers and analysts had expected. Although it removed many postwar obstacles to normal relations between countries, the structure of international relations nevertheless became more perplexed; many problems of the earlier period still existed, and new ones undoubtedly emerged.

Although some conflicts of the Cold War era have in fact disappeared, numerous new hot spots have emerged, including in the territories of the former Soviet Union and in Russia proper, as well as in the former Yugoslavia. The international community for the most part has appeared to be ill-equipped to resolve conflicts of that magnitude through international organizations, beginning with the United Nations, despite a meaningful expansion in the roles of those institutions. National and ethnic contradictions and clashes became a persistent trait of international life and in many cases were not adequately controlled by governments. Terrorism assumed a grave and worldwide character, demanding not only a high level of cooperation of the world community but also subtle and ingenious interaction of the revelant bodies of many countries.

There has been no decrease in the threat from the proliferation of weapons of mass destruction and their long-range delivery systems, including missiles that could be launched from regions of serious political-military conflict to hit targets in the territories of the Russian Federation and its allies. Defusing this threat requires engaging both national and international resources.

Although Russia turned out to be the country that greatly initiated the processes of changes of the late 1980s and the early 1990s, it was at the same time painfully and variously affected by them. The new international setting that emerged as a result of these changes also presents more serious challenges for Russia than for many other countries and requires a radical turn in many attitudes and approaches. Problems of national security, assessment of the threats and character of potential conflicts and warfare, and requirements of defense are the urgent points of the present-day Russian agenda. The answers to all these points are still to be found and substantiated. The sooner the process gains momentum the better. Otherwise we cannot meet the challenges we are facing now and shall be facing in the next century.

Present-Day Dimensions of the National Security Problem

The concept of "national security," widespread in the practice and theory of international relations, is only now becoming part of our political lexicon. As the above chapters show, during the Soviet period the official doctrine was that the national element of security was secondary, subordinate to the social-class and international elements. The Stalinist conception of state socialism puts the state above the individual and above the nation, regarding it as an end in itself. That is why the term "national security" was not part of the Soviet debate, the cornerstone of which was the concept of state security, interpreted primarily as the defense of socialism and its gains inside and outside the country.

The resulting narrowly ideological understanding of security deprived the state's actions of flexibility, diminished the prospects of warding off complications in the international arena, hindered the correct evaluation of gains and losses in various military security efforts, and did little or nothing to ensure genuine security for the country. To correct this and to develop a sound concept of "national security," one has to properly evaluate the conditions in which this concept has to function. What are the main elements of this evaluation now?

There is a danger that territorial claims may be made on various parts of Russia's periphery. Presently, such claims are only being voiced by marginal political groups in the countries bordering on Russia, but they could certainly develop into the focus of international debates or even clashes.

Russia attaches particular importance to the quality of its relations with the territories of the former Soviet Union, particularly with Ukraine, Belarus, and Kazakhstan. Admittedly, the prominence of the Russian-Ukrainian relationship transcends the boundaries of the Commonwealth of Independent States (CIS) and even Europe as a whole. World politics to a large extent depends on the status of that relationship.

Russia's security policies will be significantly influenced by how the process of reintegration develops in the territory of the former Soviet

Union. The requisite sociocultural, economic, and geopolitical conditions to speed up that process are there for all to see. Through decades of living together in a single country, most of the peoples of the Russian Federation and the Soviet Union had come to form a sort of superethnic community integrating both Slavs and non-Slavs.

It is safe to assume that some kind of a new Eurasian political entity will emerge in the territories of the former Russian Empire and disintegrated Soviet Union, with the Russian Federation serving as a systemic core attracting other nations to come together on an equitable and mutually beneficial basis.

However, the potential for reintegration will not be realized automatically without dedicated efforts on the part of politicians and public figures held accountable to their constituents, and the leaders of the newly emerging market economy. The formation of such a political entity will to a large extent determine the needs of Russia's national security, including defense.

This entire process could be undermined by a whole array of acute conflicts and crises capable even of endangering the territorial integrity of the Russian Federation. However, according to the overwhelming majority of analysts, Russia is not likely to be confronted with the threat of a nuclear or large-scale conventional war. No alarming political or economic preconditions for such a conflict have been evident to date.

Overall, conflicts on the world stage now primarily focus on domination in the areas of economics, finance, science, and technology, with the Soviet Union having nearly been kept out of that race over the last ten to fifteen years of its existence. Thus, as Russia scrambles to join in that global competition, Russia appears to be much more disadvantaged in comparison not only with the developed Western nations and Japan, but also with a whole range of the newly industrialized states. Still, it would be inappropriate to rate Russia in line with the less developed countries given its relatively high educational, cultural, and industrial standards.

One of the key levers that Russia can use to secure status in the hierarchy of nations and avoid simply existing on its raw materials at the margins of the global economy is provided by the defense industrial complex, which for decades attracted the nation's best minds and the investment of huge resources. Unfortunately that lever has never been fully activated because of serious blunders in defense conversion policies and a lack of a long-term national industrial vision.

One cannot help noticing that the term "conversion" does not adequately describe, and in many ways even misrepresents, how Russia's defense industrial complex is to be transformed. What most needs to be emphasized is the diversification of defense industrial enterprises. A good many domestic and foreign experts have on numerous occasions underscored that defense industries simply cannot be converted on a "purely market basis." When World War II ended, many U.S. defense industrial facilities were just closed down, which proved to be a sound solution. But that was successfully achieved because the United States had a highly mobile labor force, a rapid rate of growth in the civilian sector of the economy, a social insurance network that resulted from President Roosevelt's New Deal policy, and other factors that contributed to this result.

Meanwhile, Russia and the other former Soviet republics created a different kind of culture and economy, and by the early 1990s, at least seventy cities were almost totally dependent for their livelihood on the defense industry.

Under the Soviet Union's rigid system of centralized planning, the old-fashioned conversion strategy practiced in the late 1980s had a fair chance of success. Defense plants and design bureaus were charged with creating products for the food industry and manufacturing consumer electronics and other equipment, and the orders were integrated in the existing systems of pricing and demand. Many of those assignments were diligently fulfilled, though at some cost. Despite a general slump in the Soviet industrial output for 1991, the production of conversion durables—refrigerators, television sets, stereos, and the like—registered a meaningful increase. However, in early 1992 there was a great readjustment in prices, and production costs skyrocketed after decades of having the prices of building materials and parts kept artificially low. The jump in prices of both defense-related and civilian products produced by the defense sector was steeper than the increase in the prices of goods produced in the civilian sector of the economy. In the past, a "defense" ruble produced much more value than a ruble invested in, say, a civilian machine building. A ruble expended to build battle tanks or combat aircraft once delivered eight to ten times as much value as the U.S. dollar, according to research findings. Many Russian industrial plants tried to adapt to the pricing shift, and some even succeeded in increasing the production of consumer goods. Unfortunately those goods were increasingly stockpiled in warehouses because of a sharp drop in consumer demand. Compounding these problems, Russia's domestic market appeared to be open to an unconstrained influx of imports.

At this point, it should be underscored once again that the key asset of the Russian defense industries is the highly skilled labor force. The educational system Russia inherited from the Soviet Union should not be underestimated either.

Along with economic, financial, and political factors, the crucial role of military power should also be appreciated as one of the major elements in the international competition for influence. Along with political and other measures, Russia's sufficiently powerful military force should be viewed as a major deterrent of aggression against Russia and its allies. Given Russia's large arsenal of nuclear weapons, above all strategic weapons, Russia remains, despite the disintegration of the Soviet Union, a military superpower.

The power to deter an adversary from attacking continues to hinge upon the capability to inflict devastating damage on the aggressor in response to any option it might choose to take, including a surprise disarming and decapitating strike. Both Russia and the United States possess hundreds of nuclear warheads that are, for purposes of deterrence, ready to be launched against targets that would result in tremendous destruction and snuff out tens of millions of human lives. The recognition of the inevitability of reprisal, of the danger of exterminating vast numbers of people, is certain to make pointless any of the political goals that might be pursued by a side willing to unleash war. This awareness is the keystone that stabilizes military-strategic parity.

As has been emphasized above, the concept of nuclear deterrence, the political role of nuclear weapons in achieving national security aims, and moves to build nuclear arms that are predicated on deterrence should be at the center of the work of political and defense-related experts.

Efforts by one side to build a strategic defense system able to radically degrade the other side's retaliatory strike capabilities pose a major threat to strategic stability. Thus, the 1972 ABM Treaty continues to play a crucial role in assuring strategic stability in today's world.

As has already been noted, the available nuclear arsenal and the low risk of a nuclear or major conventional attack on Russia in no way rule out the threat to Russia's interests posed by regional and local armed conflicts and wars. Moreover, there is some risk of large-scale conflicts erupting in various parts of the world, and while they might not affect Russia and its closest allies directly, they could dramatically unsettle the global status quo.

The nature of armed conflicts and wars in which Russia is likely to become involved will largely be affected by the prevailing trends in the development of weapon systems. In this regard, achieving informational superiority in managing troops and weapons has become increasingly important. Competition in the information sector continues in peacetime even between allies belonging to the same political-military blocs. Understandably, in wartime that struggle is likely to escalate into large-scale special operations in which command of the air and domination in firepower will be determined by the outcome of the information technology competition.

The integrated use of troops and weapons from all the armed services has become increasingly common. In World War I, victory in combat and in battle generally resulted from superiority in battlefield weapons, in that case, field artillery. They were used to either clear advance routes for the infantry or, if the enemy were on the offensive, to check the attacker's advance. In World War II, achieving superiority in firepower on the ground to support effective infantry operations remained important, but securing command of the air became the top priority on the battlefield. Today, while none of those missions has been phased out, they are all now secondary to establishing superiority in the field of information handling.

This is where efforts should be increasingly targeted in order to equip the Russian armed forces with the right hardware and develop and test the tactics and techniques needed to mount even large-scale operations should they be required. Corresponding efforts to provide Russia's armed forces with the requisite materials should be undertaken to accomplish this task.

Nonlethal weapons designed to incapacitate both troops and equipment of the belligerents will increase in importance in the course of armed conflicts.

Victory or defeat in current and future wars are and will continue to be decided not only by combat operations supported by appropriate political and economic instruments, but also by increasing coverage of hostilities in the media, which already have a global reach. This in turn places its own requirements on the armed forces, techniques, and means of warfare. A fitting example to prove that point is provided by the 1991 operations of the coalition of forces against Iraq in the Persian Gulf area, including Desert Storm, when numerous battle scenes were televised live for the whole world to watch.

The evolution of the system of international relations has not resulted in the world's "bipolar configuration" being replaced by either a superpower "condominium" dominated by Russia and the United States or some kind of "global concert" of major world powers, i.e., the permanent members of the UN Security Council. Nor is any substantive progress evident in the roles played by major world institutions like the United Nations and the Organization for Security and Cooperation in Europe (OSCE), though when compared to other world bodies in the past, their influence on world politics has grown quite significantly.

Attempting to take advantage of the current state of international relations, NATO appears to be desperately trying to prolong its existence even though the Cold War has ended and the Warsaw Treaty Organization, its principal adversary, has disintegrated. Obviously, NATO itself is not a monolithic organization, though it has spent decades developing and testing assorted arrangements and vehicles to iron out differences and secure consensus, which have occasionally been quite effective. The alliance is now clearly attempting to gain control over the processes under way in areas of vital interest to Russia and its allies. The enlargement of NATO runs counter to the idea of an all-European security system.

However, one should not remain oblivious to the fact that the Western European Union that is both NATO's partner and rival has gradually begun to expand its influence all across Europe. The Nordic countries, which have their own regional organization, have also become more active. The Visegrad Group in Central and Eastern Europe has survived the "divorce" of the Czech Republic and Slovakia as well as radical shifts in the leadership of individual countries, including the social democrats coming into power in Hungary. At the same time, since the end of the bipolar confrontation, France, Germany, Italy, and a number of other nations have been preserving their international standing and even increasing their influence.

Similar trends can also be observed in other world regions, where individual states and coalitions continue to play their roles and maintain enduring power centers even as global and regional bodies are rising in importance.

In this context, the military dimension of Russian national security policy has to take into account a multiplicity of factors. The international context in which Russia is operating simply cannot be underestimated or oversimplified; otherwise Russia would not be able to take advantage of numerous emerging opportunities in order to support its national interests.

These opportunities are Russia's options for becoming actively involved in the overall effort to create sub-regional, regional, and global balance-of-power arrangements that would be beneficial to Russia's national interests and supportive of the goals of the world community. The more Russia's foreign policy is grounded in its pragmatic and concrete interests, the more effective it will be. Under current conditions, Russia's interests would be well served by a flexible policy of diverse partnerships with individual countries or groups of countries interested in building ties with Russia. Such an approach would give Russia more room for maneuver on a global scale. Selecting strategic allies should necessarily be in line with the nations' interests. In choosing a nation's allies, the leadership should not allow itself to be motivated by illusions, as had been the case with the former Soviet leadership. More often than not, the

Soviet Union's attitudes toward its allies and partners had been a whimsical mix of cynicism and idealism, which led to a tremendous squandering of resources, with true friends turning out to be very few in number. Those policies were among the reasons for the collapse of the Soviet Union and the coalition of its allies.

Without diminishing the central role of U.S.-Russian relations, the importance of Russia's ties with China and India in Asia and its efforts in Europe to resume its traditional relationships with France and Germany should be highlighted. French and German efforts in the post-war period to eliminate the deeply rooted schism that divided France and Germany for centuries have benefited Russian politics as a whole. Russia's relations with such countries as Bulgaria, Slovakia, and Yugoslavia, as well as Cuba, Mongolia, and other states, are also crucial.

In the 1990s, the world found itself with only one superpower and immediately sought changes in the international order so that this unipolar arrangement would not last for too long. By the early 1990s, many U.S. economic growth indicators had declined. The decades of the Cold War, in which the United States competed with the Soviet Union and ultimately achieved a dubious victory, had left an impact on America as well. Meanwhile, new centers of power were increasingly coming into the limelight of world politics, mainly as a result of their industrial, financial, and cultural capacities.

Russia's international objectives should be targeted toward identifying and effectively utilizing its options for participating in assorted alliances and coalitions, learning to operate in a multidimensional environment while being governed by its own long-term national interests, and firmly sticking to its chosen course of policy. One major policy instrument available to Russia is international military and defense industrial cooperation. Russia's achievements in the development and production of a multitude of major weapons systems have been winning broad recognition worldwide, and, given the right direction, they could become a crucial tool for building balance-of-power structures in the Pacific Rim, the Persian Gulf, the Middle East, parts of Latin America, and other areas. High on the military cooperation agenda are programs to educate and train foreign uniformed personnel at Russia's higher military schools, where the trainees would also absorb the best of Russian culture and learn to speak Russian, one of the official UN languages.

Building National Egoism

The concept of Russian national security derives from the conception of national development of the country as a whole and its status in the global hierarchy of industrialized nations. Developing a new political-military and strategic vision and building up the Russian armed forces appear to be inseparable from this kind of national self-identification. Russia's sovereignty and genuine security cannot be assured unless a powerful economy, high-capacity industries, and stable finances are achieved. Russia cannot secure the appropriate armed forces unless the effort hinges on a focused, long-term industrial policy. A profound understanding of the country's national interests and national goals is one of the crucial prerequisites for drafting Russia's industrial policy. Russia is a country with a long and eventful tradition of searching for self-identity on the world stage. Most Russians deeply sense the grandeur of their country, and there is nothing to be ashamed of in that kind of feeling.

The Japanese people had somewhat similar sentiments following their defeat in World War II. Although they were hurt and humiliated, the Japanese refused to succumb to those feelings, and they scrambled to show the world, and above all the United States, that Japan could rise to be at least at par with the United States in economic terms, and they established Japanese society and culture as a global role model.

The Japanese post-war experience has quite a few common features with those of Germany, France, Spain, and South Korea as they rebuilt their economies. Taking into account national specifics and ethnic idiosyncrasies, each of these countries accomplished the most important task—achieving the proper degree of public trust in the long-term national ideal, which encompassed both individual and group interests.

In the late 1980s and early 1990s, while displaying our endemic Russian urge to go to extremes, we rushed from messianism and self-glorification to self-humiliation and banishment of everything that was good in our society, even by the best world standards. Hopefully, the time will come when Russians will come to their senses nationwide, restore their self-respect and love for their country's culture and history, no matter how dramatic and tragic it has often been.

As a multiethnic society headed by Russians, Russia needs to build up a number of qualities, including an enduring sense of national egoism laced with a healthy ambition and desire to prove to the world that Russians can be just as well off as West Europeans or Japanese without having to sacrifice their cultural authenticity, indigenous features, and genuine sovereignty.

I cannot refrain from reiterating that France has been motivated by precisely that kind of vision in its struggle to preserve the French national identity and restore France's genuine grandeur. Meticulous work to gather and build up their cultural heritage also helped Germany, Japan, and Italy, utterly defeated in World War II, to resist the unprecedented onslaught of American mass culture, firmly stand on their own feet, and achieve outstanding results in the economic, manufacturing, and social welfare sectors.

The Russian language can play an important role in Russia's drive to rebuild its nationhood and search for its legitimate and solid niche in the world. Fostering the Russian language, above all its literary version, should be one of the principal thrusts of the state's cultural policy. However, that policy should in no way infringe on the rights of Russia's ethnic minority communities seeking to cultivate their own languages or dialects, and it certainly should not be suggestive of a Russification campaign similar to the one pursued under Tsar Alexander III.

The sustained trend to simplify and even vulgarize the living language poses an enormous threat today, which is eroding the capability to adequately evaluate and describe the increasingly complex world. Not for the first time in this century, "newspeak" presents a huge threat to Russian culture. In the realm of national security, particularly in dealing with political-military matters, where subtleties and shades of meaning can often spell life or death, especially in acute crises, the clarity and explicitness of the language used are of paramount importance.

Cultivation of the Russian language, the key component of national culture, appears to be a most productive way to preserve Russia's unity and territorial integrity and to secure Russia's influence not merely in the "near abroad" but also in many other regions of the world. The Russian language should receive particular attention in the education of the officer cadre of the armed forces. One should recall that one of the accomplishments of Cardinal Richelieu, the great builder of a unified France, was the establishment of the Institute of the French Language and the promotion in every possible way of French authors and playwrights to foster a single national literary language. The creator of Russia's modern literary language, Alexander Pushkin, has done more for the unity of Russia and the enhancement of its global role than thousands of high-ranking policymakers and generals.

Today, like Germany and Spain, Japan or South Korea, Russia badly needs unifying ideas. This task is already recognized by the more alert segments of Russian society—politicians, scientists, media people, public figures, political party and union leaders, business managers, and, of particular importance, industry executives and progressive workers. It is up to these parts of society to formulate national goals and define national interests on the basis of the concepts of public concord and incorporation, thereby enabling Russia to follow the path of stable democratic social development.

One of Russia's top (if not the top) national goals is to provide acceptable living standards, which would allow Russia to take its place among the industrialized nations. Comparative research on Russia's current prospective capacities allows one to conclude that, in the near future, in terms of socioeconomic and science-technology standards Russia could become one of the three or four most developed countries, rather than merely joining the G-7.

In order to secure a worthy niche in the international hierarchy, Russia must stake a firm hold in the global market for high technology. Russia's best engineering minds undoubtedly constitute part of the world community's small elite who are equipped to develop and operate super-sophisticated technological systems that are only possible with hundreds of highly organized and closely integrated production plants, research institutions, and design bureaus to develop and support them.

For Russia's domestic industries to grow more efficiently, appropriate industrial policy needs to be drafted and national consensus on the matter must be achieved. Leaders in the high-tech sector could include the aviation and aerospace industries that are linked to a whole range of high- and mid-level technologies and advanced building materials. This is an area in which Russia can boast of world-class achievements, for example, in the field of UHF electronics. Admittedly, there have been weaknesses and even flops in the process, but overall, these industries can serve as "locomotives" to pull along Russia's entire economy.

Russia also desperately needs a strategy for penetrating the most lucrative markets. Achieving a worthy place in the world community will largely depend on a skillfully crafted strategy of finding a niche for Russia's products, including collaborative ties with carefully selected foreign partners. Russia's foreign policy objectives should also support this strategy to assist Russian products in penetrating international markets.

State support for Russian entrepreneurs together with reasonable and effective protectionism are essential prerequisites for general success. Given Russia's specifics, counting on large-scale private investments in the social security system is unrealistic. Therefore Russia needs state-run programs for social security.

One of the most critical sectors in which the state should actively participate is health care, and its construction effort should include the large-scale production of Russian-engineered, state-of-the-art medical equipment. Russia's top industrial goals should likewise be to develop hardware and integrated production lines dedicated to supporting the complete agricultural processing cycle, providing people with reasonably priced foodstuffs, and implementing dietary schemes that meet contemporary health care requirements. Production of environmentally safe foodstuffs that satisfy the standards adopted in most West European countries should also be undertaken. A nationwide infrastructure (transportation, communications, etc.) development program could be an extremely powerful vehicle to help execute the whole health care plan. Russia's current national infrastructure badly needs to be updated as soon as possible, since it is also called upon to ensure the unity of our country primarily by maintaining full-scale cultural, economic, and financial links between the Far Eastern regions and the rest of Russia.

Russia is currently faced with a severe shortage of assorted transportation vehicles, means of communication, and television equipment. In domestic production plants and shipyards, large numbers of finished aircraft, ships, locomotives, and satellites sit unused. Even in the most developed market economies, the state invests either directly or indirectly in transport, communications, and power engineering as well as education, science, and culture, and the national budget has a flexible deficit ceiling. If the paper policies were pursued, government investment would eventually produce lower tariffs. State-initiated investments in infrastructure are by no means grants to loss-producing enterprises. Rather, such appropriations are certain to set things in motion and can be recouped by the state within a few years. By building up infrastructure, the state provides multiple incentives for the market to grow.

Russia's industrial policy should stipulate measures for creating powerful financial-industrial corporations able to compete as equal partners with the world economy's giants. This drive has been launched in Russia, including a humble contribution by this author, and it is now attracting companies from the "near abroad."

In discussing the creation of viable production companies and joint-stock financial-industrial groups, one must underscore that this is a long-term effort that is difficult to implement. No matter how irresistible the temptation might be at times, quick-fix solutions and hopes for a miracle must be abandoned. If appropriate long-term goals have been devised, the nation is accordingly activated, and the people believe that the country's strategy is being soundly charted, then society's most civic-minded segment must create the conditions in which the given tasks can be executed.

However, industrial giants alone cannot effectively build a booming economy and create an enduring social security network. There is an evident need to promote the growth of small and medium-sized entrepreneurial businesses with links to large production facilities and major financial-industrial structures. This trend, in fact, emerged in Russia in the late 1980s, when major production plants and design bureaus started to spawn small businesses.

The development of small and medium-sized businesses, integrated into Russia's comprehensive industrial vision, should be targeted to foster the growth of a solid middle stratum of the population, the "middle class," without which no solid democracy or developed domestic economic market can be built. Russia also requires a certain number of relatively apolitical technocrats, who, while engaged to consolidate the state, should espouse the tenets of cost-effectiveness and dedicate themselves to securing the best yields in industry and in the economy as a whole. In general, the rise of social classes and strata, as the great Russian historian V.O. Kliuchevsky so aptly remarked, is a "two-sided affair" [*dvoyakoe delo*] founded on political and economic bases, with the government working on top and economic conditions at the bottom. It is the middle class that is expected to be the source for increasing the Russian officers corps.

Russia's powerful national industrial base is the principal provider of defense equipment to adequately outfit the armed forces. Given fierce competition in the markets, civilian products have started to outclass comparable defense products in many industrialized nations. In the late 1980s, civilian technological advances in the United States and other developed countries increasingly began to be utilized for defense research, engineering, and production purposes, rather than vice versa.

The New Armed Forces for Russia

Five crucial points will be addressed about "building" the Russian armed forces ("building" is a better term than "reforming," which, like the term "converting," generally confuses the reader).

First, the military recruitment system should be altered. A gradual transition to a mixed recruitment system is a major element of the current effort to build the Russian armed forces. Unfortunately, many enlisted men do not yet meet the professional standards of the military. The entire Russian officers corps, including top-ranking officials, now serves on a contract basis, which represents a phenomenal shift. Admittedly, the state cannot always meet its commitments to members of the armed forces. Although the contract-based recruitment system is not yet fully recognized, it will certainly be understood within the next five years. Military officers now being signed up by the state are becoming more in tune with the civil society that is developing in Russia. In this regard, it is extremely important that the state should live up to its commitments.

Second, the military educational system should be improved. Russia has top-notch military academies with their own schools of thought and many world-class scholars and researchers, both uniformed and civilian. Those academies are especially valued by Russian officers because they provide not only excellent specialized training but also a good education in the humanities. However, many of Russia's lower-level military schools are very different. It seems that the time is ripe to expand the network of cadet, Suvorov, and Nakhimov schools, in which only one out of eight to ten applicants are enrolled. Opening more of such schools would be a crucial step not only for the army and navy but also for the whole of Russian society. They could be extremely instrumental in selecting the smartest and most energetic young men. Particular attention should be focused on training lower-level leaders in order to create a body of professional sergeants and master sergeants in field units, which would undergird the officers' leadership.

Third, the force structure and system of management should be modified. The Russian Ministry of Defense has inherited a tangled and unwieldy system of armed forces management. When it was activated, the new Russian Ministry of Defense had no time to alter management structures: the mission of the day was to avoid losing control over the armed forces. There was a point at which many were perplexed by the very idea that such a huge war machine equipped with nuclear, chemical, and vast numbers of conventional weapons and delivery vehicles might either disintegrate or lose its bearings in totally new political and ideological circumstances.

Reducing the number of combat forces and weapons now appears to be unavoidable. However, this task is not as simple as many who are not directly involved in it might be tempted to believe. Above all, this task requires major cuts in the troop management and supply structures, and these changes will necessarily demand tremendous expenditures.

The Russian Ministry of Defense has been evolving into the armed forces' political, administrative, and logistical management body, operating through a number of dedicated central structures and main commands. The country's armed forces are governed by the Ministry of Defense via the General Staff—the principal operational management agency. The General Staff is expected to manage troops through multi-service strategic commands by zones and functional areas. This kind of force structure will conform to the nature of future wars and armed conflicts. Depending on the specifics, the main commands of the armed forces will have administrative and operational management powers beyond those belonging directly to the General Staff.

Measures to reform combat forces and weapons should largely be carried out with due regard for the existing management structures. Incidentally, many planners propose radical reductions in the current levels of combat equipment at the fronts (the rationale is that trench warfare, in which frontal groupings of forces used to be part of the established command levels, is now a thing of the past), as well as alterations in the army, corps, division, and brigade-level command structures. The armed forces would mainly include armies (flotillas) and corps (squadrons) with actual war-fighting capabilities.

Strategic nuclear forces will remain the backbone of Russian deterrence; they are intended to prevent either a nuclear or large-scale conventional war against Russia. At the same time, tactical nuclear weapons, particularly air-launched ones, will also play a crucial role in deterring aggressors.

Fourth, the military's logistical system, which is a direct structural outgrowth of Russia's economic system, should be updated. In the Soviet era, the rigid centralized management style had been applied when, say, supplies from the Soviet Far East were transported to destinations in Ukraine via storage bases in the Moscow military district, and vice versa. In 1992–95, much of this was changed, and mandatory military acquisitions and deliveries are now more adequately distributed between the central structures and those of military districts, fleets, air forces, air defense units, and strategic missile forces. But most of the task remains to be completed. The new distribution system, which is less centralized, warrants better oversight of appropriations, and requires local pricing policies to be taken into consideration whenever products and services are involved.

Today, the military is becoming integrated in Russia's emerging market economy, with all kinds of positive and negative effects fully in evidence. Admittedly, the drawbacks are often fertile soil for the corruption that infests Russia.

Finally, military-to-industry links should be reviewed. In the Soviet era, nine industry-managing ministries, dedicated divisions in Gosplan (the State Planning Committee), the Commission for Military and Industry Matters with the Council of Ministers of the USSR, not to mention the relevant departments of the Central Committee of the Communist Party, operated as brokers between the nation's armed forces and industrial facilities. There had been instances when the old system made the military accept things they did not need. But then recipients of state prizes and

Hero of Socialist Labor awards included members of the armed forces. In the meantime, high-cost weapon systems, though not fully surged, would nonetheless be commissioned. There were numerous deferrals in infrastructure development projects, particularly in the navy. For example, having been accepted for active duty, the heavy missile cruiser *Kirov* required several years to be completely outfitted and become a fully combat-capable ship. In the air force, several aircraft types had similar experiences.

At present Russia is building the kind of military-industrial relationship that is generally practiced in all civilized countries. Companies and enterprises, their form of ownership irrelevant, have been increasingly doing business with customers within Ministry of Defense structures. To date, things have been far from perfect in this area. Military-industrial arrangements definitely need to be better researched and supervised, and cross-departmental oversight should be activated. The armed forces are also confronted with difficulties that come from the as-yet uncompleted restructuring of the nation's industries. Many industries continue to have design bureaus separated from their production facilities, the odd result being that those related agencies sometimes turn into rivals in world markets. Then, too, prospective purchasers of Russian defense products are often kept ignorant of whom they have to deal with.

On the whole, the building and reforming of the Russian armed forces has been set in motion, though progress has not yet been as fast or substantive as would be desirable.

History has given Russia only so much time to reform the military; it would be foolish to believe that Russia has all the time it needs. The greatest challenge to reform is the issue of funding. Unlimited resources authorized for defense would hardly speed up the reform, but the acute lack of funds that Russia is now experiencing surely serves to keep the whole reconstruction effort frozen. In general, it would only be right at this juncture to underscore the fact that building the Russian armed forces is the task not only for the Ministry of Defense, but for the nation as a whole.

The army is an instrument of state policy, since the military is a state institution. For hundreds of years, armies in various countries have also been used to carry out tasks related to domestic politics. But over time, the duties of the army, the police, the gendarmerie, and the national guard became more clearly defined. In today's world, in which many national armies have turned into massive forces, any "body movement" (*telodvizhenik*) displayed by a modern military force is viewed as a major event. In Russia and other nuclear-armed countries, the armed forces also have to shoulder the very special responsibility of safeguarding weapons of mass destruction and preventing their unauthorized use. The entire ideology of the military is predominantly aimed at driving back external aggression. Nonetheless, even in the industrialized nations, extreme domestic circumstances have occasionally demanded that the army should help the police and other forces to restore public order.

Unfortunately, in recent years various political forces have been attempting to appeal to the army and pull it in their direction. Obviously, that is a dangerous game. The army has a rather rigid and conservative culture, and it should embody the concept of stability both internally and nationally. The army is built around an ironclad framework of command levels in which the supreme command authority is clearly defined. This arrangement stems from the very nature of military forces.

A system of civilian management and supervision of the Russian armed forces is still being molded, but some critical components have already been put in place. The powers of the president of the Russian Federation as supreme commander-in-chief, as well as those of the government, have been enacted, and the role of the State Duma in devising the defense budget has also been delineated. However, a multitude of other questions relating to civilian oversight of the military remain to be tackled. The system of civilian oversight of the armed forces and other uniformed forces is needed not only for the sake of Russia's political stability, but also so that defense funds will be appropriated efficiently and fitting strategies for building the combat services will be drafted.

Index

ABM (Anti-Ballistic Missile) Treaty, 176, 183, 197
Abyssinia, 91
Academy of the General Staff, 19, 27, 50, 69
active means of defense, 174
Adaridi, N., 27
aftermath of nuclear war, 136
aggressive fascist states, 92
aircraft carriers, 159
air force. *See* aviation
air supremacy, 88–89
Akhromeyev, Sergei F., 134, 137, 142
Alafusov, 47–48
Aleksandrov, A.R., 79
Aleksandrov, V.V., 136
Alexander I, Emperor, 156
Alexander III, Tsar, 202
All-Russian General Headquarters, 68
Altfater, V.M., 14
America
  first strike potential, 182
  role in war scenarios, 84
  violates military-strategic parity, 144
  See also United States
Ammosov, S.N., 160
analyzing past wars, 100–104
Angola, 4
annexation in war, 108
Anti-Ballistic Missile (ABM) Treaty, 176, 183, 197
Anti-Comintern Pact, 91
anti-missile defense, 175

deployment, 176
anti-Soviet coalition, 82–85
anti-tank artillery in Great Patriotic War, 101
Arab-Israeli War, 129, 138
Arbatov, Alexei, 145
Arbatov, Georgy, 144
Argentine-British war, 138
Arkhangelsk, 96
armed forces system of management, 206–207
arms race, 127, 140, 141, 176
army motorization and mechanization, 88
artillery in Great Patriotic War, 101
art of war, 135, 155
Artsimovich, L.A., 182
atomic attack on Hiroshima and Nagasaki, 113–114
atomic blitzkrieg, 113
atomic submarines, 116
attrition strategy, 151
Aurora (naval cruiser), 78
Austria falls, 92
Austrian-Prussian War, 24
Austro-Hungarian Empire, General Staff of, 39
aviation
  importance of, 97
  in initial phase of war, 88–89
  and tanks support socialist mission, 90
Avksent'evsky, K.A., 16

Bagramyan, I.Kh., 42
Bagration, P., 156
ballistic missiles, 116
Barbarossa Operation, 166
Batitsky, P., 177
Belitsky, S.M., 160
Belli, V.A., 79
Bellingshausen, F., 130
Beneš, Edvard, 41
Beria, Lavrenty, 44
Bering, V., 129
Bernhardi, 52
besieged fortress, 66–67
Bialystok, 150
Big Soviet Encyclopedia (*Bol'shaya Sovetskaya entsiklopediya*), 36
bipolar configuration, 198
Biryuzov, S., 49, 122
Bismarck, 21, 24, 26
Black Sea Fleet, 78
Blagovolin, S., 145
Blukher, V.K., 16, 41, 90
Bol'shaya Sovetskaya entsiklopediya (Big Soviet Encyclopedia), 36
Bolsheviks, 33
Borisov, V.E., 27
bourgeoisie
  and proletariat struggle, 64–66
  types of, 84
Brest, 150
Brezhnev, Leonid, 55, 129, 182
Britain. *See* Great Britain
British-Argentine war, 138
Brown, Harold, 181
Brusilov, Aleksei A., 15–16
Brusilov, Alexis, 68–69
Brusilov breakthrough, 15
Budennyi, Semen M., 17, 43–44, 75–76
Budker, G.I., 182
building Russian armed forces, 205–209

Cannae (battle), 155
Cannae model, 149
capitalism vs. proletarianism, 64–65
Carter administration, 140
Caspian Sea, 83
Catherine the Great, 129
Cavalry Congress, 75

cavalry
  role in future wars, 74–77
  supporters, 75–77
  units, 98
Central Powers, 152
Chelomei, V.N., 182
chemical weapons, 138
Cherednichenko, M., 125
Chernavin, V.N., 131, 143
Chesma (battle), 130
Chiang Kai-Shek's forces, 70
Chicherin, Georgi, 80
Chile, 4
China and Soviet Union relationship breakdown, 125
civilian management of armed forces, 209
civilian specialists contribute to political-military thought, 144–145
civilian strategists, 134–135
class enemies, 66
Clausewitz, Carl von, 22–24, 53
  on integral military leadership, 39
  On War, 22, 154
  waging war, 152
Clausewitz's formula modified in 1980s, 58–61
cold steel doctrine, 28–29
Cold War, 111, 200
collapse of capitalist system projected, 114–115, 117
commissar's right to control, 12
Committee of Soviet Scientists for Peace and Against the Nuclear Threat, 141–142, 183
Commonwealth of Independent States (CIS), 6
Communist International (Comintern), 64
Communist Party
  praised for military achievements, 55
  principles, 117
  See also Party
communists support wars of national liberation, 125
comparative troop strengths in eastern and western countries, 81
composition of mechanized corps, 162–163

conventional war in the nuclear age, 136–140
conventional war vs. nuclear war, 132–140
counteroffensive battles, 170
critics of revolutionary military councils, 18–19
cultivation of Russian language, 202
cult of personality (Stalin), 37, 39–40, 172
Czechoslovakia, 92
  fall of, 93

Danzig corridor, 82
debates on offensive and defensive strategies in 1920s, 147–157
deep battle, 160–163, 177–180
deep operations, 160–163
defense
  as a means to launch a counteroffensive, 153–157
  and offense defined tactically and strategically, 174
  and offense in early 1980s, 180–183
  in strategic context, 150
defense conversion policies, 195–196
defense industrial complex, 195–196
Delbrück (military theoretician), 151
Demidkov, G.I., 178–179
demilitarization in late 1980s, 6–7
Denikin, Anton I., 16
Desert Storm, 198
destruction strategy, 87, 151
détente, 132
dialectics of defense and offense in the nuclear sphere, 175–177
disarmament, 157–160
disarmament policies of capitalist states, 80–81
Dnieper line, 83
domestic culture, 6
Dumenko, B.M., 17
Dushenov, K.I., 78
Dzerzhinsky, Feliks, 67
Dzhordzhadze, I.I., 178–179

effects of technology on conventional warfare, 139–140
Eideman, R.P., 16, 88

Eighteenth Party Congress, 92
Eighth Party Congress, 12, 14
Eikhe, T.Kh., 16
Elchaninov, A.G., 27
Eleventh Party Congress, 148
  definition of unified military doctrine, 32–34
emerging opportunities in Russian national security, 199
Emilius, Paul, 155
Empress Maria (battleship), 47
encirclement, 171
Engels, Friedrich, 13, 71
enhanced role of offensive operations in 1960s, 172–175
Entente, 63
entrepreneurial businesses, 204
era of pacifism, 157
Estonia, 81–82
European and Japanese troop strengths, 81–82
events leading to World War II, 91–93
evolution of unified military doctrine, 26–38
export of revolution, 63–65

Far Eastern and Zabaikals fronts offensive missions, 166
fascist bloc, 95
feasibility of destroying German troops, 99
Fed'ko, I.F., 16
fiftieth anniversary of Soviet armed forces, 124
fighting a surprise attack, 122–124
fighting on two fronts, 105–106
Filatov, 163
Finland, 81–82, 85. *See* Soviet-Finnish War
Finnish Democratic Republic (FDR), 93–94
five types of war, 126
Five-Year Plan for reconstruction of Red Army, 161
five-year plans, 73–74
flexible response strategy, 124, 125
forecast of World War II, 95–96
former tsarist officers in Red Army, 13–17

formulation of national goals, 202
France, 81–83
Franco, Francisco, 91
Franco-Prussian War, 24, 90
French military doctrine, 30–31
frontier warfare, 109
frontline armies, 97–98
front line movement, 102
Frunze, Mikhail V., 29–30
  on besieged fortress, 66–67
  on class enemies, 65–66
  defines unified military doctrine, 32–33, 36
  on German military doctrine, 30
  military reforms, 36
  offensive strategy proponent, 147–150
  as "Soviet Clausewitz," 29
  on strategic cavalry, 74–75
  two dimensions of military doctrine, 30
Frunze Military Academy, 48, 50, 161, 170
future war probabilities and threats to Soviet security, 63–146
  continuity and revolution in 1980s, 132–146
  Great Patriotic War, 98–111
  initial phase of war
  and surprise attacks, 122–124
  theory, 86–89
  in late 1940s and early 1950s, 111–115
  local and limited wars, 124–126
  maneuverability and strategic cavalry role, 74–77
  Nazi era political and military situation, 89–98
  new role of the navy, 129–132
  political-military conditions in late 1950s, 116–122
  political-military situation
    during détente and stagnation, 126–129
    in late 1920s and early 1930s, 80–85
  revolutionary and national wars, 65–74
  role of the navy, 77–80
future wars as foreseen by Svechin, 70–73

future war scenarios, 70–73, 82–83, 172–173

G-7 (Group of Seven), 203
Gai, G.D., 16
Gamarnik, Ia.B., 12
Gareyev, Makhmut A., 55–56, 137
General Conference for the Reduction and Limitation of Armaments, 89, 157–160
genius of Stalin, 44–46
Genoa Conference, 80
German aggression (pre–World War II), 90–93
German Democratic Republic, 171
German military
  doctrine, 30–32
  leaders, 21–22
  machine, 22
German-Polish War, strategy of destruction, 102–103
German preparedness in Great Patriotic War, 109–111
German strategy of destruction, 102–103
Germany, 82
  as an adversary, 89
  establishes officer training in Soviet Union, 31–32
  and ties with Poland, 92
Ginzburg, A.S., 136
global political-military situation, 80–82
Golikov, F.I., 45, 110
Golitsyn, G.S., 136
Golovko, A.E., 45
Golushkevich, V.S., 44
Gorbachev, Mikhail, 58, 140–141
Gorbatov, A.V., 41
Gorodovikov, O.I., 17
Gorshkov, Sergei, 131
Govorov, L.A., 42
Grachev, N., 59–60
Great Britain, 81–84
great devourers of space (*prostranstvo*), 156
Great Patriotic War, 98–111
  bears out Svechin's forecasts, 156
  initial strategic operations, 165–169

mistakes in, 172
offense and defense issues post-war, 169–172
Soviet command revised objectives, 167–168
Soviet victory, 3
See also World War II
Grechko, A.A., 128–129
Grishanov, V., 130–131
ground forces, 177–180
Gusev (Drabkin), S.I., 12, 33

Hannibal, 149, 155
Hart, B.H. Liddell, 158
health care sector, 203
Heydrich, Reinhard, 41
highly precise conventional weapons, 138
high-tech sector, 203
Hindenburg, Paul von, 21
Hiroshima and Nagasaki bombing, 113–114
Hitler
  and chemical weapons, 138
  and Czechoslovakia, 92
  imperialist plans, 90–91
Hoover, Herbert, 158

ICBMs (intercontinental ballistic missiles), 175
Impact of Stalin's Purges (1937–1938) on Military Command Personnel (table), 43
Imperial Guard, 37
imperialist camp, 118
imperialist states plot aggression, 117–118
Imperialist War, 89. See also World War I
Imperial Russia, 4–5
increased militarism under Reagan, 141–143
Indonesia, 4
industrial policy, 204
information technology development, 197–198
infrastructure development program, 204

initial phase of war, 122–124
  in the 1960s, 123–124
  theory, 86–89
initial strategic operations for Great Patriotic War, 165–169
  Soviet command revised objectives, 167–168
Institute of Military History, 58
Institute of USA and Canada Studies (ISKAN), 145
integral military leader concept, 38–40
intercontinental ballistic missiles (ICBMs), 175
"International Life" (journal), 59
invasion army, 103
invasion group tactics, 97
Isakov, I.S., 79
Israeli-Arab war, 129, 138
Isserson, G.S., 7, 101–103, 110, 160
Italian aggression, 91
Italy, 81
  used toxic agents, 91
Ivanov, S., 125
Izrael, Iu.A., 136

Japan, 81, 89
Japanese aggression, 91
Japanese press overstates effects of atomic bomb attack, 114
Julius Caesar–class battleships, Italian, 164

Kakurin, Nikolai, 69
Kalinovsky, A.K., 160
Kamenev, Serge S., 14, 41
Kapitsa, Pyotr, 135
Kapustin Yar proving ground, 175
Karaganov, Sergei, 145
Khalkhin-Gol, 42, 70, 100, 104
Khrushchev, Nikita S., 46–50
  administration, 117–119
  defines three categories of war, 124–125
  formulated military policy, 46
  future vision of war, 117–118
  on ICBMs, 175
  initial phase of war, 117–118
  on modern warfare, 117

Khrushchev, Nikita *(continued)*
  praised for modern military doctrine, 49
  troop reduction, 118
  visits United States, 118
  on warships, 118
  and Zhukov, 45–47
Khrushchev era of politics and military leaders, 46–53
Kiev, 150
Kingston-McCloughry, Edgar J., 53
Kirov (missile cruiser), 207
Kirov, Sergei M., 12
Kirshin, Yu.Ya., 59
Kisun'ko, G., 175
Kliuchevsky, V.O., 205
Kokoshin, Andrei A., 145
Kola Gulf, 45
Kolchak, Alexander, 29
Kon, F.Ia., 67
Kondratkov, T., 54
Konev, I.S., 42, 45
Konstantinov, B.P., 182
Korean War, 111–112
Kork, A.A., 14
Kornilov, Lavr, 16
Korolev, Sergei P., 116
Kortunov, Andrei, 145
Kostyayev, F.V., 14
Kosygin, A.N., 176
Kozlov, Svyatoslav N., 54
Krivtsov, E., 27
Kronshtadt mutiny, 78
Krusenstern, I., 130
Krylov, N., 123
Kuibyshev Military Engineering Academy, 55
Kulik, G.I., 101
Kulikov, V.G., 126, 141
Kulish, B., 51
Kun, Bela, 12
Kurasov, V., 46
Kursk (battle), 40, 168–169, 173
Kutuzov, 156, 170
Kuusinen, Otto, 93–94
Kuznetsov, N.G., 47, 79, 164

lack of proletariat support from other countries, 99

Lake Khasan armed conflict, 70, 92, 99, 104
Langovoi, A., 160
Lapchinsky, A.N., 88, 96, 160
Latvia, 81, 82
Lazarev, M., 130
League of Nations, 158
Lebedev, P.P., 14
Leer, G.A., 87
Lenin, V.I.
  adds to Clausewitz's war views, 23
  Marxist perspective on war, 23
  on New Economic Policy, 64
  praises former tsarist officers, 13
  proletarianism vs. capitalism, 64–65
  thesis on world politics, 64–65
  three relationships between politics and armed struggle, 23
  on war, 71
  "war is a continuation of politics," 34
Leningrad, 72, 93, 96
lessons of warfare, 101
Leval, Jules Louis, 21
limited nuclear war concept, 133–135, 141
Lisyansky, Yu., 130
Lithuania, 93
Lobov, Vladimir, 145
local and limited wars, 124–126
localized armed conflicts involving the Soviet Union, 70–71
Lomov, N.A., 51, 122, 124
loss of purged officers impacts Great Patriotic War, 110
Ludendorff, Erich, 21, 25, 34
Ludri, I.M., 77–78

MacArthur, Douglas, 115
Maginot Line, 159
Main Military Council, 103–104
Malenkov, Georgy, 115
Malik, Ya., 114
Malinovsky, Rodion Ya., 42, 48–50, 175
  military power to deter United States, 119
  on Soviet superiority, 120–122
  on United States' vulnerabilities, 120–121

management relationship between policy and strategy, 55
Manchuria, 157
maneuverability in future wars, 74–77
Mao Zedong, 5
marketing Russian products, 203
Markhlevsky, Iu.Iu., 67
marshals of tank forces, 138–139
Marxist-Leninist ideology, 147
Marxist theory, 144
massive retaliation strategy, 124
McNamara, Robert, 181
mechanized corps, 100–101, 162–163
Mekhlis, L., 100
Melikov (Svechin disciple), 148, 151
Meretskov, K.A., 41–42, 106
middle class development, 6
Middle East, 126
Mikhnevich, N.P., 20, 152
militarism, inherent feature of imperialism, 144
Military Academy of the General Staff, 20, 51
military
 buildup, 2–3
 command purges, 40–44
 doctrine in the United States, 29
 educational system, 205–206
Military Encyclopedic Dictionary, 134
Military Herald (Voennyi vestnik), 35
military-industrial relationship, 208
military leader concept, 38–40
military leaders in the Khrushchev era, 46–53
military opposition, 14
military logistical system, 207
military recruitment system, 205
military specialists, 114–115
 analyses, 103–104
military-strategic parity with U.S., 57, 197
military strategy as component of doctrine, 51
military superiority downplayed, 133
military technology, 56
military-to-industry links, 207–208
Miliutin, Dmitry, 36
Minsk, 150
Mironov, F.K., 14

MIRVs (multiple independently targeted reentry vehicles), 177
mistakes in Great Patriotic War, 172
Miyasnikov, G.A., 64
mobilization
 issues due to size, 111
 leads to war, 87–88
 readiness, 128–129
Moiseyev, M.A., 142, 163
Moiseyev, N.N., 136
Molotov, Vyacheslav, 94, 114
Molotov-Ribbentrop Pact, 110
Moltke the elder, Helmuth von, 21, 24–25, 34, 154
Mongolia, 6, 42
Mozambique, 4
Mozhaisk strategy, 151
Muklevich, Romuald A., 20, 79
Multiple independently targeted reentry vehicles (MIRVs), 177
Munich conference, 93
Murmansk, 96

Nagasaki and Hiroshima bombing, 113–114
Napoleon, 31
 power of an army, 152
 Russians retreat, 156
Napoleon's Egyptian campaign, 70
national and revolutionary wars, 65–74
national egoism, 200–205
NATO, 124, 142, 198–199
Naval Academy, 79
naval
 achievements, 129–130
 forces questioned, 78–80
 independence, 77–78
 strategy
  Stalin's offensive, 164–165
 warfare
  types of craft needed, 79–80
Navarino (battle), 130
navy
 attains higher status in 1960s, 129
 as a deterrent, 132
 in a future war, 77–80
 independence from army, 77–78

navy *(continued)*
  mission in 1980s, 183
  post–Great Patriotic War, 171–172
  See also tsarist navy
navy's mission, 120
  in World War II, 166
navy's new role, 129–132
navy's role in 1950s, 120
Nazi era political-military situation, 89–98
New Economic Policy (NEP), 2, 64
new generation of Soviet military leaders, 42–44
new methods of warfare ignored in Great Patriotic War plan, 109
Neznamov, A.A., 27–28, 33, 148, 152, 168
  on military doctrine, 28
  on strategic defense, 153
Nikolayevskaya Military Academy, 15, 20, 27, 30
Nikolayevich, Prince Konstanin, 36
Nimitz, A.B., 15
no-first-use pledge, 180–181
nonaggressive democratic states, 92
nonoffensive defense, 174
non-support of the proletariat in wars, 99–100
Northern Fleet, 78
"Notes on the Mobilization in Germany" (Intelligence Department), 110
no victory in nuclear war, 140
Novikov, A.A., 45
Novobranets, V.A., 110
Novorossiisk (battleship), 47
nuclear deterrence, 4, 197
nuclear submarine, serial production, 120
nuclear war, continuation and instrument of policy, 53–55
nuclear war vs. conventional war, 132–140
nuclear weapons
  impact on strategy, 3–4
  and relationship between policy and strategy, 53–55
  suggested in Korean War, 115
nuclear winter theory, 136

Obysov, I.P., 161
Ocean (*Okean*) (naval exercise), 130–131
October Revolution, 1, 27
offense and defense
  defined tactically and strategically, 174
  in early 1980s, 180–183
offense and defense in early 1980s, 180–183
  no-first-use pledge, 180–181
  Strategic Defense Initiative (SDI), 141, 181–183
offense and defense in Soviet military strategy, 147–192
  background debates in 1920s, 147–157
  development of deep battle theory, 177–180
  dialectics in the nuclear sphere, 175–177
  in early 1980s, 180–183
  enhanced offensive operations in 1960s, 172–175
  General Conference for the Reduction and Limitation of Armaments, 157–160
  immediately after Great Patriotic War, 169–172
  initial strategic operations pre–World War II, 165–169
  new relationships and defense sufficiency, 184–192
  Stalin's naval strategy offense, 164–165
  theory of deep battle or deep operations, 160–163, 177–180
offense and defense issues after Great Patriotic War, 169–172
offense in Stalin's naval strategy, 164–165
offensive operations in 1960s, 172–175
offensive orientation of Soviet military leaders in World War II, 167
Ogarkov, Nikolai V., 55–57, 134–135
  international tensions diminished, 142
  questions new conventional weapons, 138

Ogorodnikov, F., 27
Okean (Ocean) (naval exercise), 130–131
OMG (Operational Mobile Groups), 179
Operational Mobile Groups (OMG), 179
Operation Barbarossa, 166
Order No. 55, 112
Ordzhonikidze, Sergo, 12

Panzer tanks, 101
partisan sentiments, 17
Party, on world revolution, 63–65
Party Congresses
  Eighteenth, 92
  Eleventh, 148
  Seventeenth, 76, 89–90
  Sixteenth, 74
  Twentieth, 115, 121, 172
  Twenty-first, 120
  Twenty-second, 119, 175
  Twenty-seventh, 141
Party goals in 1939, 93
patriotic sentiments during Soviet-Polish War, 68–69
Pavlenko, N.G., 16, 44
Pavlov, A.V., 16
Pavlovsky, I.G., 120, 132–133, 177
  importance of tank forces, 138–139
peaceful coexistence
  Lenin, 64–65
  Tukhachevsky, 66
peacetime initial phase of war, 96–97
Peking leadership, 127
People's Republic of China, 127
perestroika (reconstruction), 132, 143
permanently operating factors of war, 112–113, 116
Peter the Great, 129, 149–150
Petrovsky, D., 35
plan for strategic deployment, 105–107
  See also Great Patriotic War plan
Poland, 81–85. *See also* Soviet-Polish War
Polaris submarines, 120
polemical strategy (*polemostrategiya*), 38

policy and nuclear war, 53–55
policy and strategy in 1980s, 55–58
policy and strategy relationship in Soviet military doctrine, 11–61
  Clausewitz's formula modified, 58–61
  evolution of unified military doctrine, 26–38
  genius of Stalin, 44–46
  integral military leader, 38–40
  during Khrushchev era, 46–53
  new generation of military leaders, 40–44
  nuclear weapons and, 53–55
  purges of 1937–38, 40–44
  revolutionary military councils and political commissars, 12–19
  Soviet art of war, 44–46
  supremacy of policy over strategy, 19–26
policy defines political mission of war, 52
policy's dominance over military strategy, 56
Polish-German War. *See* German-Polish War
Polish Kingdom, 68
Polish-Soviet War. *See* Soviet-Polish War
Polish threat of 1920, 15
political department (*politotdely*), 12
political-military conditions
  future of tanks, 119–120
  imperialism, 117–118
  Soviet superiority in military development, 121–122
  strategic rocket forces (SRF), 116
  troop reduction, 118
political-military situation during détente and stagnation, 126–129
  United States-Soviet détente, 126–127
political role of nuclear weapons, 59–60
politics in the Khrushchev era, 46–53
politotdely (political department), 12
Poltava model, 149–150
Popov, V.M., 54
post–Great Patriotic War toast by Stalin, 169

potential enemies of Soviet Union, 80, 85
potential World War II enemies, 95–96
Povaly, M., 52, 124
praising Soviet armed forces, 120–122
preemptive attack, 181
premobilization period of war, 86–87
preparatory operations of war, 87
present-day national security issues, 194–200
pre–World War II concepts of initial strategic operations, 165–169
  shock group formations, 166
Pripyat River, 96
probable adversaries (post–Great Patriotic War), 111
Proektor, Daniil, 60
proletarianism vs. capitalism, 64–65
proletarian state defeat, 84–85
proletariat strengthens armies, 67
proponents of defensive strategy, 148–150, 152–156
proponents of offensive strategy, 147–148, 150–153
prostranstvo (great devourers of space), 156
Provisional Revolutionary Committee of Poland, 67
Prukhnyak, E.Ia., 67
Prussia, 22
Prussian-Austrian War, 24
public consciousness about wars, 145
Punic Wars, 155
purges of 1937–38, 40–44
  compared to Germany's, 3
Pushkin, Alexander, 202

qualitative disarmament, 158–160

Rattel, N.I., 14
reactionary forces in the west, 143
Reagan administration, 57
Reagan, Ronald, 181
  Star Wars, 181–182
Red Army, 31, 65, 93
  birth date, 11
  cavalry, 75–77
  decisions based on Spanish Civil War, 100–101

leaders, on world revolution, 63–65
loses prestige after Soviet-Finnish War, 40
mission, 65, 67, 73–74, 83, 99
and navy, 77–78
purges by Stalin, 40–42, 43 (table)
and Soviet-Polish War, 8, 67
technological gap, 73
theory of strategy and management, 39
Red Fleet, 77, 93
redoubts, 150
reduction and limitation of arms, 157–160
reduction of Soviet armed forces
  by Gorbachev, 143
  by Khrushchev, 118
relationship between policy and nuclear war, 58–60
resources squandered on three empires, 5
restricted use of nuclear weapons, 125–126
retreat and defense in 1941–42, 169–170
revolutionary and national wars, 65–74
revolutionary military councils, 12–19
Revolutionary Military Council, 73, 77, 96, 161–162
revolution by bayonets (*revolyutsiya na shtykakh*), 66–67
Rhineland, 91
Richelieu, Cardinal, 202
Rokossovsky, Konstantin K., 41–44
Romania, 81–85
Romanov monarchy, 13
Rotmistrov, P.A., 49, 123–125
Russia as a military superpower, 197
Russia joins in global competition, 195
Russian armies retreat in Napoleonic War, 156
Russian Civil War, 84
  description of, 2, 11–12
  strategic cavalry, 74
  See also civil war
Russian colonies, as war rewards, 84
Russian Federation, 4, 193, 195

Russian military strategists, expertise lost, 7–9
Russian national goals, 200–205
Russian navigators, 129
Russia's national security and military power, 193–209
  building national egoism, 200–205
  new armed forces, 205–209
  present-day issues, 194–200
Rybalko, 45
Rychagov, P.V., 41

St. Petersburg Technical Institute, 29
Salmanov, G.I., 138
Samsonov's army, 103, 153
Sary Shagan proving ground, 175
Scharnhorst-class, German battle cruisers, 164
Schellenberg, Walter, 41
Schlieffen, Alfred von, 24, 52
screen forces, 86
SDI (Strategic Defense Initiative), 141, 181–183
second Cold War, 132
Second Punic War, 149
Sedyakin, A.I., 160
Seventeenth Party Congress, 76, 90
Shabanov, V.M., 139–140, 182–183
Shaposhnikov, Boris M., 14, 50
  on bourgeoisie, 85
  deep battle proponent, 160
  identifies potential World War II enemies, 95
  on integral military leadership, 39
  on mobilization, 87–88
  supports cavalry, 75
  World War II on two fronts, 95–96
Shilovsky, E.A., 160
Shilyag, V., 54
shipbuilding program, 164
shock groups in World War II, 166
Shtemenko, S.M., 45, 119
Simonov, Konstantin, 169
Sino-Soviet split, 5, 125
Sixteenth Party Congress, 74
Sklyansky, E.M., 15
Smilga, I.T., 66
Smirnov, M.V., 179
Smirnov, V.M., 14

Smushkevich, Ia.V., 41
socialist and capitalist harmony, 66
social science evolution, 8
sociopolitical dimension of military doctrine, 56
Sokolovsky, V.D., 45, 49–50, 125
Sokolov, S.L., 140
Sorokin, Ivan, 17
southwestern sector deployment in Great Patriotic War, 107–108
Soviet art of war, 44–46
Soviet atomic weapons, 115
Soviet battleships
  Kronshtadt-class heavy cruisers, 164
  Soviet Belorussia (*Sovetskaya Belorussiya*), 164
  Soviet Russia (*Sovetskaya Rossiya*), 164
  Soviet Ukraine (*Sovetskaya Ukraina*), 164
  Soviet Union (*Sovetskii Soyuz*), 164
Soviet Belorussia, 151
Soviet-Chinese Nonaggression Treaty, 91
Soviet dependence on defense industry, 196
Soviet-Finnish War, 40, 70, 93–94, 104
  demonstrates non-support of proletariat, 99–100
Soviet foreign policy, post–World War II, 4
Soviet-German Nonaggression Pact, 98, 105
Soviet miscalculations in Great Patriotic War, 111
Soviet navy. *See* navy; tsarist navy
Soviet no-first-use pledge, 180–181
Soviet plan for Great Patriotic War, 105–108
Soviet-Polish War, 67–70, 74, 94
Soviet security threats and probability of future war, 63–146
  continuity and revolution in 1980s, 132–146
  Great Patriotic War approaches, 98–111
initial phase of war
  and surprise attacks, 122–124
  theory, 86–89

Soviet security threats and probability of future war *(continued)*
  in late 1940s and early 1950s, 111–115
  local and limited wars, 124–126
  maneuverability in a future war, 74–77
  Nazi era, political-military situation, 89–98
  new role of the navy, 129–132
  political-military conditions in late 1950s, 116–122
  political-military situation during détente and stagnation, 126–129
  in 1920s and 1930s, 80–85
  revolutionary and national wars, 65–74
  role of the navy, 77–80
Soviets underestimate German preparedness and strength in Great Patriotic War, 109–111
Soviet tactics in overtaking countries, 94
Soviet Ukraine, 151
Soviet Union
  controls Finland, 93–94
  homeland of the world proletariat, 99
  and nuclear blackmail, 57
  troop strengths, 81
Soviet Union's potential adversaries, 127
space-based anti-missile system, 182
Spanish Civil War, 91, 104
  pushed Stalin to build up navy, 164
Stalin, Josef, 12, 44–46, 89, 100, 169
  on bourgeoisie politicians, 89
  cult of personality, 37, 39–40, 172
  and Eighteenth Party Congress, 92
  feasibility of destroying German troops, 99
  inaugurated shipbuilding program, 164
  integral military leader, 39–40
  as a military genius, 45–46
  permanently operating factors of war, 112–113
  protects USSR's vital resources, 108
  purges Tukhachevsky, 40–41

Sixteenth Party Congress, 73–74
ten strikes, 170
unprepared for World War II, 40
war of engines, 76
Stalin's dictatorship, 40–41
Stalin's purges of Red Army, 40–44
State Duma, 209
state socialism, 194
Stenchikov, G.L., 136
Stepanov, 47–48
Steppe front, 168
Stern, G.M., 41
strategic and tactical issues, 102–103
strategic approaches to future wars based on World War I and Russian Civil War, 65
strategic defense concept, 154–155
Strategic Defense Initiative (SDI), 141, 181–183
strategic defense in modern warfare, 173–174
strategic offensive operations, 170–171
strategic options in nuclear war, 54
strategic rocket forces (SRF), 116
strategic stability to avert war, 141–142
strategic surprise, German assault on Poland, 102–103
strategy and policy in 1980s, 55–58
strategy and policy relationship in Soviet military doctrine
  See policy and strategy relationship in Soviet military doctrine
strategy of attrition, 71–72, 151
strategy of destruction, 71–72, 87, 102–103, 151
struggle for the straits, 79–80
supremacy of policy over strategy, 19–26
Supreme Court of the Military Collegium, 48
surprise attack, 122–124
Svechin, Aleksandr A., 7–8, 50, 72, 96, 168
  advocates defensive strategy, 148–149
  examines defense and offense together, 153–157
  on future wars, 70–73

on German military machine in World War I, 31
initial phase of war, 86–87
military career and publications, 19–21
on offensive and defensive strategies, 153–157
politics over strategy views, 26
premobilization period, 86
revolutionary war not likely, 70
on role of general staffs, 26
Soviet Union technologically behind the west, 83
strategy of attrition, 71–72
on studying strategy, 25–26
Svechin and Tukhachevsky opposing views, 19, 21
Svechin school of military thought, 84, 150, 154, 166
Sweden, 82, 85
Swedish army, 149–150

tactical and strategic plans, 171
Talensky, N., 113
tanks
  and aviation support socialist mission, 90
  in nuclear age, 119–120
  reconsidered in modern warfare, 129
  under Khrushchev, 119–120
targets of anti-Soviet coalition, 82–83
technological gap in Red Army, 73
technology impacts conventional warfare, 139–140
Tekhachevsky, 160
Telegin, N.F., 45
ten strikes of Stalin, 170
Terrentius, 155, 168
territories of former Soviet Union, 194–195
terrorism, 193
theory of deep battle or deep operations, 160–163, 177–180
thermonuclear war as a crime, 57
third world war predictions, 114–117
threat assessments to Soviet security, 63–146
three-dimensional battle concept, 178–179

three relationships between politics and armed struggle, 23
Timoshenko, S.K., 17, 103–104, 106, 109
toast by Stalin, 169
Tolbukhin, F.I., 42
Tolly, Barclay de, 156
Tomin, N.D., 17
Transcaucasia nationality issues, 82
threats to Soviet Security, 111–115
Treaty of Versailles, 31
trench warfare, 206
Triandofilov, V.K., 83, 160–162
troop reductions in 1960, 118
troop strengths, 82
Trotsky, Leon, 12–13, 33–36
tsarist
  fleet, 77
  military theory ignored, 100
  navy, 77, 78, 165 (see also navy)
  officers, defense over strategy, 152
  officers in Red Army, 13–17
  Russia's cavalry force, 75–76
Tsar Nicholas I, 5
Tsar Nicholas II, 27
Tukhachevsky, Mikhail N., 16, 19, 24, 34, 50, 83
  blames Stalin for military failures, 41
  clashes with Voroshilov, 38
  criticizes Svechin, 72–73, 151
  on frontline armies, 97–98
  offensive advocate of strategy of destruction, 150–151
  offers polemical strategy, 38
  revolution by bayonets, 66
  supports cavalry, 76
  threat assessment, 90–91
Turenne, 31
types of bourgeoisie, 84

Uborevich, I.P., 16, 28, 160
UHF electronics, 203
unified military doctrine for the Red Army, 26–38
unintentional, accidental nuclear war, 57
United Nations, 193, 198

United States, 82, 120
  aggressive forces and nuclear weapons, 59–60
  main military threat to Soviet Union, 117
  and nuclear blackmail, 57
  troop strengths, 81
  See also America
United States and British imperialism, 111
United States imperialism, 126
United States–Soviet détente, 126–127, 132
United States successor of German fascism, 111
United States' vulnerabilities, 120–121
Unshlikht, I.S., 66, 67
Urals, 72
U.S. and Soviet physicians on aftermath of nuclear war, 136
U.S. Civil War, 130
use of chemical weapons, 91, 99
U.S. military buildup (1980s), 142–143
Ustinov, Dmitry, 133, 180

Varennikov, V.I., 177
Varfalameyev, N.E., 160
Vasilevsky, Alexander M., 31–32, 42, 45, 106–107
  at Main Military Council, 104
  proponent of strategic defense at battle of Kursk, 168–169
  Stalin and World War II, 40
Vatsetis, I.I., 14, 28–29
Vatutin, N.F., 107
Velikhov, E.P., 135, 182–183
Ventsov, S.I., 86, 96, 160
Verkovsky, A.I., 7, 148–150, 168
victory by traditional war methods, 133
Vietnam, 126
Volkogonov, Dmitry A., 11
Voronov, N., 45
Voroshilov, Kliment Y., 12, 36–38, 40, 80–82, 162
  analyzed global political-military situation, 80
  clashed with Tukhachevsky, 38
  created Stalin's cult of personality, 37
  on Mozhaisk strategy, 151
  services to the nation, 46
  on Red cavalry, 76
  supported Frunze on unified military doctrine, 33
  belittled former tsarist officers, 16
  Voroshilov and Tukhachevsky clash, 38
Voroshilov Military Academy, 137

war becomes obsolete in nuclear age, 59
war mobilization, 86–88
war of engines, 76
war on two fronts, 90, 95–96
war probabilities. *See* future war probabilities and threats to Soviet security
Warsaw Treaty Organization, 6, 199
wars of national liberation, 124–125
Wehrmacht, 3, 100–101, 110, 150, 168
western assessments of the aftereffects of nuclear war, 128
White Army, 13, 15–16, 29, 63
Workers' and Peasants' Army, 68, 162
working people of all countries, 93
world revolution debates, 64
World War I
  initial phase of war, 86
  mobilization, 86–87
World War II
  Directive No. 3, 167
  initial strategic operations, 165–169
  offensive orientation of military leaders, 167
  Soviet strategic defense neglected, 168
World War II shock groups, 166
Wrangel, Baron, 15–16, 29

Yakimychev, A.M., 79
Yakovlev, A.N., 144
Yakubovsky, I., 124
Yanushkevich, R.R., 27
Yazov, Dmitry, 133, 140, 142
Yegor'ev, A., 160
Yegoriev, V.N., 14
Yegorov, A.I., 14, 41, 96–97, 160–161

Yeremenko, A.I., 42, 170
Yevseyev, A.I., 137
Yurpol'sky, I.I., 178–179
Yushkov, 75

Zaionchkovsky, A.M., 148
Zaionchkovsky, L., 7, 27
Zakharov, M.V., 50, 104
Zaporozhets, A.I., 99
Zav'yalov, I., 175
Zhdanov, Andrei A., 99–101
Zhlob, D.P., 17

Zhukov Georgy K., 42–45, 107–111
  and Directive No. 3, 167
  and Khrushchev, 46–47
  at Main Military Council, 104
  proponent of strategic defense at Kursk, 168–169
  Soviet miscalculations in Great Patriotic War, 111
Zhukov's persecution by Stalin, 44–45
Zhurkin, Vitaly, 134–135, 145
Zodenstern, von, 109

The Robert and Renée Belfer Center for Science and International Affairs

Graham T. Allison, Director
John F. Kennedy School of Government
Harvard University
79 JFK Street, Cambridge MA 02138
(617) 495-1400

The Belfer Center for Science and International Affairs (BCSIA) is the hub of research, teaching, and training in international security affairs, environmental and resource issues, and science and technology policy at Harvard's John F. Kennedy School of Government. The Center's mission is to provide leadership in advancing policy-relevant knowledge about the most important challenges of international security and other critical issues where science, technology, and international affairs intersect.

BCSIA's leadership begins with the recognition of science and technology as driving forces transforming international affairs. The Center integrates insights of social scientists, natural scientists, technologists, and practitioners with experience in government, diplomacy, the military, and business to address these challenges. The Center pursues its mission in four complementary research programs:

- The International Security Program (ISP) addresses the most pressing threats to U.S. national interests and international security.

- The Environment and Natural Resources Program (ENRP) is the locus of Harvard's interdisciplinary research on resource and environmental problems and policy responses.

- The Science, Technology, and Public Policy (STPP) program analyzes ways in which science and technology policy influence international security, resources, environment, and development, and such cross-cutting issues as technological innovation and information infrastructure.

- The Strengthening Democratic Institutions (SDI) project catalyzes support for three great transformations in Russia, Ukraine, and the other republics of the former Soviet Union—to sustainable democracies, free market economies, and cooperative international relations.

The heart of the Center is its resident research community of more than one hundred scholars: Harvard faculty, analysts, practitioners, and each year a new, interdisciplinary group of research fellows. BCSIA sponsors frequent seminars, workshops, and conferences, many open to the public; maintains a substantial specialized library; and publishes a monograph series and discussion papers. The Center's International Security Program, directed by Steven E. Miller, publishes the CSIA Studies in International Security, and sponsors and edits the quarterly journal *International Security*.

The Center is supported by an endowment established with funds from Robert and Renée Belfer, the Ford Foundation, and Harvard University, by foundation grants, by individual gifts, and by occasional government contracts.